1977

Calderón and the Seizures of Honor

Calderón and the Seizures of Honor

Edwin Honig

Harvard University Press, Cambridge, Massachusetts, 1972

To William L. Fichter

In the conflicts of this century, I have felt close to all obstinate men, particularly to those who have never been able to abandon their faith in honor. I have shared and I continue to share many contemporary hysterias. But I have never been able to make up my mind to spit, as so many have done, on the word "honor" — no doubt because I was aware and continue to be aware of my human weaknesses and the injustices I have committed, and because I knew and continue to know instinctively that honor, like pity, is the irrational virtue that carries on after justice and reason have become powerless.

Albert Camus in *The Reporter,* vol. 17, no. 9

Body: it was a white field ready for love,
On her body's field, with the gaunt tower above,
The lilies grew, beseeching him to take,
If he would pluck and wear them, bruise and break.

Eyes talking: Never mind the cruel words,
Embrace my flowers, but not embrace the swords.
But what they said, the doves came straightway flying
And unsaid: Honor, Honor, they came crying.

Importunate her doves. Too pure, too wise,
Clambering on his shoulder, saying, Arise,
Leave me now, and never let us meet,
Eternal distance now command thy feet.

Predicament indeed, which thus discovers
Honor among thieves, Honor between lovers.
O such a little word is Honor, they feel!
But the grey word is between them cold as steel.

from *The Equilibrists* by John Crowe Ransom

Preface

These chapters grew out of two books of my own translations, *Calderón: Four Plays* (1961) and *Life Is a Dream* (1970). The practical problems of translating the plays touched off speculations about their meaning and intention, which in turn incited various attempts, early and late, to test my ideas in print. Some appeared as introductory material to the translations. Others grew into essays on the inner life of each play and the working alliances of several themes common to all five. The essays have now become the central matter of this book.

Most of my commentary was written after close work with the texts and without recourse to any of the pertinent scholarship. I turned to the scholarship only after deciding to shape the material into a connected literary argument. How much I subsequently profited from my readings is made clear in the notes and in the course of the essays. Where I differed with prevailing opinion, even of scholars who had edified me, seemed a matter worth discussing in detail. But because the aim of this book is to make Calderón better known to English-speaking readers of drama and not to debate with the specialists, there are no polemics in the main chapters. The bulk of theoretical considerations is put last where it more naturally serves to sum up the lines of argument developed in the discussion of individual plays in the main portion of the book.

Translations from Calderón in this book are my own and are taken from my *Calderón: Four Plays* (New York,

Hill and Wang, 1961) and *Life Is a Dream* (New York, Hill and Wang, 1970). Parts of Chapters 2 and 3 are adapted from the Introduction to the first of these volumes. Other versions of this material as well as much of Chapter 5 first appeared as "The Seizures of Honor in Calderón," *Kenyon Review*, 23 (1961), 426–447; "The Concept of Honor in the Dramas of Calderón," *New Mexico Quarterly*, 35 (1965), 105–117; and "Calderón's Strange Mercy Play," *Massachusetts Review*, 3 (1961), 80–107.

Chapter 4 is drawn from "Calderón's *Secret Vengeance:* Dehumanizing Honor," in *Homenaje a William L. Fichter*, ed. A. D. Kossoff and J. Amor y Vázquez (Madrid, Editorial Castalia, 1971), pp. 295–306.

"Calderón's *Mayor:* Honor Humanized," *Tulane Drama Review*, 10 (1966), 134–155, provides the substance for Chapter 6.

Chapter 7 derives from "Flickers of Incest on the Face of Honor: Calderón's *Phantom Lady*," *Tulane Drama Review*, 6 (1962), 69–105.

"Reading What's in *La vida es sueño*," *The Theatre Annual*, 20 (1963), 63–71, the original source for Chapter 8, was later modified to serve as Introduction ("The Magnanimous Prince: *Life Is a Dream*") to my translation of the play.

To the editors and publishers of these materials I am deeply grateful for the permission to reprint and adapt all the sources cited above.

A word regarding titles. Since this book is intended mainly for the reader who has little or no Spanish, I have consistently translated play titles rather than use the original, except where each title is first mentioned. I have also provided in an appendix the Spanish original of all passages excerpted and emphasized in the discussion of the plays. Where not otherwise noted, I have silently translated other quoted materials from the French and the Spanish.

I am grateful for grants of money and time from the John Simon Guggenheim Memorial Foundation, the National Institute of Arts and Letters, and Brown University. On various occasions over the years I have profited immensely from the astute advice of Professors Bruce W. Wardropper, Cyril A. Jones, Alan S. Trueblood, and Eric Bentley.

Contents

Calderón and the Seizures of Honor

1 A Beginning

In stature and influence Calderón as often equals Shakespeare and Jonson as he excels Racine and Corneille. He belongs in the forefront with these and other giants of the age who sought the freedom of imagination to chart the range of consciousness from an individual's daily struggles toward manhood to a nation's growing recognition of its special aspirations. Like the best minds of his century Calderón was engrossed with many of the ideals that still shape the modern conscience and mirror its distortions and diseases. Yet no comprehensive study of his works exists that would establish him once and for all as the universal dramatic genius he is.[1]

Considerable obstacles lie in the way. First, the immense bulk of his writing. Over two hundred dramatic pieces exist, an output greater than any serious reader, let alone audience, can think of digesting in a lifetime. But even Shakespeare and Jonson, whose plays when put together comprise a bare fourth of Calderón's total *oeuvre,* are not often read entire. Like theirs, his particular gifts quickly emerge on getting to know half a dozen of the plays. Yet whether the greater part of his best work — say, thirty or forty *comedias*[2] and *autos*[3] — will ever come to be read by those who would enjoy them, seems as questionable today as it was in the late seventeenth century.

Another obstacle derives from his peculiar gifts as a master of poetic forms and an experimenter with dramatic styles. Calderón's verse, more than Racine's, certainly more than Corneille's, is quite flexible, more wide-ranging in diction, and more formally varied in meter. It is distinctive for drawing maximum effect from standard patterns of imagery and for a trope system stressing the symmetrical balance of argument, inventions partly influenced by Góngora's so-called conceptist style and partly by classical rhetoric used in debate. Yet, though the diction is varied, it is also constrained by a curious three-way verse convention which Lope de Vega and other immediate predecessors used in order to make simultaneously recognizable the tone of a dramatic speech, its characteristic subject, and its figurative make-up. The dramatic poet, for example, would be expected to master a variety of at least six metrical and linear patterns: *silva, décima, romance, quintilla, redondilla, octava.*[4] Although conventions of this kind help to make Calderón's verse appear more lucid as dramatic writing than even Racine's (not to mention Shakespeare's and Jonson's), the effect is often more artificial, certainly more *contrived* — as we say when wishing to show that craft is respected but not craftiness. Consequently, his characters sometimes appear to obey the requirements of the particular verse types imposed upon them, like a colony of Procrustes, sooner than they do the more usual criteria.

To such questionable virtues add that Calderón was by temperament an allegorist who liked puns,[5] even bad ones, for their concentrative effect, and that he indulged the age's weakness for highflown rhetoric and casuistical dialogue, and you have a dramatic writer almost anathematic to Anglo-Saxon tastes. But being an allegorist interested in ideas does not exclude an interest in character. Like Henry James, Calderón believed that ideas are bound to character because character is the prime means for enacting them. In effect, what a man *says* — the things he reasons about and quarrels with — identifies him more than what he *does*. What he does issues from what he thinks he must be — an instrument of fate proceeding from the typological idea which activates his dramatic role. What he does, then, is absorbed or ritualized by his role, duty, and status in the play. In this sense he is like a company of *toreros,* going through his paces, engaged in fighting bulls according to prescribed stages or acts, until the dénouement when the matador finally delivers the *coup de grâce.*

Not only are the characters ritualized, but the complicated plots which accompany them also look like exemplifications of fate. Intrigue calls for long soliloquies, set speeches, as well as quick exchanges, expletives, and outcries, all more or less conventionalized in the drama of the time. In Calderón these aspects of the play seem to have more to do with working out the implications of the honor impasse, with its insult-and-revenge motif, siege of jealousy, and personal anxiety, than with any simple psychological determinism.

One does not expect such a dramatist to stick to rules of decorum or to the unities. In fact, he will expressly show his disregard of them, as when he says in the *auto* version of *El pintor de su deshonra* (The Painter of His Own Dishonor): "Here there are no real human characters, / and the allegorical type can / squeeze centuries into hours." Nor can a dramatist of this sort be trusted to keep comic subplots separate either; to be sure, Calderón mixes for his purposes within the problematic fabric of the main action strands of inanity and tonal discordances that often make us doubt his intention to be taken seriously.

From such virtues turned into handicaps the nearly implacable view is derived that Calderón is essentially a parochial writer. Even his defenders sometimes help to spread this view. The first modern promulgator may have been Marcelino Menéndez y Pelayo, the absolute Saintsbury of Spanish historical scholarship, who in *Calderón y su teatro* (1888) sees him as a failed humanist, disabled by an outmoded theology and, born in the wrong century, having no grasp of any liberal ideology. Oddly enough, even Calderón's craftsmanship is attributed to his religious disposition, when beneath its baroque surface the elaborate structure of his drama is said to frame a guiding rationale based on a few explicit church dogmas. Then the complex verbal and structural techniques, finding analogues in the dramatic development of his arguments and paradoxes, are seen to emanate from Aquinas and Suarez. From this it follows that his dramatic exploitation of the honor formula was an outcome of his Jesuit training in dialectics and homiletics, which induced him to turn plays into disguised theological exercises on the old oppositions of free will and predestination, duty and love.

The trouble with this view is that it makes Calderón's uniquely religious cast of mind seem dull, against the plain fact that even such a doctrinal play as *Devoción de la cruz* (Devotion to the Cross) comes alive to a modern reader in fresh and basic human terms. One can not deny Calderón's religious preoccupations, nor that after he became a priest, he took his religion seriously enough to write two morality plays (*autos sacramentales*) yearly for the last thirty-one years of his life. Among the best of their kind ever written, these short plays resort variously to traditional Catholic doctrines. But it is not the doctrine that makes them interesting. They are interesting because they enact the drama of human conscience in a new way and in a new form, showing us what we are in what we are not. The same ethical vitality fills his great secular plays, *La vida es sueño* (Life Is a Dream), *A secreto agravio, secreta venganza* (Secret Vengeance for Secret Insult) and *El príncipe constante* (The Constant Prince).

Making Calderón seem parochial when he is not is also obscurantist. To insist that he is a *religious* dramatist (Lope de Vega and Tirso de Molina were also priests but for some reason are not thought of as religious) seals him off from the thriving humanistic involvements he shared with his English and French contemporaries. It gives him second-class honors by explaining the problematic nature of his plays in terms of doctrine so that they seem convincing as arguments, not as plays. The notion also inhibits an appreciation of his contemporaneity, his continuing interest to our own time. By concentrating on one type of play, it neglects to account for the extraordinary range of Calderonian drama. Plays about Biblical, historical, and mythological subjects are no more numerous in his work than plays about events and personages significant to his own time. He has fewer plays on problems of doctrine than on matters of sexual anomalousness, psychological frustration, the life of anarchy, and disbelief. His drama repeatedly proposes that for most men, who are not saints, the demands of duty, too scrupulously followed, defeat the hero's humanity instead of ennobling it, while the pursuit of individualism, in testing the limits of freedom and erotic curiosity, including murder, rape, and brigandage, may be the road to salvation. To recognize such conditions and themes puts a different face on Calderonian drama than the one it is usually described as wearing.

These essays are mainly about five plays that dramatize alternative views of the honor problem, where honor is a trope as well as a basic theme. Calderón is thus seen through a wider lens, particularly one validated by aspects of contemporary experience of which his work has silently become a part. For the concern with honor which touches off his best plays is not only at the heart of the humanist tradition in Renaissance drama: subject to a few modifications of feeling and thought, it is also basic to the strong moral imagination we admire in Camus, Faulkner, Pirandello, and Pasternak. Like them, Calderón saw in honor both a self-imposed obstacle and a self-imposed goal. He understood that while honor as duty often turns into a force that oppresses and degrades its champion, honor as the assertion of belief in action may at times be the only means a man has to preserve his personal identity. But what made Calderón a great dramatist is that he further saw the paradox: in any given instance where honor as obstacle depends on honor as goal, the issue must be the destruction of life and human pride.

In each play the honor theme receives a different emphasis and leads to a significantly different resolution. Thematic variations and structural developments go hand in hand, either sustained through symbolic patterns or deliberately interwoven with mythical material. What keeps the theme alive is the impression the plays give of an author who is constantly examining and revising his own, and hence our, view of the dramatic possibilities of the honor code according to increasingly more humane resolutions.

In *Devotion to the Cross* and *La dama duende* (The Phantom Lady), where the principles of mercy and freedom triumph, there is a continual testing of the ground on which the honor principle stands: authoritarian law and paternalistic custom. Calderón seems to be trying to find out how far one may go in rectifying, with some ameliorative action, the self-degrading and socially destructive effects of the code on the honor-bound man, even while knowing there is always a cruel price to be paid for earnest infringements of the code, whether by individual or by society. In *El alcalde de Zalamea* (The Mayor of Zalamea), where the most auspicious social resolution of the problem occurs, it is at the expense of the culprit nobleman, who is garroted. In *The Phantom Lady* and *Life is a Dream*, where the pursuit of freedom concerns a disattached woman having to assert herself, the plot complications ring with near-incest reverberations, reminding us that such mixed developments in Calderón often crop up where psychosexual frustrations are indeterminate. Other tests of honor's monolithic law involve father-son conflicts, brother-sister oppositions, old man-young wife deceptions, invariably culminating in acts of rebellion, incest, adultery, and wife murder.

In these instances, and despite the depredations of family and state on individual self-realization, a positive light begins to glow after the doomed struggle and defeat. We begin to make out how difficult it is to be — or attempt to be — human, even when the ameliorative principle wins out, as, for example, in *Life Is a Dream* and *The Phantom Lady*, where possibility masters fate. Awesomely wasteful and debilitating, as most wars are, the battle almost always ends in a total loss. Still, it is only when we know what the odds are that we can glimpse the promise of a new dispensation, the emergence of some possibly humane order overcoming the impersonal, mechanical injunctions which victimize the honor-bound man and his society.

Unexpected consequences follow from these Pyrrhic victories and conscientious defeats. One is that whatever the word *comedia* was intended to mean from Lope to Calderón (when the term was loosely applied to any full-length play), one feels there is something inappropriate about an unrelieved tragedy or a crushing pathos run through a dramatic production where man's fate is publicly resolved by human actors before a human audience. *Comedia* as comedy is necessarily human in its resolutions, however destructive they may be. Tragedy, on the other hand, is abstract, theological, concerned mainly with nonhuman orders of being — saints, heroes, gods. From this a second consequence emerges in recognizing how much the intolerable aspects of ideality may still come to be accepted among one portion of the society (as audience), which is otherwise, in real life, victimized by it. We see that a growing contiguity exists between the ludicrousness of the protagonist's impasse, especially where the honor situation is bleakest, as in *Secret Vengeance*, and the open, fun-making freedom which comes of mocking the taboos in comedy, as in *The Phantom Lady*. The opposite effects of near-ludicrous pathos and sentimental near-tragedy are acceptable because in neither play can the tragic implications, under whatever guise, be more than momentarily tolerated as the answer to the living question being proposed on the stage. Looked at in another way, one solution to too much ideality that seems headed toward tragedy may be comic farce; a tragicomic admixture allows for a "riper"-seeming dramatic conclusion. Honor then becomes acceptable, strangely enough, when it is least tolerable. And this may be what Camus had in mind when he said "that honor, like pity, is the irrational virtue that carries on after justice and reason have become powerless."

2   Honor Seeks Its Own Level

Something impenetrable about the Spanish temperament has always put off the foreigner. Spaniards themselves are confounded by it, and the best of them, when driven to explain the matter in print, have often had to leave or be put out of Spain in order to do so. The long list of illustrious prisoners and exiles is headed by Cervantes, Luis de León, and Quevedo, and in modern times, Unamuno, Ortega y Gasset, Américo Castro, and Salvador de Madariaga. Explaining Spain, the last resort of outraged affection, becomes the morbid pastime of writing about the Spanish temperament as if it were a double-headed Minotaur or a beautiful mistress by whom one had unforgivably been jilted.

How is the temperament usually described? As a nest of contradictions, a mixture of boundless candor and inflexible reserve. Self-criticism bordering on despair and a cynical distrust of new ideas, the motives of foreigners, liberalism, continentalism. Pride, gallantry, religious fervor; egotism, libertinism, contemptuous anticlericalism. An unquenchable passion for life and the joys of the senses; an obsession with death and a medieval veneration for the spiritual life or any career dedicated to a lost ideal. A nationalism that scorns internationalism; a local and provincial pride that makes light of nationalism and takes the form of political separatism and anarchism. Adapting each culture to which they submitted in turn — Phoenician, Greek, Roman, Visigothic, Christian, Hebrew, Moorish — Spaniards grew into the habit of supporting these cultures more zealously than their conquerors could. Then, when the time came for it, Spain was as zealous in driving out its conquerors as it had been in adapting their cultures. Such lines of contradiction are so intrinsic to the Spanish temperament that paradox seems to be the only certain word to describe its peculiar durability. Coming to Calderón, "the monster of ingenuity," every reader soon finds a toughly abiding pattern of paradox to reckon with. In fact, unless he is willing to reckon with it patiently, Calderón's best work is bound to make very little sense to him. And the pattern is nowhere so apparent as in the plight of the proud man who suddenly feels that his identity is about to be extinguished because his honor has been threatened.

Of course this literary representation of paradoxical pride — fierce, glorious, absurd — does not start with Calderón. It goes back at least as far as the Cid, hero of Spain's first and greatest epic poem. As a medieval man, the Cid is innocent of Calderón's psychologically harassed hero's plight. He has more calm, more aggressive heroism in his nature — naturally, since he reflects the confirmed aspirations of the early Castilians. His knowing how and when to act under adverse circumstances is his crucial asset.

The Cid is seen first as an obscure soldier-squire, who is tricked and banished by powerful noblemen; then he vengefully returns to become a rich conqueror who sees his enemies punished and his daughters married to kings. This archetypal Christian warrior, whose ideals have been steeped in a mixed bath of Visigothic, Hebrew, and Moorish honor, later conquers the New World, spreading his anachronistic version of militant Catholicism, at once zealously mystical and egregiously imperialistic. When we come upon him again in Don Quixote, with all his ideals chastened by defeat, his persistent absurdity wrings a momentous Pyrrhic victory from his misadventures. Paradoxically, in this way he revives the standard of Spanish pride so successfully that he becomes a sort of secular saint — the counterpart to the only other Spanish saint whose *order* endures, Ignatius Loyola.

In Spanish Golden Age drama something further happens to heroic pride. Methodized and internalized, it becomes the conscientious resource of heroes who feel themselves estranged from society, often because they have in some way violated its unwritten code of honor. Yet they proceed to act strictly according to the axiomatic tenets of the code based on vengeance. The honor code lends itself to the intolerably burdened conscience, the embattled condition of outraged pride, a state of personal fear mirroring society's dread of contamination and the assault against its autocratic rule. As reflected in the stock-taking speeches of the honor plays, the burdened conscience resorts to a desperate ultrarational dialectic, a kind of private Inquisition or legalistic tourney, justifying the precise means involved in regaining lost personal honor. Within these means are often mixed the medicine of hypocrisy in order to bring about the catharsis, the shedding of the burden in murder, whereby the social law is preserved and the individual is sacrificed. Even where alternatives appear in frenzied aggressive acts justified by religious devotion and supernatural mercy, the redeeming action seems almost as hypocritical, self-defensive, and criminally directed as the vengeance principle it is meant to combat. Whatever his cause may be, the hero is thereby induced to perform acts of violence and sadism as grim as the traditional *auto da fé*.[1]

One reason for this paradoxicality of pride may be sought in the nature of Spanish society where the ideal of honor became an intense, ritualistic concern. For almost four centuries, since the death of Philip II, Spain has been, except for brief intervals of foreign domination and liberal governments, an authoritarian state, a society closely ruled by king and church, and when the king was weak or had disappeared, ruled by an oligarchy together with the church. In such a society, external forms (public ceremonies, class distinctions, social behavior) take precedence over matters of the individual conscience. The conscience, in fact, must express itself in a social guise, the oldest form of which is called *pundonor,* the code of honor.

Stemming from feudal customs, honor — a virtue built on pride, obedience, fealty, adoration, and self-sacrifice — was turned into a combative ideal to preserve caste society. In the Spain of the Counter-Reformation, an imperialistic theocracy, the medieval concept of honor was fervently reinforced and rigidified. The need to preserve gains wrested in military-religious missions gave honor both a repressive and an idealistic character. The three Spanish synonyms for gentlemen — *señor, hidalgo, caballero* — suggest as much. *Señor* also means God, lord, sir, sire, and owner; *hidalgo,* the member of a privileged class, a nobleman; *caballero,* a squire, horseman, rider. These are the figures of authority who actively sustain the rule of honor. The word *hidalgo* (a contraction of *hijo de algo*[2] — "son of something") also suggests the patrilinear law of inheritance. The term thus carries certain implications of polygamy derived from Moorish society where the sequestration of women in a harem insured the breeding of numerous sons. The sons inherited portions of their father's vast lands; and because each son held exclusive dominion over his portion through pure-blooded affiliation with the patriarchal lord-owner, he could be expected to defend it to the death against any foreign or extrafamilial encroachment.

One aspect of honor is that it traditionally shows itself less as a private virtue than as the socially nurtured exhibition of self-esteem, which may be asserted only when challenged or assaulted by some antagonist. It is the precarious just cause daily safeguarded in the cold war of social life, awaiting the trespass of a lurking enemy. One's honor depends on someone else, as Lope de Vega pointed out. No man is honorable alone and by himself; he becomes honorable by means of another person. Having a sense of one's merit, or being virtuous, is not the same as being honorable; honor is achieved by successfully overcoming attacks against one's social status or reputation, one's pride of ancestry.[3] Understood in this way, honor feeds the central paradox in Calderón's drama, where, like Richard Lovelace's avowal to his lady, it must become his "new mistress," "the first foe in the field," superseding all other attachments, since "I could not love thee, dear, so much, / Loved I not honour more." For the hero, honor is a continually exigent ideal, a cause to die for. For the playwright, it is a practical matter, a dramatic convention. "Incidents concerning honor," as Lope de Vega put it in *The New Art of Writing Plays in the Present Day* — a partly ironic seventeenth-century manifesto for dramatists — "are preferable because they move all people forcefully." Serving his inclusive thematic and dramaturgic purposes, honor becomes the prime mover in Calderón's most chillingly resolved plays.

In plays taken up with questions of duty and conscience, the need to be true to a standard of right, though not necessarily Christian, behavior, honor hinges on an ethical principle and a moral action. The principle assumes a relationship with another person — friend, mistress, wife, sister, father — to whom one is responsible and in whose behalf one must be prepared to act. The consequent action has to do with safeguarding the social or sexual status quo. To judge right and wrong behavior and to weigh the necessity of direct action, honor requires the ability to perceive — not so much correctly as opportunely. The need to make the action fit the principle sets up the existential equation: who I am and how I act give me the right to decide matters of life and death; when my reputation is at stake, I am obliged to act because on my reputation depends the health of society, which must be safeguarded at any price. The formula is often stated through the hero's collapsed view of his own beseiged situation: I fear, I am jealous, I must be revenged — so that the society upon which my well-being depends may be satisfied.

In a closed society any transgression is actually or potentially a crime against the system, but particularly against the absolute figure of authority: an autocratic God or his representative, the king. Saying or believing that one's honor or reputation must be defended means that a man is conscious of being himself a symbol of society and is therefore eternally vigilant of the forces which threaten its authority. Self-centeredness threatened by antagonistic forces is a state of mind which makes for the bleak hysteria of heroic consciousness. The honor-struck man, fearing a possible assault on his reputation, works up an intolerable tension which nothing short of force, an act of vengeance, can relieve. The attack on his honor is an injury that touches off sexual jealousy, which in turn constricts his sense of personal liberty. Feeling himself deprived of a vital possession, he shrinks in the eyes of God and his fellow men; his essential identity is in question until he has somehow found the means of striking back. In striking back, he redeems the lost object and thereby restores himself to a society whose image he must preserve.[4]

Traditionally, the attack on one's honor may be provoked in any of three ways: by adultery or seduction, a physical blow, a verbal insult. Reparation for the latter two is fairly immediate; the aggrieved man responds — like thunder after lightning, as Calderón puts it — by attempting to kill his antagonist on the spot. One's honor is cleansed in the blood of the offender, though the act may sometimes have to be repeated, as Don Juan in *Secret Vengeance* discovers when he feels provoked enough to kill a gossiping misinterpreter of his original act of vengeance. With adultery or seduction, retaliation is far from immediate. A chasm of doubt opens; one is not sure. The violation may only be a figment of the wronged man's fearful imagination. It will take a while to find out. And then, there are the customary remedies. If the woman in question is seduced and unmarried, family honor compels her to marry the real or would-be seducer, to retire to a convent for the rest of her life, or to be killed along with her seducer. The woman's father or brother carries out the acts of vengeance. If the woman is married, she is put to death by her husband, who is likewise obliged to kill her lover, unless the latter happens to be of royal blood.

If, however, the insult has not been noticed publicly, the pragmatic act of vengeance runs into complications requiring special skills to resolve. The wronged man must first assess his injury — perhaps even first seek proof of its existence — before he manufactures the means of revenge that will make his victim's death appear accidental. This is the burden of Don Lope's, the aggrieved husband's, "secret vengeance." That the avenger himself may be psychologically diminished or victimized by his actions does not affect the rationale for such actions, nor that they are later accepted, praised, and even rewarded by the highest prevailing authority. But clearly the approval of authority is indispensable if the honor code is to be upheld. In an extreme case (*Devotion to the Cross*), the assaulter-turned-victim is in the end redeemed by divine intercession. In another (*The Mayor of Zalamea*), the King approves the peasant's exceptional departure from the letter of the law, when he executes a nobleman, by making the peasant permanent mayor of the town.

Two vivid historical instances from contemporary writers cited by Norman Maccoll, the nineteenth-century Hispanist, illustrate that actual events of the Calderonian era were probably no less incredible than fictional events in Calderonian drama. The first is drawn from the *Memoirs* of the English gentleman traveler and friend of Ben Jonson, Sir Kenelm Digby.

The well known adventure of Sir Kenelm Digby, when he followed Charles, Prince of Wales, to Madrid in 1623, shows that a Spanish gentleman could plan to have all the advantage on his own side in a personal encounter. Sir Kenelm was returning late at night from the English embassy in company with a relative of Lord Bristol's, whom he calls Leodivius, and another Englishman, when they were attracted by the sight of "a gentlewoman in a loose and night habit that stood in an open window (supported like a gallery with bars of iron), with a lute in her hand, which, with excellent skill, she made to keep time to her divine voice . . . Only there seemed to sit so much sadness on her beautiful face, that one might judge she herself took little pleasure in her soul-ravishing harmony." While they were listening fifteen men fully armed rushed on Leodivius, and he, after striking the foremost blow on the head which would have been fatal had the Spaniard not been protected by a steel cap, went off to the embassy to obtain assistance, leaving his companions to deal with the assailants as best they could. They remonstrated, but the leader of the band told Sir Kenelm, "Villain, thou hast done me wrong which cannot be satisfied with less than thy life, and by thy example let the rest of thy countrymen learn to shun these gentlewomen where other men have interest." Sir Kenelm managed to run his antagonist through the body, and on seeing their master fall, the Spaniards "attended to succour their wounded lord. But all too late, for without ever speaking he gave up the ghost in their arms. The next day the case of this quarrel was known, which was that a nobleman in that country having interest in a gentlewoman that lived not far from the Ambassador's house, was jealous of Leodivius, who had carried his affections too publicly, so that this night he had forced her to sing in the window where Leodivius saw her, hoping by that means to entice him to come near to her while he lay in ambush to take his life with him."[5]

The second instance is drawn from a contemporary Spanish account by Pellicer.

Don Luis de Trejo, a soldier of distinction and a man highly connected, who had paid his addresses to a widow in good positon — *dama principal y de porte* — was appointed to the command of a regiment in Italy, and, during his absence from Madrid, Don Diego Abarca Maldonado, who had spent some years as a captain of infantry in Italy and Flanders, because he had

been involved in the slaying of the son of the governor of Aran-
juez, became the lady's lover. On his return Don Luis paid her
a visit, and a few days after, Abarca going to her house *a des-
hora,* met a man coming from her apartment, whom he forced
to confess that he was a servant of Trejo. Two days afterwards
the rivals encountered each other in the street, and Abarca,
"with all civility and politeness," begged Don Luis to desist
from his attentions to the widow. Don Luis declined, and said
the matter could only be settled by the sword; and, as Abarca
was alone, he requested three gentlemen who were with him
(Don Luis) to leave him. The pair proceeded to the *Prado,*
and in the combat that ensued Abarca ran his adversary
through the body. He helped to carry Don Luis to the Clérigos
Menores, and while he was knocking at the door the three
friends of Don Luis appeared on the scene, and, seeing the
state in which he was, wished to fall on Abarca; but Don Luis
prevented them, saying his opponent had acted like a gentleman, and had endeavoured to save his soul by bringing him
to the monastery. Abarca had his own bed removed to the
monastery for his wounded adversary, provided for the safety
of the lady who had been the cause of the duel (*puso en salvo
la dama*), and, after staying till the next day and making some
highly civil speeches to the dying man, whose debts he offered
to pay, he took refuge in the English embassy. Don Luis, not
to be outdone in courtesy, begged the King in his will to pardon
his adversary, and expired, surrounded by his relations, "with
great tokens of sorrow for his sins" (*con grandes muestras de
dolor de sus pecados*).[6]

Reading this suggests Calderón's personal involvement in
a similar episode in 1629. His brother José had been
wounded by Pedro de Villegas, an actor, who then escaped
and hid in a convent, where Calderón pursued him, molest-
ing and insulting the nuns — according to contemporary
reports — while searching for his brother's assailant.

The popularity of the honor theme goaded writers to
exploit it — Cervantes, Lope de Vega, Tirso de Molina,
Mira de Amescua, and Rojas Zorrilla, who are the leading
Spanish dramatists of the time. Honor plays were popular
for their acts of violence, contortions of jealous rage, in-

fringements on sexual taboos, and much highflown language aimed at a chilling ethic which, however battered, could never be overthrown. This convention, offering itself to Calderón at the start of his career, was enormously fruitful. He was a man temperamentally disposed to the psychological and esthetic treatment of the subject. His Jesuit training may have prepared him to exploit its implications, while his penchant for a complex allegorical view of action would have incited him to shape his plays with great subtlety. Yet theological training and dramaturgical astuteness should probably be thought less crucial to his rapid development than his inexhaustible ability to dramatize the paradox of honor as a universal figure for invincible necessity. An allegorist more by temperament than by training, Calderón created a typological variety of character and situation in his secular plays and developed the sacramental *auto* into an essential dramatic form.[7] To do this, however, he had to overcome severely limited materials and the effects of pursuing an unattractive ideology.

But it was his coping with and exploiting of these limitations which made Calderón a major dramatist. On the one hand, the honor situation gave him a pattern for working out certain modes of characterization appropriate to his dominant themes during his early career. On the other hand, the experience of shaping his plays according to the exigencies entailed by that process led him to develop tragicomic distortions that would have been possible to discover in no other way. In effect, we recognize that the spring of action in all of Calderón's honor plays derives from the hero's need to find release from a conscientious impasse, and that this in turn makes for a temperamental type and a set of attitudes which are at once melancholic, anarchic, conformist, hypocritical, schizophrenic, and dehumanized. The determinism behind the type, which views life as cheap, evanescent, and transitory, perpetuates both the rapacious imperialistic designs of the state and the deathbound consolations of religion. And this tragic view of the Calderonian hero, subsisting in an all-or-none credo, is perfectly represented in those dramas where the motives of church and state coincide.

Then, as if to mitigate the austerity of this view, Calderón presents the more humane principle of the freedom of the soul, the right of the individual conscience to choose its own destiny against the dictates of an authoritarian code. In this type of play, the lifting of the strictures of the honor code permits both some cushioning of its devastating impact and the opening of an alternative view in types of pastoral ethic and romantic love which momentarily revive the unfallen state of man's Golden Age. To make this more humane view feasible, Calderón had to sharpen comic and romantic characters in his plays, and he had to create admixtures of seriocomic types and situations which, though never verisimilar or realistic in the nineteenth-century sense, could embody his principled thinking, his consuming sense of life as a play, a stage, a dream.

Calderonian honor, then, is less a profession of belief in a theme for cautionary morality than an aspect of method and development in dramatization. Its variability for dramatic use taught Calderón to be a playwright, as perhaps the soldier's, the prizefighter's, and the bullfighter's codes taught Ernest Hemingway to be a story writer. It gave the young writer something admirable and intriguing to work with, to invent upon, to perfect — and, eventually, something to leave behind him in his pursuit of other themes and techniques. It is the close working sense of that variety in his treatment of the honor theme which concerns us now.

3 Honor and the Comic Subversion

In *No hay cosa como callar,* 1638–1639 (There's Nothing Like Keeping Still), a play which he regards as "a masterpiece," A. A. Parker sees the conventions of comedy used for a tragic purpose, "so that the 'happy ending' resolves the dramatic conflict on the level of honor but does not restore happiness to the heroine, who is compelled to forsake the man she loves and suffer in silence, unable to tell him why." In addition, Parker notes the recurrent pattern of Calderón's themes and situations from play to play, making the plots often seem so similar. Thus the overlapping of *Life Is a Dream* and *Devotion to the Cross:* "If Segismundo had been killed in the vain attempt to recover his freedom while Basilio had been forced to see him die before his eyes as the price of retaining his throne, the Curcio-Eusebio situation would have been exactly paralleled."[1]

Another critic, Prosser Hall Frye, notes something similar about Calderón's characters who are "like the shadings of a watered or changeable silk in which the figure is continually losing itself and reappearing more or less uncertainly or elusively like a shadow on the surface of the stuff." In any half dozen Calderón plays, he goes on to say,

notice the resemblance, if not the identity of the essential traits or lineaments, see how the one person repeats himself again and again, until you turn your attention from the personality to its affection. In other words, the character remains a constant in every equation; once admitted, it is negligible and neglected.[2]

Calderón goes over the same ground again and again, as if wishing to show a multiplicity of choices without effecting the tragic dénouement. In *Secret Vengeance,* the husband kills his possibly faithless wife and burns the house down where he has left her body. In *El pintor de su deshonra,* 1648–1650 (The Painter of His Own Dishonor), the husband rescues from the burning house his guests as well as his wife, only to kill her later. One solution is the dramatic alternative not faced but proposed and followed through in another play. Both husbands are happy, older married men to begin with. Both have been married by proxy. Both are supremely self-centered, with young wives who were loved before by younger men believed to be dead who are suddenly returned in secret. In both plays there is the same beach scene where the wife's lover crucially reappears. But in *Secret Vengeance* the husband strangles and drowns the lover; in *The Painter,* the lover makes away with the wife. The parallelism begins to fade subsequently, though it is still faintly apparent when in *The Painter* the husband, with his fortune reversed, appears in the last act as an impoverished artist, and so recalls in this guise the humiliated friend of the husband in *Secret Vengeance.* This doubling effect, or the overlapping of characters from play to play, calls attention to itself and seems to be telling us something about the nature of Calderón's design.

What is the design? It is, at least partly, the overall sense of what may be used of the comedic and tragic conventions to validate a serious subject like honor and yet to imply various criticisms of it. The workings of the design may be traced in some of the plays which will later concern us in detail.

In comedy there is the special thrill, seldom available in tragedy, that comes from the broad freedom to mock taboos. Comedy indulges in this freedom as though it had just walked into the Garden of Eden. It wants us to enjoy the near miss, the hot breath of approaching disaster. We know at the start that this is the kind of thrill Calderón is preparing when Doña Angela, in *The Phantom Lady*, appears, breathless, running away from her own brother-turned-swain. Quavering, temptingly veiled, she solicits the protection of a stranger, Don Manuel, then disappears.

"Was that a lady or a whirlwind?" asks Manuel's servant, Cosme, the play's great comic exhibitionist. And the question tumbles us right into the lap of the mystery.

What is this mystery?

Part of it may be better understood by asking two further questions. Can the whirlwind be made to materialize? If it does, will she stop being a wildly pursued erotic force and become human, a real woman? To complicate such possibilities here, as elsewhere in Calderonian drama, there is an underlying assumption that women, like poets, madmen, and devils, are as fascinating as they are dangerous and disruptive. They must be handled gingerly and put away, unless they can be placated by marriage. Women subsist on the margins of the serious life; they have nothing to do with the business of living in a world charged with purpose, patrimony, and passionate missions. They are sirens, temptresses, something to pick up, enjoy, and abandon along the way. Love 'em and leave 'em, as they perennially say in the world's armies.

In *The Mayor of Zalamea*, with its half-comic, half-revolutionary solution to the honor question, where the dishonored peasant father judicially kills the offending officer, we see woman presented with a clear set of alternatives: either be loose or be strict. Let the woman be jolly and companionable, let her enjoy herself, and she is cast in the role of the camp follower, La Chispa (The Spark):

> I love to sing, and where
> other women burst into tears
> over any little trifle,
> I myself burst into song.

To this the plain alternative is the rich peasant's young daughter, Isabel, who must be sequestered from all rapacious eyes. For unless she is hidden, she is too apt to succumb, as all virgins must, to any lingering male, of whatever age or rank. So her existence must be kept secret; if it gets out that she is there in an upstairs room, she becomes fair game to Captain Álvaro's excited Don Juanism. Then he must seduce her, or else he is not a real man. As he says,

> Now perhaps if she were here
> and quite available,
> I wouldn't care two pins about her.
> But just because the old man's
> locked her up, so help me, he's made me
> want to get at her up there.

Even the zany, out-at-elbows knight Don Mendo must make his flourish at her. He swears the peasant's daughter is the undying object of his affection, but when asked why he doesn't marry her, his reply is realistic:

> Aren't there nunneries enough
> where I can drop her if she bores me,
> without my marrying the girl?

But not every available woman is raped, at least not immediately. There is a code, a safeguard against assault, that will usually work in broad daylight. Yet the code, of course, is made to be broken, especially at night, when it demands that the gentleman be nobler than he can ever swear to be by day. Even Don Álvaro temporarily subsides when he is reminded of it by the peasant's daughter, whom he will rape later:

> Gentlemen like yourself
> are duty-bound to honor
> womankind, if not because
> they're individuals,
> then because they're women.

But the point is, no woman can be free if no man is free. This is proven by what actually happens in a military society, frankly portrayed in *The Mayor of Zalamea* — though it seems at the end that there is little difference between a military and a civilian society if the same prohibitions, inhibitions, and violent assaults against women prevail in both.

And so the humanity of all characters in the honor plays is severely reduced, often annihilated, almost accidentally. Typically, a vanished lover suddenly reappears in disguise to reclaim the newly married wife; when he persists, the slowly aroused husband must kill them both. A woman may not be touched — often marriages are by proxy; she may not even be seen without serious consequences for the beholder. For once glimpsed by another man may mean once loved, hence adulterated. From this there follows the need for stratagems, undercover manipulations, clandestine meetings, walls, and darkness. Hence too, the need for protection by a father, or, where there is no father, by a brace of brothers, as in *The Phantom Lady*. Double protection may not be enough; the lady is never safe. In fact, the safeguard itself may lead to exposure. Isabel is forced to dematerialize, become a phantom, partly to escape her excited brothers, for whom the appearance of Manuel, a potential male threat in the house, seems to provide a ruse, an excuse for their predatory activities.

So the woman is a whirlwind, part of untamed nature, a destructive force.

But in an age of allegory, emblematic writing, and baroque symbols, the whirlwind has a special power, an additional appeal that may broaden the theme of a play. In Calderón the figure of the wind recurs from play to play where woman is fatally involved. At the start of *Life Is a Dream* there is the famous hippogriff and the destructive wind it symbolizes. The mythic beast is invoked by Rosaura who must regain her lost honor, but to do so can travel freely only when disguised as a man. Out of this whirlwind issues the rebellion of Segismundo against his father, King Basilio, so that the power he wrests away can be used to reconcile the principle of inner freedom to the principle of a balanced social order. But this can occur only when Rosaura's honor and womanhood are restored to her. In effect, then, the whirlwind, hinting at anarchic destruction, is tamed and redirected by the human power to love and conciliate.

There are other winds — winds that drive lovers away and drown them, or only seem to. A wind may return, bringing the lover back, as though resurrected, to pick up the adverse chain of events that will lead to the tragedy. Such a wind appears in *Secret Vengeance* and in *The Painter of His Own Dishonor*. There is also the tempest wind in the Faustian play, *El mágico prodigioso*, 1637 (The Wonder-Working Magician), a whirlwind out of which Lucifer reveals himself to the scholar Cipriano, so that he in turn may invoke and materialize Justina, the woman Cipriano yearns for.

Even the premonition of a whirlwind carries symbolic force, as in *The Mayor of Zalamea* where it augurs the violence that will sweep away the Mayor's daughter. The foreboding comes to the Mayor out of a scene of peace and plenty as he regards his own ripened fields. The ominous wind the Mayor fears will arise, the tempest wind of Cipriano and Lucifer, and the whirlwind that casts Rosaura into the bleak wasteland where the captive Prince is chained, are of the same element belittled by the impatient Don Lope, awaiting his bride across the waters at the beginning of *Secret Vengeance:*

> *Don Lope.* . . . I'd be happier still
> if I could only fly
> away today.
>
> *Manrique.* Like the wind.
>
> *Don Lope.* That would not help me much.
> The wind's a sluggish element.
> But if love would only lend
> me wings, I'd be borne away

by passion's fire. He who'd use
the wind must go by way
of wind's unsteady wallowings.
But the course that Love would choose
requires fiery wings.

Don Lope's impatience hints at a fault that will grow. His preference for fire, abetted by an unexpected wind, will lead in the end to his burning down the house in which he has just slaughtered his wife.

In *The Phantom Lady* Isabel maintains her reputation as a whirlwind because it is part of her job, she must spend a lot of time finding her way through solid walls. As Cosme, the play's arch interpreter, puts it, since only devils and phantoms can do this, she is obviously one or the other. The point is that as long as she remains the center of a mystery she can be mercurial, magical, desirable, while those who seek her, including her dragooned lover-protector and her two brothers, appear heavy-footed, ludicrous.

Walls that separate, walls that divide, underground passageways in the dark, mazes, falls from parapets, and stony heights secretly aspired to in the night by luckless lovers — Calderón is full of such ominous emblems in crucial situations. These appear in both his comic and serious dramas. Whirlwinds, fires, walls, labyrinths, confrontations in the wilderness are the paraphernalia of magic and mystery. They keep an audience alert and in suspense; they keep it diverted. Neither pure nor impure, their effect is to move at first centrifugally away from the main plot interest and thematic center. And since they occur in comic as well as tragic scenes, their use appears to be thematically and tonally disinterested. But once put in motion there is a moment when they begin to work centripetally back toward the main theme of the play, as if to sustain, reinforce, and extend the play's meaning. Whether moving outward or inward, or merely held in suspension, such devices are inseparable from the elements of intrigue in a play. For what is intrigue but a name for the constant proliferation of illusion issuing from the initial metaphor and mystery, such as the phantom lady? And so the question, "Was that a lady or a whirlwind?" frames the theme and sets up the metaphoric base from which all complications arise.

As noted earlier, the intermingling of violent romantic actions (that is, of potentially tragic elements) with comic elements was not invented by Calderón. Anyone who has heard of the Renaissance critical insistence on decorum knows why it was made and how often and far the great writers strayed from the principle. Stated baldly, the idea was that elegant and low styles should never share company in the same work because such a mixture would keep the work from being taken seriously. But the exceptions leap to mind, not the rule: the Porter at the gate in *Macbeth,* the play within a play in *Hamlet,* and so on. It seems more natural to suppose that mixed styles make for variety, and variety stimulates interest — and without such interest there is no drama in the theatre. Since examples of such disparity crop up in almost every play of Calderón's, one is led to suppose that the typical Renaissance contribution to the drama may be tragicomedy, the mixed type that grew out of the morality, the mystery play, the fabliau, as well as Seneca's revenge play.

The mixing of genres and the mixing of tones, though a feature of popular medieval practice, is heavily marked in all sophisticated Renaissance art and literature. When St. John of the Cross wants to express religious joy, he puts together the symbolism of pastoral poetry with that of the Song of Solomon. Christ is a shepherd sacrificing himself for his beloved, the human soul; or Christ is the bridegroom, while the human soul is the bride. The intermingling of profane and divine love is another commonplace in Renaissance poetry. This development suggests that while Eros is being rediscovered the glorification of God is being envisaged in a new way. As the fears of hell are thrust back, man finds himself aggrandized, and the human personality begins to understand its limitless potentialities in a suddenly expanding world. Lope de Vega writes a play about Columbus and the discovery of the new world, and the play glows with its own fascination for a new kind of man, the Indian. A hundred years earlier there is the lover's heretical cry in the *Celestina,* "In your beauty I see the glory of God!" In the Faust plays of the time there is the discovery that the power of God may be transcended by the range of human intellect. The same experimental view sets off the clash of motives and loyalties, the strangely eruptive energies in Calderón's plays. In *Life Is a Dream* and *The Phantom Lady* we sense a new possibility, a new way out of the bleak fate of the hero trapped in the honor impasse. The avenging man, the sufferer, need not be dragged down with the victim he hardly even knows; he need not be blinded by society's legalistic impositions on his conscience. And with the new dispensation appears a possibly new human order that may overcome the mechanical, inhuman order of the revenge and wife-murder plays.

The new order brings about an overwhelming interest in speculative doodling, strange physical and psychological combinations, paradoxes. This is a hallmark of the baroque style in painting and literature. Essays, poems, portraits, emblematic and allegorical designs treat the monstrous and the fatuous, the mirror and the object, the painting and the reality, grotesque and ideal, dream and reality, faith and doubt, the rare and the plausible. There is a serious popular literature of the journey, of shipwrecks and far-off lands, of werewolves, astrology, and witchcraft. Cervantes, a fine craftsman, speaks of creating the sense of a disordered order which would bring greater truth-to-life in art. Like Calderón, who learned from him, Cervantes was interested in discovering human beings in all their complexity, not in misleading or cheapening their nature as readers or as audience. He believed that if the absurd were to be accounted for, it must be present to balance the real, to make it life-like. For the absurd, according to Cervantes, becomes more credible the more it is documented — as though everyone had accepted it, as though it were not absurd at all.

Admiratio is the seventeenth-century critical counter for the absurd made fictively plausible. It is the third element in art, which includes pleasure and instruction as well. The neo-Aristotelian critic, Alonso López Pinciano, discussed *admiratio* in a well-known treatise of the time, *Filosofía antigua poética* (1596), a book which Cervantes probably read. The term embraces the wondrous and the marvelous in language, characterization, and action. When controlled, it allows for a channeling of inventive energy so that the unexpected, the inconceivable, the patently crazy thing, becomes feasible instead of bathetic or simply ludicrous. *Admiratio* would include awe, the pleasurable surprise, something between tears and laughter. Speculating on these effects in a famous passage of the *Quixote,* Cervantes observes,

the falsehood is better the truer it looks, and the more it contains of the doubtful and the possible the more pleasing it is. Fabulous plots must be wedded to the reader's intelligence, and written in such a way that the impossible is made easy, enormities are smoothed out, and the mind is held in suspense, amazed, gripped, exhilarated, and entertained. (I,47; iii, 349)[3]

In Cervantes, Calderón, and others, such admixtures show up in the hyperbolic address to ladies: the Petrarchan compliment, the absurd and delirious comparison. Woman is not only put on a pedestal but is elevated in orbit around the moon, as though her seducer, having convinced her she was up there, could thereby benumb her so that she could do nothing but throw herself at his feet. As in an ecstasy, she must be verbally transformed and magically made to stand outside herself, not knowing herself. The swain, intoxicated by his own hyperboles, doesn't seem to be there either; he is a disembodied mouth-piece, a medium for the supernal message he happens to be delivering. Nobody human can rape an angel, as the Bible tells us — unless the angel has been so caught up in the belief he is an angel that he isn't looking.

But Calderón's romantic ladies know all about mys-teries that turn into miseries. They know that to be over-praised is to be dehumanized. They have all read *Don Quixote* and know that Dulcinea is what she is — not what the Knight says she is. To save themselves they must cut short the swain's hyperbolic praises. They must continually fight to make a human confrontation pos-sible, so as not to be victimized by idolatry, whose real name is seduction. As objects of attraction and agents of reality, they embody a mixture if not a clash of life styles.

There are further uses of *admiratio* in Calderón. He enjoys, for example, the double-talking sonnet, addressed simultaneously to two different persons, to each of whom it conveys an appropriate message. His plays grow heavy with the soliloquies of the victim or murderer indulging in the fantastic pyrotechnics of conscience display, while setting forth the hideous legalities of the honor dilemma he has fallen into. There are the labyrinthine entrances and exits, underground tunnels, obscure passages through gardens and nunneries, where anyone may turn out to be somebody else. There are the repartees, the verbal pirouettes of the servant gagsters. If nothing else, Cal-derón's *graciosos* are technicians par excellence. Since they are never emotionally involved, they can be expert strategists and escape artists. In this way they become counterparts in action to the hyperbolic swains, their masters.

Engaged by the honor and courtly love conventions, *admiratio* apparently functions to undermine both. Cer-vantes himself, best known for mocking conventions he is half in love with, forces a confrontation with them. This gives an unexpected, sympathetic insight into them.

Dulcinea is appalling the first time she appears in the flesh. It does not matter how much we favor realism — we find ourselves backing away, preferring the Knight's luminous hallucination to the real thing. Over against the visibly gross peasant girl, Quixote's hallucinative image is warmer, more generous and believable, even when the reader is allowed to see through it, with the author's complicity: "The beauty of Dulcinea demands to be depicted on tables, marbles, and bronzes, by the brushes and burins of Parrhasius, Timanthes, Apelles, and Lysippus, and lauded with all the rhetoric of Cicero and Demosthenes" (II,32).[4] The burlesque encomium works; it takes us in even while we share with the author the knowledge that we are being hoodwinked. Perhaps in some sense the romantic is always anticipating the ironic, and the ironic, after it has done its work, looks lingeringly over its shoulder at the romantic. At any rate, in this instance, as elsewhere in Cervantes, the romantic and the ironic, much more than anticipating one another, are actually interchangeable. The notion has interesting implications for tragicomedy with its comic subversion of too strenuously held ideals, like honor.

One way of describing the heroic fault in Calderón's wife-murder plays is to think of it as the result of tragic *hamartia*.[5] The husband, once a strong or influential man, is blinded by credulity so that he cannot see his own shortcomings. The blindness makes him vulnerable, but also leads to a course of action that ends in multiple murder and often suicide. In *Secret Vengeance* the injured man — the husband who thinks himself wronged on circumstantial evidence — is triply impelled to his vengeance. First, because the blight on his honor (whether real or imagined cannot finally be determined) must be redressed in blood, an act required by the honor code. Again, since others may begin to wonder at his uneasiness, the vengeance must be accomplished in secret; that way the murder will either look accidental or not be revealed at all. Finally, because as a possibly cuckolded man he must fight another man's usurpation of his wife as well as the imagined imputations which the wife-theft brings up regarding his own potency. But even after accomplishing his vengeance he has no satisfaction. He is reduced in stature; he is almost dead. What is possibly worse, he looks ludicrous.[6]

Now, if one thinks of the cuckolded husband in comedy, say the old man in the Cervantes interlude *El viejo celoso* (The Jealous Old Husband), it appears that the ludicrous core of the situation is precisely the element the dramatist exploits. Here is the characteristic *hamartia,* the same human failing at work as in the serious play; the protagonist is an elderly man, like Don Lope of *Secret Vengeance* or Don Juan of *The Painter of His Own Dishonor.* Like them he is blind to the fault he passionately regards as a strength in himself. Like them he thinks he is invulnerable to his wife's would-be seducer, even though others know she is going to deceive him. But in the interlude the old man never learns that he has actually been deceived. The dramatic irony triumphs, the husband is kept in the dark. This is one way of punishing him for his cupidity. The implication is that he cannot be further reduced by the revelation of the fact of his wife's infidelity. For if it were revealed he would have to embark on a course of vengeance — something he would be incapable of doing. It would also be out of character for him to do so, for then we would have to take him seriously. On the contrary, he is meant to be ludicrous and laughed at — that is his punishment. By the same token, we cannot laugh at the man who because he believes himself wronged seeks vengeance; for in accomplishing his vengeance he punishes himself as well. Opposites though they seem to be, the injured man who acts and is thereby revealed and reduced by his own blindness subsists in the same world as the comic cuckold whom we laugh at.

Beyond this crossroad, where the comic and the problematic meet, we seem to be headed toward middle-class realism, where the modern novel begins. Pathos displaces laughter or tears as we watch the downward progress of the debilitated hero, victimized by circumstance, who becomes the class-determined, anonymous, naturalistic man.

But if this later deterministic hero develops at one end of the tragicomic spectrum, it is the personified hero, the abstract man of the moralities, that we recognize as his ancestor at the other end. For it is out of the church plays and the *commedia dell'arte*, with their simpler typological characters, that the Renaissance dramatic heroes emerge. Dramatists, in order to cope with a more sophisticated view of experience, adapt the earlier conventions in the comic subplot and in the idealized behavior of the protagonist of the main plot. In the subplot the exemplary action of the main plot is underlined by opposition. The trouble is that the opposition is strictly maintained throughout; it is never bridged. And this is not life-like. The reconciliation of opposites, so often sought in tragicomedy, fully occurs perhaps only in *Don Quixote* — a novel, if anything, and not a drama at all. There, what begins with the typical kind of splitting, on the allegorical principle that characters must be made to represent oppositional or complementary moral elements, is turned around; what ensues is a merging, even a transposition of types, as when Sancho becomes more like Quixote and Quixote more like Sancho.

Something of the sort is made to happen, though not completely, in Calderonian comedy, possibly with Cervantes as the model. In *The Phantom Lady* Manuel, the master, and Cosme, the servant, infect one another, as they never would be permitted to do in a tragic play. But Cosme's effect is to weaken his master by playing on his superstition, his fear of ghosts, devils, women — in a word, by attacking the rational faculty that Manuel is so proud of possessing. (It is just this rational faculty, overused and all-encompassing, which becomes the weapon the honor hero turns against himself in the vengeance plays.) But now Angela, at the other extreme, works by a mixture of white magic, love, and counter-rationality, like a Shavian heroine, to innoculate Manuel and to free him from an honor seizure into which she too has almost fallen. He must accept her, her gifts, and her other remarkable attentions, in order to save them both. But because he is kept ignorant and does not know what is at stake, he cannot understand this until the end of the play. Once he has accepted her, everything is magically reconciled. Honor is regained, the incest threat is put down, and the phantom becomes a real woman. This is the triumph of love.

Things turn out rather differently in *The Mayor of Zalamea* and *Life Is a Dream.* The reconciliation in these plays does not embrace everybody. The Mayor's daughter, because she has been raped and the culprit legally executed, has no recourse but to live out her life in a nunnery. The point of honor is what her father gains when the King justifies and even rewards him for garroting the gentleman seducer. In the *Dream* play, Rosaura does not marry Segismundo, who loves her, but the Duke, her cousin, who wronged her. And the ringleader of the revolt which Segismundo successfully led against his father the King is permanently imprisoned in the tower. In tragicomedy, as often in real life, someone must pay the price of freedom. This is no black-and-white morality but the dim gray ground of the problematical, which is much closer to human experience and human possibility.

The ground in Calderonian drama is not always dim and gray. It can be luminous and scintillant, too. In fact, once a truly human order struggles to assert itself, the degree of its triumph may be measured by the type of situation or character alternative set up in the plays. And these matters generally work themselves out according to one of three principal solutions.

First, the pastoral solution. Though provisional and incomplete, it indicates a new view of possibility in allowing the individual conscience to assert itself against the social stratifications of class or rank. This is what the victory means when it comes to the Mayor of Zalamea; a peasant may josh a *comendador* of Spain as an equal and speak to the Spanish emperor man to man, and justice will be awarded him even under the tyrannical dispensation of the honor code.

Secondly, the romantic solution. This seems somewhat more complete, perhaps because it is more elusive — a case of poetic justice being superior to the legal variety. It works in *The Phantom Lady* as the reconciling principle of love and of woman's right to assert her own choice in love. Still, when the victory occurs it does so only by very narrowly escaping the voracious claims of honor, summarily and magically appeased at the end.

Finally, the ironical solution that turns up mainly in the vengeance plays. The typical hero is cut down by his own machinations, impelled by the insane legalities of a code which demands an eye for an eye. Here Calderón most openly criticizes the tyranny of honor. With the other solutions the claims of honor are temporarily assuaged as the disrupter of the human order. It is almost as if honor were then converted and put to work upholding the newly emergent principles which the human order nourishes. We are thereby given to understand that while the justified peasant and the triumphant woman rise in stature, the anguished hero-victim declines and sinks, even to absurdity. Peasant and woman seem to gain their identities, the honor victim only loses his.

The strangeness of honor in Calderón is that out of an impossibly negative code, a tight and hemmed-in law, it creates an unexpected redemptive effect — the vision of a totally different possibility. By using honor in this way Calderón seems to allow humanity the minimum choices it needs in order to overcome the oppressions of outworn, dehumanized systems it cannot otherwise cope with. And in making for a *reductio ad absurdum,* which is the ludicrous effect of his tragicomedy, Calderón in his use of honor establishes, paradoxically enough, a dramatic way of pointing toward the difficult ascension of the human, the discovery of what it means to be a human being.

4   Dehumanizing Honor:
Secret Vengeance for Secret Insult

A secreto agravio, secreta venganza (Secret Vengeance for
Secret Insult) is Calderón's definitive honor play. His autocratic hero gains a brief respite from despair but loses
everything in the complicated course of the vengeance he
undertakes in order to safeguard his honor. Full of dialectical soliloquies and discourses on the fine points of
conscience, it is not a simple play. Culminating in a
heavily rationalized wife murder, it is not an attractive
play either. Among Calderón's bleakest works, *Secret Vengeance* is unique: it is the only one in which the hero's
humanity is completely devastated from within.

Don Lope de Almeida is scarcely married to Doña
Leonor when he finds reason to suspect her fidelity. He
employs elaborate devices that only assure him there are
grounds for his suspicions. Consequently, the play is given
over to the process by which he plots and concludes his
vengeance against his wife and her former lover. No infidelity is actually committed, but because Lope's stratagems are so provocative they bring the pair, Leonor and
her lover Luis, to the verge of enacting his suspicions.
After drowning the lover and burning down the house
where he has stabbed his wife, Lope's only comfort is that
he is able to serve his king with a clear conscience. Since
both King Sebastian and Don Juan, Lope's friend, sympa-
thize with him and even praise his actions, it would seem

that hypocrisy and clandestine murder are the approved means of recapturing one's lost honor. Read by realistic criteria, the play seems absurd. Read symbolically, by following Calderón's dramatic development of his theme, the play points to a conclusion which is anything but absurd.

Don Lope's first speech sets up the dual nature of the honor code: the demands of love and peace oppose those of war and duty. Although he is the king's chief commander, Lope must ask to be excused from accompanying Sebastian to war so that he may join Leonor, whom he has married by proxy. When permission is granted, Lope views the prospect impatiently, though with some apprehension: she is a bride he has never seen. Impatience and apprehension are twin aspects of his doomed condition that are reiterated throughout the play in metaphors of fire, water, wind, and earth.

As love fights duty, the conflict touches on other oppositions: sea and land, sun and cloud, happiness and misfortune, certainty and doubt, honor and disgrace, insult and vengeance, day and night, Castile and Portugal, false (that is, counterfeit or proxy) and true, speech and silence, public and private spheres, word and sword. As such oppositions emerge in the rationale of dramatic action, they give Lope's personal problems a larger, at points even a cosmic, dimension. So the theme is symbolically transformed; the literal action of the play and its moral questions are pressed into a figurative matrix which seeks to universalize them.

To accomplish this, inset and foreshadowing devices typical of allegory are employed. In an early speech his servant Manrique's jocular warning against Lope's haste,

> . . . if the day
> you are to marry, you elect
> to be impatient of the wind,
> what's left to do, reflect,
> the day you are a widower?

foreshadows Lope's situation at the end of the play. Manrique's playful, half-cynical courtship of Leonor's servant Sirena provides inset situations which define Lope's impasse with Leonor. His clumsy love sonnet to Sirena parodies an earlier one of Lope's addressed to Leonor. The parody also makes fun of the seriously intended Venus-Mars opposition, introduced in Lope's first speech to the king, and with its references to Orpheus and Eurydice also points to the pathetic consequences of Lope's final vengeance. Another of Manrique's speeches, his fanciful parable on the tokens of love, parodies Luis's (the lover disguised as diamond merchant) earlier solicitations of Leonor. Marriage is "a very grave affliction"; "the lady I love must be a liar" who "must deceive and mock me, / make me jealous continually." The same lady's duplicity is shown in her eyes: "One eye weeps boiled honey, / and the other olive oil"; and there is, finally, the reference to "a house . . . where two midgets dwelt but never / met each other."

Calderón thus sharpens the conventional use of the *gracioso* — the buffoonish servant. The servant provides comic relief, with his comforting reassurances about the normal world in a tragic play, while he also serves an allegorical purpose. Don Lope's friend Don Juan, appearing early as well as having the last speech in the play, serves in a similar way. As a foil to Lope he supplies crucial insets, wherein he details his own experience and thus reveals a course of action parallel to Lope's. These insets instigate Lope finally to his secret vengeance, and alternative he adopts in order to avoid the disastrous effects of Juan's public vengeance.

Other aspects of the honor theme are developed allegorically. One concerns Lope's need to maintain his identity, or — since he feels he may have lost it — to regain it, as a man of substance in society, particularly as a member of the body politic, the king's right hand. Since Calderón assumes a basic split between love and duty, Lope's haste in turning from the king toward Leonor, even with the king's permission, suggests a rupture of allegiance. Both the object of authority and Lope's identification with it are thereby displaced. This "treason" remains covert and more a matter of imminent psychological dread than one of fact, for the honor code, which follows courtly tradition in this instance, does enforce the husband's fealty to his beloved, and as yet unseen, wife. King Sebastian indicates as much in exempting Lope from fighting a war so that he can consummate his marriage. At this point Don Lope would not be able to say, as the typical Calderonian hero might, with Lovelace, "I could not love thee, dear, so much, / Loved I not honour more," since he has yet to prove his love. And he is only imminently about to become heroic in the honor-bound sense. But evidence soon accumulates to show that he will be incapable of proving his love. He is a man consumed by his own choler, not by love for another — a fact which Manrique's satiric sonnet emphasizes. To safeguard his reputation Lope must ultimately preserve the literal and official view of his wife's chastity. Instead of bringing the report of love's consummation, he can only ask the king to imagine Leonor lying dead, "her blood / staining the sheets of that / still unviolated bed."

This is in decided contrast to Lope's exclamation, "Loving is no duty," after his first meeting with Leonor. A formal, complimentary statement in its context at the end of Act One, the ironic implications emerge when Don Lope shows himself incapable of acting except in terms of duty. What qualifies him as a soldier disqualifies him as a lover. Duty obsesses him even before the obsession is transformed into an anxiety about his honor. The exact point where the one shades off into the other occurs just past the beginning of Act Two, in his aside, "Bright honor, how much must / still be done on your account."

Leonor has been shown attempting to dismiss Luis, her former lover. By the end of Act One, one has also been made aware of her lover's intention: "And blast all honor, for I must / have Leonor at any price, / though I pay for her with my life." Now, in conversation with her servant, Leonor tries to cope with the imminent disaster:

> *Doña Leonor.* For Heaven knows, if he does not go
> away, he forfeits both our lives.
>
> *Sirena.* I shall tell him all you say,
> if I can only find him.
>
> *Doña Leonor.* When is he not lingering
> somewhere along this street?
> But do not speak with him outside.
> If you meet, go to the inn instead.
>
> *Sirena.* Madam, you are very daring.

It is at this point that Don Lope enters with his aside about honor. Since there has been no indication of infidelity, Lope has no grounds for suspecting Leonor. We must assume that his having noticed Luis "lingering / somewhere along this street" must also make for a certain foreboding in him. He cannot yet surface what he feels; he can only display an uneasiness which he calls melancholy, and which Manrique helps him to focus by bringing up the imminent departure of the king for the war in Africa. His duty to Leonor will not let him join other gentlemen in the court going off to battle. One duty conflicts with another; the interests of Mars and Eros cannot be reconciled. He dreams of military glory, of panegyrics celebrating his name. Manrique's own disavowal of glory ("possibly I'll go . . . but surely / not to kill my fellow man / and vainly break the law of God") is received without comment. Yet it is clear that Lope's annoyance with himself and others, his sense of an approaching impasse, is increasing. This shows in his testy reply to Leonor's warm greeting, when he accuses her of "flattery and fine phrases":

> Spoken like the very lady
> of Castile you are! Do
> put aside the flattery

and fine phrases. Note that
we Portuguese prefer
the feeling to its explanation,
for the lover by his very words
devalues all he feels.
If your love is blind, my love
must be mute.

The speech now frames his real prejudicial quandary:
his inner conflict with regard to love, the Castilian manner
as against the Portuguese, the duplicity of words and feeling. Next, he turns morosely on Manrique, who before
leaving has helped Lope give voice to his unhappiness.
Having now reached the kindling point, Lope's anxiety
brings on a highflown speech about "heritage and duty"
crying out "shrilly to my conscience / to awake from this
slothful peace / and this forgetfulness / where my propri-
etary / laurels lie in dusty sleep." The speech concludes
with an appeal to Leonor to release him so that he may
join the king.

I wish, of course,
to join the King, yet since
I am but newly wed, I cannot
offer him my services
until, my dear Leonor,
your own lips grant me leave.
I now must seek that favor of you,
in granting which you honor me
and place me in your debt.

It seems clear that he wants to escape the demands of
love, with its impasse-making threat to his honor, by taking up again the more familiar role of soldier. But when
Leonor astutely tells him the decision must be his own, he
is surprised, though he covers his surprise by praising her
courage. Then, when Juan, his closest friend, is asked for
an opinion and simply reaffirms the king's and Lope's own
prescription of being dutiful to his wife first of all, Lope's
frustration gives way to jealousy. He is hurled full force

into the impasse he has been avoiding. The long soliloquy which follows describes his predicament, surfaces his sense of split allegiance, and turns him into an advocate of vengeance. Frustrated by the king's official word releasing him from war's duty in order to confront love's duty, and now unable to fulfill the demands of Eros, he discovers a new master in honor, the requirements of his superego, which he is temperamentally capable of following. In the name of honor he can now proceed to wage a private war against Eros and the suspected advocates of passion-in-love, Leonor and Luis.

But, as it turns out, this warfare on the grounds of honor is fraught with difficulties, illusions, and deceptions, the least of which inflicts shattering blows to Lope's self esteem. The path ahead requires the submergence of his personality, frequent yielding to humiliations, intolerable prolongations of a forebearance he can hardly stomach, and a frozen-faced calm. Lope becomes an underground man, the creature of a superrational machine, the machine of honor. In such a campaign he must seem to be someone he is not, proceeding "with silence, / skill and cunning, forewarned, / and on my guard, solicitous, / even obsequious." He must seem to be all things to all men: to Manrique, a blind and hounded man; to Leonor, a prudent and abashed husband who "so enjoys the sense / of being disabused / that he's turned it into love"; to Don Juan, a pitifully proud but courageous friend; to Sirena, a master full of despair; to Don Luis, a chillingly arrogant, but easily deceived, rival. Yet while he passes muster before them in a variety of roles, he is still all the time manoeuvering "in sufferance, / silence, and dissimulation" with the fixed resolve of vengeance, as though awaiting some inflexible command from high headquarters to tell him when "the moment's ripe." Until that moment he can only confide his terrors and misgivings, his doubts and confusions, to the inner court of his conscience.

In this light each of his lengthy soliloquies is dramatically necessary: they fully document the inner struggle which the honor quandary provokes. He is the besieged man on trial before an invisible jury in honor's court; but he is also prosecutor and defense attorney as well, gathering and mulling over the reports of silent witnesses — Don Juan, Leonor, and the rest. Each of the soliloquies presents a dialectical interplay of the oppositions underlying the honor problem, beset with legalistic ambiguities. In this bleak, portentous court Lope is far from being a confident executioner of honor's cause. While he sees himself as a man insulted by his wife's infidelity he is seen by us as a self-insulted, retentive man, stewing in his own choleric outrage. "Ever loath to mewl complaint," he would punish his own tongue for admitting jealousy, and yet "must wheedle . . . like a snake." Only once does he openly hint at the towering proportions of the rage he is suppressing, the split person he has become. This is when he answers, in Act Three, Juan's fictitious parable about "an injured man" and the duties of a friend who tells such a man that his honor has been lost. His infuriated reply reveals the extent of his extreme isolation as a victim:

> why, I say it
> again: as God is my witness,
> if I so much as dared tell myself
> such a thing, I'd kill myself at once,
> I who am myself my oldest friend.

His nightmare, both self-imposed and imposed upon him by the honor code, breeds an intolerable schizophrenia. Compelled by duty, he is still unable to act freely without some clearly accepted surrogate. In flight from passion and the act of love, he must enroll himself in the cause of honor. Honor, then, becomes his surrogate. Yet the subtleties of his case, burdening him with a guilt he cannot name (although others imply it is the guilt of unreciprocated love), carry him beyond the usually straightforward cause-and-effect directive of honor's laws. Honor becomes a tangled emblem of "the world's insane legalities," victimizing him in his deluded conscience. There he can recognize its potential destructiveness.

> Honor, are there further subtleties
> to learn, still unpropounded?
> more torments and more burdens,
> more sorrows and suspicions,
> more fears to hound me with,
> more insults to drown me in,
> more jealousies to confront me with?
> There cannot be, and unless
> you've greater means at your disposal
> to destroy me . . .

One must be careful to turn its eruptible force outward, away from oneself. "I must dissimulate / or else be thought the victim / of the very fear I scorn." Still, wherever one turns one is never far from the possibility of being entrapped by honor.

> Honor outmanoeuvers me:
> doubt deployed by doubt; this way
> madness lies: compelled to speak
> about my own condition
> as though it were another's.

It is not until the middle of Act Three, when the king (a former surrogate of whom he has been deprived) questions Lope's urgency to escape to the wars — certainly understood by now as an act of despair — that Lope can measure out his full cry against the laws of honor.

> Honor, you are greatly in my debt.
> Come closer, listen to me.
> Why do you complain of me?
> Tell me how I have offended you?
> To that courage I inherited
> have I not brought full measure
> of my own, and by it lived my life

and scorned the greatest dangers?
Honor, since I would not subject you
to the slightest risk or fault,
when have I not been courteous
to the humble, friendly
to the gentleman, generous
to the poor, fellow comrade
to my soldiers? And as a husband
now, alas, how have I failed,
and of what am I to blame?
Was not the wife I chose
of noble blood and ancient stock?
Do I not love my wife?
Do I not respect her?
If I have been at fault
in none of these, and if
my conduct has not given rise
to viciousness of any sort,
whether out of ignorance
or malice, why am I exposed
to insult? Why? By what tribunal
must the innocent be so condemned?
Can there be punishment
without a crime, a trial
without an accusation read?
and penalty where there is no guilt?
Oh, the world's insane legalities!
That a man who has ever labored
in the cause of honor cannot know
if he has been insulted!
When the evil consequences
of another's actions
are visited upon me,
then never has the world misprized
virtue more. Again, I ask:
why is goodness less esteemed
than misdemeanor, in whose hands
its proud fortress is surrendered
so supinely, and merely
in response to the blandishments

of appetite? Who put honor
in a glass so fragile,
then, totally inept in physic,
made such crude experiments in
that retort? But let me now be brief.
An injured man will hurl
cries endlessly against
blind custom's cudgelings.
I cannot lessen them a whit,
and this is all men's fate.

Honor, the prerogative of the gentleman, the heroic ideal in society, prescribes a rational framework, a set of laws dependent on the agent's own discretion and interpretation of them. It is the law of the superego devised to punish, extralegally, crimes against one's status and self-respect, essentially crimes of impulse and passion. But as Lope exhaustively discovers, there is really no rational means by which an injury can be assessed. As doubt meets doubt, so passion must meet passion. The machine of the honor code, then, becomes a huge, frustrating, self-contradictory extension of the private conscience. If Leonor is guilty by intention, then by such intention she eventually will succumb to Luis's seductive designs upon her. And so it happens. Luis is on the point of accomplishing them when he is drowned by Lope.

The passion of love like the passion of jealousy is a madness; one cancels out the other. Leonor was once in love with Luis, before she knew of Lope; she was never in love with Lope. When Luis returned, she resisted his advances. But then, having successfully, as she imagined, put to rest her husband's possible suspicions, her interest in Luis was rekindled, and having no real or imaginary surrogate, as Lope did, to appeal to, she had no way of avoiding Luis's persistent offer of love. In this state she was not a person but an abandoned trophy on the male-dominated battlefield of honor, the condition of many Calderonian heroines. So there is no triumph of satisfaction in her final situation — only the sense of having been perversely used, as a simulacrum, a pawn of killed passion, who can only react perversely herself.

> Thus when I was loved by
> Don Luis, I felt that I
> disliked him; when that love
> was guiltless, I seemed to fear it.
> And now (what utter madness!),
> I neither love my being loved
> nor fear my guiltiness.
> I began to love when I felt
> I'd been deserted and offended.
> Now my love is guilty,
> I become more daring.
> And while Don Lope himself
> goes off on my behalf today
> to join the King, I've written
> Don Luis to visit me,
> and give my love away at last,
> for it belongs to him.

If the play's underworld of honor is the refuge which Lope, partly assisted by the example of his dishonored friend Don Juan, comes to inhabit in order to engineer his vengeance, then the normal world by contrast is limited to the zany, undebatable realism of the servants, Manrique and Sirena, and to the briefly enchanted twilight vision of the departing, soon-to-be-defeated King Sebastian. Yet both these foreshortened spheres, following Calderón's allegorical treatment of the honor theme, serve mainly to reflect, define, and offer variations upon that theme. Manrique's speeches and flirtation with Sirena are explicit renderings of the hidden duplicities in Don Lope's underworld — a sort of boastful, satirical fabling on the sick psychology of love, the abortions of romantic springtime, the myths of the re-arisen phoenix, the incompletely resurrected Orpheus and Eurydice, the "house afire like another Troy." These mythological and symbolic allusions re-echo the theme of duty against passion throughout the play. And at the end, even the king's brief lyrical invocation of the hushed evening scene, coming just before Lope kills his wife and sets his house afire, rings with the sounds and fluctuates with the images of duplicity, a false paradise, a crepuscular landscape and seascape between truth and deception. By this time we have learned to appreciate the grave auguries of elemental symbols, the treacherous impositions seductive appearance makes upon harsh reality.

> . . . the waters seemed so sweetly
> beguiling that the sky itself,
> a blue Narcissus self-entranced,
> lingered fondly, silently above.
>
> .   .   .
>
> All those country houses
> among the trees are so enchanting
> they would rouse nymphs out of the sea,
> who seem indeed to be approaching
> now, obedient, in breathless
> quietude. And meanwhile, we appear
> to gaze upon a wandering forest
> on a moving hill, for as we view
> them from the sea, they stir
> as if to wave farewell.
> Farewell, my sweet beloved land.
> I shall return, if my cause is just . . .

Critics have seen in King Sebastian's speech the voice of pride going before an historic fall, since, as any contemporary Spaniard would have known, Portugal's mission in Africa was doomed to end in disaster. So when Lope hypocritically describes the death of his wife and adds,

> This one consolation's left me:
> I may freely serve you now,
> my duties at home all ended.
> I shall go with you to battle,
> and there may end my life,
> if indeed misfortune ever ends.

the same critics see the implication of a punishment to come after the play, not only for Lope's ruthless murder but also for the king's overconfidence and his approval of Lope's action. Perhaps such implications are present, but they are not therefore meant as a dramatic substitute for retribution. The terms of the formula, "secret vengeance for secret insult," so minutely developed through the action of the play and so firmly resolved at the end, would indicate that what is called for is an emphasis upon the triumph of personal strategy in Lope's vindication of honor, not retribution in any particular sense. And this is what is offered in Lope's self-congratulatory speech which begins,

> It well becomes a man
> to silence insult, and even
> seem to bury his revenge.
> This way he comes eventually
> to requite his wrongs, who
> waits and suffers patiently.
> Honor, we have pursued
> our course assiduously,
> and now silently repay
> dissimulated insult
> with dissimulated vengeance.

Lope's momentary exaltation is that of a skillful mechanic who has made a big stalled machine suddenly work.

> How well I grasped the chance
> occasion offered when
> I cut away the mooring
> and took the oars in hand
> to push us farther off
> while pretending I meant
> to draw us back to shore.
> How well my plan succeeded,
> for I killed the man (as this
> dagger is my witness) intent
> on my dishonor and disgrace,
> and hurled him, a glassy monument,

upon his raging tomb.
How well I managed when I
crashed the boat against the shore,
for now the act lends credence
to my tale and so dissuades
suspicions of complicity.

As he goes on to say, he has acted strictly "in conformance with the law of honor," whose champion he has been, despite all the anguish of his misgivings. He is the model of the dutiful man who has pushed himself through a subterranean world of unimaginable self-loss to emerge into the wan daylight clutching the trophy of honor, his restored self-respect, tightly between his teeth, as it were. No wonder he is given this brief moment of exultation and then another one to nail down the point of it all, when he tells his friendly interpreter and negative example, Juan,

And you, my valiant friend,
Don Juan, tell him who seeks
advice of you, how a man
must be avenged and not permit
a living soul to know of it;
for vengeance now no more reveals
what the offense no more conceals.

These are Lope's final words — his last possible words.

In some way Don Lope's last speech reminds one of the end of Don Quixote: the sad demise of a man who has been true to an ideal which instead of exalting destroys him when it is practiced wholeheartedly in the real world. But where Don Quixote returns to sanity, chastened and aware, Don Lope can only reiterate that he was a dutiful man, having served the cause of honor, tyrannical though it was, instead of war or love — or the pleasures of his own imagination, as Don Quixote did. For the sheer magnitude of Lope's hurt is undiminished by any vengeance, no matter how secret, that he has been capable of. He is literally a wreck, his humanity has been totally destroyed.

The impressive thing about all this is that, as in *Othello* or *Hamlet*, we are allowed to see the situation almost exclusively through the hero's eyes — a typically solipsistic view. And so, if we read *Secret Vengeance* as the case of a man haunted by a deep, personal inadequacy which is intimately tied to the cause of honor, as well as a cautionary study in solipsism, we are in line with Calderón's intentions, as far as these can be determined by a close reading of the play. For what the dramatist keeps hammering at from beginning to end, in the strongest symbolic patterns, is the cosmic decline of honor through the example of a singularly scrupulous military man, forced to become its creature and finally its victim. What clearer proof is needed than the moral drawn at the end: that in order to satisfy honor to the letter, the spirit of man is killed?

5 A Strange Mercy Play:

Devotion to the Cross

In *Secret Vengeance*, where honor's agent is the king and its instrument is Don Lope, "membered to the body" of the state, the action is largely internalized through Lope's soliloquies. The legalistic development of the theme proceeds appropriately in secret, through definition of his state of mind, implemented by his conscientious strategy. Symbolic counterparts to this action appear in the critically realistic speeches of his servant Manrique, through the recurrence of elemental symbolism throughout the play, and through the various inset actions and witnessings which other characters introduce. Dramatically we are aware of a constant balancing and symmetry of processes; the play's highly schematized structure, based on the allegorical treatment of theme, makes for sharp but discrete doubling effects, like sounds counterposed to echoes and images counterposed to mirrored reflections.

No such thing occurs in *La devoción de la cruz*, 1633 (Devotion to the Cross). For here is a play in which the honor theme is eclipsed by an incest situation and transcended by an act of supernatural mercy. What seems more prominent is a blurring of dramatic action, an impression of structural imbalance, together with a thematic resolution which shocks belief. One reason for this difference between the plays is that the action of thought in *Devotion* is largely externalized; there is no nice thematic complementariness set up between auxiliary characters and the principal agents. And since the allegory is revealed in what the main characters do, the course of action must be viewed more generally; it must be taken as a continuous analogue to an archetypal situation of man's fall and redemption.

Although the play is structurally ragged and esthetically less satisfying than *Secret Vengeance,* it is more moving. As with *Hamlet* or *Doctor Faustus,* the dramaturgic failure is somehow overcome by the play's resonant tone of outrage and by the depths of implication at its center. The gross melodrama enforces a pathetic and strategically delayed action of self-realization, and this is achieved by a flouting of the very credibility which the play insists upon in order to make its point.

For us the play is problematic; for Calderón's contemporaries it was perhaps mainly a religious thriller, a lesson in heavenly clemency steeped in blood and spiced with incest. Our problem is not how to swallow the melodrama with its religious message in one gulp, which is what troubled nineteenth-century critics of the play. For us as for Albert Camus, who adapted *Devotion to the Cross* in French, neither the dramatic tenor nor the morality is necessarily anachronistic:

Grace transfiguring the worst of criminals, goodness weakened by excessive evil are for us, believers and nonbelievers alike, familiar themes. But it was three centuries before Bernanos that Calderón in his *Devotion* provocatively illustrated the statement that "Grace is everything," which still tempts the modern conscience in answer to the nonbeliever's "Nothing is just."[1]

To go further: the larger problem of belief depends upon how we understand the implications of honor and incest in the play. What, we may ask, has honor to do with incest and, if a real connection exists, does this account for the resonances we feel in the play as well as the shock of poetic justice underlying the thaumaturgic actions at the end? Unless we frame the problem in some such way we must stop with a literal reading of the play, and a literal reading leads into a tangle of absurdities.

Lisardo has challenged his friend Eusebio to a duel for daring to court Julia, Lisardo's sister, without asking permission of Curcio, their father. Eusebio, as Lisardo tells him, would not qualify as her suitor anyway since he is presumably not of noble blood. So Lisardo must now redress the blight on the family honor incurred by Eusebio's rash suit, and Julia must be made to end her days in a convent. Eusebio tells Lisardo the story of his strange birth at the foot of a cross and the charmed life he has led; then, vowing to have Julia at any price, he mortally wounds Lisardo. But, in answer to Lisardo's plea to be shriven, Eusebio carries him off to a monastery. Following this, Eusebio enters Curcio's house secretly, speaks with Julia, hides when her father appears and, after the body of Lisardo is brought in and Curcio leaves, Eusebio emerges and carries on an impassioned dialogue with her over the corpse. He finally leaves at Julia's bidding, promising never to see her again.

In Act Two Eusebio is a refugee from justice and the leader of a band of highwaymen, notorious for their crimes in the mountain passes and nearby villages. Eusebio spares the life of a traveling priest, Alberto, and exacts a promise from him to be shriven before dying. Next, he breaks into Julia's convent, where he is about to rape her when he discovers that she bears the same sign of the cross on her breast which he bears on his. Now he will have nothing to do with her, and escapes. She leaves the convent to search for him, although he does not know this. Meanwhile Curcio, who has been officially directed to capture Eusebio dead or alive, leads a group of peasants and soldiers through the mountain. There he reveals the story, partly hinted at in the first act, of his mistrust and jealousy of his wife Rosmira. We learn of the ruse by which he brought her to the mountains when she was pregnant and of his attempt to kill her there. We also learn that he left Rosmira for dead at the foot of the cross where she gave birth to twins. On returning home he found her, miraculously transported there with the infant Julia, the other child having been lost.

In Act Three Julia, disguised as a man, is captured and brought before Eusebio. Left alone with him, she first attempts to kill him, then is persuaded to tell her story, which turns out to be a fantastic tale of the multiple murders she has committed since leaving the convent. She is interrupted by the report of Curcio's arrival. When Eusebio and Curcio meet they are almost immobilized by a feeling of mutual sympathy. They fight briefly without swords and are interrupted by Curcio's men who chase Eusebio, then slash at him until he topples from the cliff and falls dying at the foot of the cross — the same one where he was born. Followed there by Curcio, he is at last acknowledged as a long-lost son, Julia's twin, and dies. Meanwhile the return of Alberto the priest causes the dead Eusebio to come back to life and call out the name of Alberto. The priest confesses him and Eusebio gives up the ghost a second time in a scene witnessed by Curcio and his group and by the disguised Julia and the highwaymen. Revealing herself now, Julia publicly confesses her crimes, but as her father advances to strike her she throws herself at the giant cross, which ascends heavenward, bearing her away with the dead Eusebio.

Many readers have been annoyed with the play's hypocrisy, its crude religious propaganda, and its perverse morality which pardons the apparently devout but unsympathetic criminal. But if one recalls the allegorical patterns observed in *Secret Vengeance*, it may become apparent that there is a general as well as particular way of making sense out of *Devotion to the Cross*, despite its odd morality.

Through Eusebio, its chief character, *Devotion* represents the figurative fall and redemption of mankind. As a figure for the fallen Adam, Eusebio is redeemed by the cross ("tree divine"), which bears him heavenward, and thus fulfills his "secret cause" — a prefiguration, as Adam in the Bible prefigures Christ. At infancy he is abandoned (assumed to be "lost") at the foot of the cross where, we learn later, his mother fell under the hand of his jealous father. Having no identity, Eusebio takes the cross as a totemic object which corresponds to the talisman etched on his breast like a birthmark. This makes him a candidate for salvation, as it does Julia his twin, who is similarly marked. As Eve may be said to have been Adam's twin, and as both were victims of the tree of the knowledge of good and evil, so Eusebio and Julia share a common destiny, part of which is to be restored through grace by the cross, the tree of eternal life. The implication of incest, which underlies the act of original sin in Genesis, is here metaphysically, if not sacramentally, material to Calderón's allegory. The reason for this is that Eusebio must learn who he is, which he can do only by discovering and rejoining Julia, his other half. But to do so he must relive symbolically the primal scene in the garden, whose analogue in the play is the convent where Julia, as "the bride of Christ," is immured.

Another analogue suggested here is that of the body and the soul, the twin or complementary entities. The soul (Eusebio) seeks to be restored to the body (Julia) from which it has been separated. When Eusebio finds Julia in the convent and is about to re-enact the primal deed, he dimly senses in her talismanic sign some heavenly purpose linking her to his secret cause. This foreboding makes him reject her, much as a figure of the new Adam, forewarned of his cause, would reject the old sexual crime — incest, original sin. Yet he must suffer Adam's fall literally as well as symbolically; and this occurs when Eusebio falls from the ladder by the convent wall. In her turn Julia, the rejected body and spouse, is separated by means of the same wall and ladder from re-entering the garden-convent. In ignorance of her destiny, she follows

Eusebio and tries to destroy him. The crimes she commits on the way are, like Eusebio's earlier crimes, committed in blind outrage at having been separated from her other half.

In the worldly terms represented by the shepherds, Eusebio's and Julia's cause is criminally absurd. But since at the play's end, worldly discretion and justice are both foiled by the twins' heavenly ascension, it seems clear that it is the spiritual significance of the action, symbolically represented, which interested Calderón.

A Christian hero, Eusebio, like the heroes of all myths, is at the start unaware of his origin, though supremely conscious of some unrevealed fate he has been designated to fulfill. While still ignorant of when and how his fate will be revealed, and because he cannot know if his duel with Lisardo will end disastrously, he tells the story of his life, ticking off each miraculous episode as if to indicate his triumphs over mere earthbound, mortal forces. To Lisardo's grim reminder of Eusebio's inferior blood, Eusebio retorts, "Inherited nobility / is not superior to / nobility that's been acquired." He can say this because he knows he has a patent to act in ways that transcend a nobleman's prerogatives; his "escutcheon" is "inherited from this Cross." He has been tested and has triumphed before; he will triumph again: in the wilderness of the mountain, in the garden-convent, and finally — to his eternal reward when he dies — at the foot of the same cross where he was born. To that cross he is to speak later as Adam might have spoken to God, remembering the paradise tree: "Forgive me the injury / of that first crime against you." And again like Adam with foreknowledge of his sin, he will say, "I do not blame / my father for denying me / a cradle. He must have sensed / the evil that was in me." Eusebio's invocation to the cross at the end is shot through with transfigured consciousness:

> Oh Tree, where Heaven chose to hang
> the one true fruit to ransom man

for his first forbidden mouthful!
Oh flower of paradise regained!
Rainbow light that spanned the Flood
 and thus pledged peace to all mankind!
Oh fruitful vine, the harp of yet
another David, and the tablets
of another Moses:
Here I am, a sinner seeking grace.

Eusebio has been transformed from the human agent of his crimes into a symbolic force voicing the redemptive hope of all mankind. In this way he defeats the exactions of earthly penalties, and incidentally overcomes the harsh, tyrannical laws of honor represented by Curcio, the father who survives his wife and all his children.

Yes, but what about the honor theme which is so abruptly transcended at the end of the play by divine law? The question of honor not only bulks large throughout the play but is also curiously altered in the light of Eusebio's cause. Further inquiry tells us something about the unconscious motivations supporting the honor code as shown in the implicit incest-relationship lividly darting forth from the root situation of the play. For as they affect human motives, the impulsions and repulsions of the characters, the conventions of honor relate to certain basic though unspecified taboos concerning the sexual assault of male upon female in the same family. But we must begin with the first recorded sexual relationship, in Genesis, and then go on to the society represented in Calderonian drama.

In effect the Genesis story demonstrates an archetypal incest situation inherent in man's disobedience, his fall from God's grace, and his knowledge of good and evil. Taken as a paradigm for man's earthly condition, the sexual crime called original sin derives from a transgression against divine command, a transgression that brings with it the knowledge of guilt. Presumably instigated by Eve, man rebels against a paternal authority, Jehovah, who punishes her accordingly: "I will greatly multiply thy sorrow and thy conception; in sorrow thou shalt bring forth children; and thy desire shall be to thy husband, and he shall rule over thee." Later in Genesis (5:2), one finds, "Male and female created he them; and blessed them, and called their name Adam, in the day when they were created." The creation of man and woman out of one body, the division of interests indicated between male and female, the transgression against authority, the sorrow of sex and childbearing, and the dominance of Adam over Eve are set down as almost simultaneous events and become an archetypal situation.[2]

It is assumed, then, that Eve's transgression is congenital and innate: as woman, she will always rebel against the authoritarian principles. Eve, "the mother of all living," will be a divisive force in fallen society, just as she was in paradise. One way to counteract her innate rebelliousness is to idealize her, as the Middle Ages did: first, symbolically, by elevating the Virgin Mary as an object of worship; secondly, by lodging the image of woman as a venerated but scarcely attainable object in the tradition of courtly love. Another way is to bind her, as the prize and victim of transgression to a code of honor — a role descending from the courtly tradition and modified by the needs of an authoritarian society, typical of seventeenth-century Spain.

The peculiarly tight, claustrophobic condition of the honor code appears to derive from an already tense, anxiety-ridden view, featured in myth and religion, of woman's unreconciled position between transgressor and idol. In addition, this view is overlaid by the historical and social exigencies of an imperial Spain warring against Protestantism as it had for centuries warred against Islam. In this struggle the impossible myth of Spanish Christian purity and pure-blooded descent would have to be sustained against the millennial evidence of intermarriage with Berbers, Moslems, and Jews, not to mention cultural assimilation with other peoples of Western and Mediterranean Europe, going back to the Phoenicians. The avowal that one is an "old Christian Catholic," repeated so often in Renaissance Spanish literature, becomes a self-defensive cry; vainglorious and perversely aggressive, it reminds one of Nazi Germany's self-conscious Aryanism. Thus, where the invasion of one's honor is sexually directed, an attack on one's personal pure-bloodedness, with social and religious implications, is also immediately assumed.

In the autocratic society of Calderón's plays, every family seems to be a miniature Spain seeking to preserve itself against the real or imagined, but always chronic, invasions of lawless forces from the outside. That the laws of honor are inhuman and tyrannical — a protest constantly being voiced by Calderón's heroes — does not prevent their being fulfilled. And as they are being fulfilled, often in strictest secrecy, we are struck by the incredible, tragic strength of will involved in acting upon an impossible ideal according to an impossible sense of justice.

The fear of incest and the fear of sexual assault become one and the same thing; particularly notable in *Devotion to the Cross*, the same fear is evident in most of Calderón's honor plays. In addition, the incest barrier is complemented by the religious barrier between different faiths as well as by the social barrier between classes, and behind such barriers lurks the constant fear of contamination. Life under these circumstances is seen as warfare, catastrophe, and fatality, in which the vaguest hint of misdemeanor is as culpable as any number of overt murders. Where authoritarian justice rules, whether theocratic or monarchic, to think or to be tempted as a human being (the hero in *Secret Vengeance* exclaims, "How is it one thinks or speaks at all?") is as dangerous as to put one's thoughts and temptations into action. What makes the honor code so strange to us is that it is a reduction (often to absurdity) of an imperialistic legal structure, from its embodiment in ecclesiastical and state authority to an individual psychological problem, without any mitigation of

its impersonal emphasis. What would justify legal punishment by state or church — the impersonal need to preserve the community against assaults by criminal or heretic
— becomes bizarre when voiced as a rationale by human
beings following the letter of the honor code. They act as
though they had set some gigantic, superhuman machine
in motion, which is just what they have done. What makes
for further bizarreness is the unconscious irony with which
they speak in rationalizing their human pride as the cause
of justice while being ignorant that they themselves are
part of the machine and that their voice is actually the
voice of the machine. The pride they boast of concerns the
acts and strategies of will — their skill, their cunning;
what they do not know is that such pride is simply the fuel
that makes the honor machine run. Human pride, then,
frequently becomes a sign not of personal satisfaction but
of the impersonal glorification of the legal structure; and
the act which the human agents engineer in its name becomes a personal *auto da fé*, a self-punishing sacrifice in
the name of a superpersonal faith.

That this makes for dramatic irony in Calderón's plays
may be seen in the various views, ranging from satiric to
sacramental, with which the central character's situation
is regarded by other characters as well as the opposing
views he has of it himself. The dramatic irony is further
evident in the rapid glimpse we get of the hero's fate at the
end of the play, where he appears at best a Pyrrhic victor,
exhausted, wrung out by the machine, and hardly distin-
guishable from his victim. Dramatic irony is highly schematized in Calderonian drama, being part of, if not indeed
the instrument for creating, a larger moral irony. It is
interesting to see how the ironic form shapes the honor-
bound figure of Curcio in *Devotion*.

An aspect of the moral irony made explicit here is that
the avenger complains against the tyrannical laws of
honor, though they are the only laws he can follow in
exacting his revenge. But an even more pronounced irony

is that the object of Curcio's revenge, Eusebio, is redeemed at the end by a higher law than that of honor, so that the matter is literally taken out of Curcio's hands. Since the action of the play is allegorical, we can no more read this final turn of events realistically than we can any other part of the play. The literal meaning is apparent: Curcio is not avenged, and in not being avenged, the course of honor which he has pursued throughout is defeated. How then are we to take his defeat and, by clear analogy, since he is its implement, the defeat of honor? The obvious answer is that honor has been superseded by a miracle; the intervention of divine powers indicates that Eusebio is not to be punished, but having entered into a state of grace is, on the contrary, given his heavenly reward along with Julia. Curcio's last speech — his final remarks to the audience are simply conventional and do not count — is clearly a revenger's furious threat addressed to Julia, an intended victim: "I shall kill you with my own two hands, / and have you die as violently / as you have lived." She pleads to the cross, and as Curcio "is about to strike her," she embraces it and so is lifted heavenward with Eusebio. Curcio could not have been more plainly foiled, and to say that his vengence, including his authority for seeking it, has been superseded by divine intervention, does not seem a full or satisfactory answer. Apparently Curcio was mistaken — just as badly mistaken here, when about to kill his daughter, as he was earlier when striking at his innocent wife, who was similarly rescued by the cross. The deeper moral irony, then, is that the laws of honor, so assiduously upheld by Curcio, are indeed defeated and their justification, as enacted by their avenger here, is shown to be reprehensible on the highest possible authority.

Is honor here defeated or merely superseded? To seek a fuller answer to the question, one must rephrase it to accord with Curcio's allegorical role in the play. In what way is Curcio, the surrogate of honor and an omnipotent figure in the community, responsible for the fate which his family suffers? First, and most generally, it is evident that by accusing his wife of infidelity and seeking to kill her on admittedly groundless evidence, Curcio touches off a series of actions which ends with the death of his three children and his wife. Secondly, it is made clear that Curcio is temperamentally handicapped: he is prodigal, rash, desperate, and overweeningly proud. Some of these attributes are inherited and reinforced to his own detriment by his children, in a way suggestive of King Lear. Lisardo's brief appearance before Eusebio kills him seems at least partly intended to characterize his father.

> My father
> was a profligate who rapidly
> consumed the great estate
> his family had left him.
> In so doing, he was heedless
> of the straitened circumstances
> to which his children were reduced.
> And yet, although necessity
> may beggar one's nobility,
> it does not lessen in the least
> the obligations one is born with.

Following his inherited obligation, Lisardo must challenge Eusebio for lacking the noble qualifications to court his sister Julia. Lisardo's pronouncement concerning his sister, considering it is addressed to her lover who is also his friend, seems precipitous and mechanical, as though echoing a catechism learnt from his father.

> An impoverished gentleman
> who finds his fortune does not meet
> the requirements of his rank
> must see to it his maiden daughter,
> rather than pollute his blood
> by marriage, is taken off
> in safety to a convent.
> In all this, poverty's the culprit.

> Accordingly, tomorrow, my sister
> Julia will quickly take the veil,
> whether she wishes to or not.

Julia's subsequent report confirms the fact of her brother's anxious nature. Lisardo's face pales, drained by suspicion; he prevaricates — "snatched the key / impulsively, and angrily / unlocked the drawer," to discover the evidence of Eusebio's courtship; then,

> without a single word, oh God!
> he rushed out to find my father.
> Then inside his room behind locked doors,
> the two of them spoke loud and long —
> to seal my fate . . .

Lisardo is hardly distinguished from his father, whose purpose he is serving, before he is killed. Later, when Julia questions Curcio's decision to put her into a convent, his voice seems simply a magnification of Lisardo's catechism.

> Right or wrong, my will
> is all you need to know.
>   . . .
> My decision will suffice, and that
> has been resolved. The matter's closed.
>   . . .
> Rebel, hold your tongue! Are you mad?
> I'll twist your braids around your neck,
> or else I'll rip that tongue of yours
> out of your mouth with my own hands
> before it cuts me to the quick again.

Curcio immediately identifies Julia's rebellion with her dead mother's, now impulsively finding "proof" where later he admits no evidence existed.

> So at last I have the proof
> of what I long suspected :

that your mother was dishonorable,
a woman who deceived me.
So you attack your father's honor,
whose luster, birth, nobility,
the sun itself can never equal
with all its radiance and light.

It is henceforth apparent that Curcio, hiding his defects behind the shield of honor, is steering a course which must victimize Julia as surely as he has victimized his elder son Lisardo and his wife Rosmira. Although victimized as well, Eusebio listens to a higher law in his worship of the cross. It would be possible to show similarly that Curcio's defects of despair, pride, and simple-minded credulity also influence the course of events. And though the exemplification of such personal defects would suffice to support the action in realistic terms, this is not what we get in *Devotion to the Cross*. What we get is allegorical action, action by analogy, by symbolic counterpart. By such action Curcio is predominantly a type of vengeful Yahweh, the thunder god in Genesis, the creator and punisher of the incestuous pair who exceeded the commandment and attained to a knowledge of good and evil — as in their separate ways Eusebio and Julia do. In the Bible the vengeful God is superseded by a sacrificed human God, who comes as Christ and redeems the Adamic sin. The code of honor, one might say, is similarly transcended in *Devotion*. It is transcended and defeated as a partial truth, but without being destroyed or removed — as the Old Testament is superseded by the New.

The attraction and repulsion which lead Eusebio toward and away from Julia, and which induce her to act in complementary movements, have been discussed in terms of the Adam and Eve analogy and the body-soul analogy. Similarly, a movement from repulsion to attraction is evident in the relationship between Curcio and Eusebio, and the effect is concentrated wholly in Act Three. Two of Curcio's speeches summarize this shift:

> his chilling blood cries out
> to me so timidly. And if
> his blood were not my own in part,
> it would not beckon me,
> nor would I hear it cry.
> How I hated him
> alive; now how I grieve his death!

As soon as father and son confront one another, there is mutual affinity between them, though they do not know they are related. It is so intense a thing that Eusebio refuses to use his sword to fight Curcio. When they struggle barehanded, the sense of their combat is dreamlike — a scene reminiscent of the more famous father-son contention in *Life Is a Dream.* Unwilling to surrender to the law, Eusebio will nevertheless give himself up to Curcio, out of "respect." And Curcio, though he has long hunted Eusebio, suddenly offers to let him escape. He refuses, and when Curcio's men arrive, the father intervenes, suggesting to their astonishment the alternative of a legal trial: "I'll be your advocate before the law." But it is too late; the honor machine has already moved closer to its inexorable goal: Eusebio is mortally wounded by Curcio's men at the foot of the cross.

Despair leads Curcio to recognize the inefficacy of the honor machine and to admit a guilt he can no longer hide from himself. The mystery of the twin birth at the cross is a mystery which he, as the surrogate of honor and fallen pride, is not prepared to contend with. Mercy is not a principle which autocratic honor accepts. We witness Curcio's increasing helplessness, a condition which the avenging thunder god of Genesis might experience in confronting the imminent redemption of his "son," Adam, transfigured into Christ. But overwhelmed by the clemency of the cross, Curcio again astonishes his men by telling them to

> Take up this broken body
> of Eusebio's, and lay it

> mournfully aside till there is time
> to build an honorable
> sepulcher from which his ashen gaze
> may contemplate my tears.

They reply with the outraged disbelief of men who have also become cogs in the honor machine.

> *Tirso.* What? How can you think of burying
> a man in holy ground who died
> beyond the pale of Church and God?

> *Blas.* For anyone like that, a grave here
> in the wilderness is good enough!

> *Curcio.* Oh, villainous revenge!
> Are you still so outraged
> you must strike at him beyond the grave?
> [*Exit* Curcio, *weeping.*]

But there is still a last and clinching irony to account for. If Curcio admits the defeat of honor before the miracle of heavenly clemency, how can he suddenly revert to the vengeance principle at the end when he tries to destroy Julia? Curcio unwittingly instigates this turn and countermovement by recognizing the mercy principle, and this recognition on his part calls for Julia's confession.

> *Curcio.* My dearest son! You were not
> so wretched or forsaken
> after all, when in your tragic death
> you merit so much glory.
> Now if only Julia
> would recognize her crime.

> *Julia.* God help me! What is this I hear,
> what ominous revelation?
> Can it be that I who was
> Eusebio's lover
> was his sister too? Then let
> my father and the whole wide world,
> let everybody know about

my crimes. My perversions hound
and overwhelm me, but I shall be
the first to shout them out.
Let every man alive be told
that I am Julia, Julia
the criminal, and of all
the infamous women ever born,
the worst. Henceforth my penances
will be as public as the sins
I have confessed. I go now to beg
forgiveness of the world for the vile
example I have given it,
and pray that God forgive
the crime of all my life.

When Curcio erupts and attempts to kill her, she pledges to the cross to "atone beneath your sign / and be born again to a new life," and the cross bears her away to heaven. If we can swallow the melodrama here, Calderón's serious purpose will emerge. Desperate and defeated though he is, Curcio still incarnates the vengeance principle — a principle which survives in him, even after he has been chastened by the higher law. In this he is like Eusebio, who represents the mercy principle ordaining that he survive his own death and be revived solely to be shriven. Because he embodies the honor code, Curcio must strike out as he does, spontaneously, against Julia's offense and dishonor. And her offense in this instance is precisely her public confession of guilt instigated by Curcio's wishful remark. For according to the code, the public admission that one's honor has been wronged compounds the wrong already committed against it. And so Julia's public declaration not only constitutes the last blow against her father's crumbling defenses but also makes explicit the cruel inoperativeness of the honor code when faced with a human cry for clemency. Julia's assertion that she will make her penances public is intolerable to honor and inadmissible to a code which categorically denies forgiveness. By implication there is no forgiveness on earth but only in heaven.

If as an honor figure Curcio cannot extend mercy, he is likewise incapable, as a figure for the Genesis thunder god, of offering reconciliation to Julia. And in the final exchange between the two, we are also reminded that Julia's "crime of all my life" is, like Eve's "crime," unforgivable in terms of the old dispensation in Genesis, where the sexual act is incestuous and the original crime of the creation underlies the discovery of good and evil. Significantly, it is when she learns of the incestuous relationship with Eusebio that Julia makes her public declaration. As a type of Eve, Julia is the quintessential criminal ("of all / the infamous women ever born, / the worst"), universally damned by authoritarian law. Only the figure of a sacrificed god, according to the new dispensation, can redeem her, as Eusebio does at the end. We see, then, that honor is a form of the old, merciless, unregenerate, earthbound, dehumanized, patriarchal law, which is ultimately self-defeating. It prevails to the end and presumably will continue to exist on earth, opposing the merciful, regenerative, humane, and matriarchal law of heaven, symbolized in the cross which has vanquished it.

At the conclusion of the play, where the cross triumphs so resolutely, so providentially, and so patently as a *deus ex machina,* we are inclined to minimize its connection with the rest of the drama. Yet its function throughout is not only essential to the theme but also integral to the action. One might say that the final appearance of the cross culminates many symbolic manifestations, from the start, of an extraordinarily complex role. And that role, in fact, is to serve dramatically as a complementary mechanism, a machine working in countermotion to the honor machine.

We first hear of the cross early in the first act in Eusebio's lengthy recital of the events of his life, while holding off Lisardo. Eusebio's story is eager, rapt, proud, enthusiastic. He has been the subject of strange, benevolent miracles; he rapidly imparts his sense of wonder and mystery at these happenings—and is never so confident again. The effect of the speech, more notable for the feeling it releases than for its literal sense, is to introduce a sensation of power and authority into a tense situation. Then tension leading to an impasse is exemplified in the opening scene of the play by the peasants Gil and Menga, vainly trying to drag their stalled donkey out of the mud. When Lisardo and Eusebio arrive, the impasse is augured in their pale, silent, distraught appearance. Gil descirbes them:

> My, how pale
> they look, and in the open fields
> so early in the morning!
> I'm sure they must have eaten mud
> to look so constipated.

Whenever the cross is introduced subsequently, the effect is similarly to dispel an impasse, initiate a contrary action, or metaphorically to lend a new dimension to the scene. Eusebio's cross "that towered over me at birth, / and whose imprint is now pressed / upon my breast" is a talismanic object which he serves and which actively serves him, symbolic of his paternity, a charismatic "symbol of some secret cause, / unrevealed as yet." And its "secret cause" gradually begins to emerge in a series of significant actions.

Lisardo's dying plea "by the Cross Christ died on" deflects Eusebio's sword and makes him carry the fallen man away to be shriven, an action which later aids in Eusebio's own redemption. When Lisardo's corpse lies between the divided lovers, Julia and Eusebio, there is a curious dramatic effect which the theatricality of the scene emphasizes. Curcio's two living children seem here to form the horizontal appendages of a cruciform figure whose vertical stalk is the dead Lisardo. As the pair speak across the corpse we realize that it is the only time when the three children are joined together in the play. Joined but also divided by the visible presence of the dead brother. That one power of the cross is to join and another is to separate will appear significantly again.

At the beginning of Act Two, Alberto, the priest, is saved when Eusebio's bullet is stopped by the holy book the priest carries in his tunic. The metaphor Eusebio uses underlies the merciful power of the cross to deflect the course of violence: "How well that flaming shot / obeyed your text by turning / stubborn lead softer than wax!" By this token Eusebio releases the priest who will reappear only once, in the third act, to confess him. The next reference to the cross occurs in Curcio's soliloquy describing the miracle which saved his wife after she protested her innocence at the foot of the cross, where he thought he had killed her. There the twins Eusebio and Julia were born, though, as we learn later, Eusebio was left behind when Rosmira was rescued by divine intervention and brought home with Julia. Subsequently, when Eusebio forces his way into the convent to violate Julia, he discovers that she, too, bears the imprint of the cross on her breast and fearfully withdraws. Here the cross serves to prevent the incestuous act, and in so doing separates the Adamic from the Christ figure in Eusebio. Julia and Eusebio are not meant to repeat the paradisiacal crime under the Eden tree; they must now be separated from one another. They are only destined to be joined in an act of heavenly redemption at the cross where they were born.

As we observed, when Eusebio falls from the ladder leaning against the convent wall, he symbolically enacts Adam's fall. Of this fact he seems dimly aware on rising:

> Oh Cross Divine, this I promise you
> and take this solemn vow
> with strict attention to each word:
> wherever I may find you,
> I shall fall upon my knees
> and pray devoutly, with all my heart.

Julia, too, vaguely senses that her destiny is to follow Eusebio's "fall" by way of the ladder, though she is not impelled by heavenly signs nor aware, as he is, of the cross's "secret cause." At this point she may simply be following the Genesis prescription — "and thy desire shall be to thy husband, and he shall rule over thee" — when she says, "This is where he fell; then I / must fall there too and follow him." Or perhaps she is feeding her desire with a later rationalization: "Does not my creed tell me / that once I give assent in thought / I thereby commit the crime?" Yet when she continues in this vein, we see that she has clearly identified her destiny with Eusebio's, though she may not know what that destiny is.

> Did not Eusebio scale
> these convent walls for me?
> And did I not feel pleased
> to see him run such risks
> for my sake? Then why am I afraid?
> What scruple holds me back?
> If I leave now I do the very thing
> Eusebio did when he entered;
> and just as I was pleased with him,
> he'll be pleased to see me too,
> considering the risks I've taken
> for his sake. Now I have assented,
> I must take the blame. And if
> the sin itself be so tremendous,
> will enjoying it be any
> less so? Since I have assented
> and am fallen from the hand of God . . .

In modern terms the covert incest motive may be fused here with the affinity science has noted between closely related persons, particularly twins, causing similar behavior patterns because of similarities between their neuro-electrical activities. But in Christian terms it is clear that once Julia "falls" — that is, makes the choice to descend the ladder — she is seized by the chilling evil of the symbolic act:

> I find that my esteem for mankind,
> honor, and my God is nothing
> but an arid waste. Like an angel
> flung from Heaven in my demonic
> fall I feel no stirring of
> repentance.

With this admission she becomes Eve, the transgressor in Eden and cohort of the fallen angel, the eternal rebel against the patriarchal order of society. Her rebellion is an assault against man's contempt, the authoritarian abuse of her fruitful power to love and to heal the divisive prohibitions which sacrifice individual men to its order:

> I am alone in my confusion
> and perplexity. Ingrate, are these
> your promises to me? Is this
> the sum of what you called your love's mad
> passion, or is it my love's madness?
> How you persisted in your suit —
> now by threats, now by promises,
> now as lover, now as tyrant,
> till I at last submitted to you.
> But no sooner had you become
> master of your pleasure
> and my sorrow than you fled
> before you had possessed me.
> Now in escaping you have
> vanquished me entirely.
> Merciful Heaven, I am lost
> and dead! Why does nature provide
> the world with poisons when the venom
> of contempt can kill so swiftly?
> So his contempt will kill me,
> since to make the torment worse
> I must follow him who scorns me.
> When has love been so perverse before? . . .
> Such is woman's nature that
> against her inclination
> she withholds that pleasure
> which she most delights to give.

The capacity to sin is no different from the capacity to hurt and be hurt, perversely, against one's inclination. But to tell one's hurt, confess one's sin, and be forgiven are to triumph over the corruptions of evil enforced by social law. As Julia says, this forgiveness can be extended by the restorative power of providence.

> faith teaches
> there is nothing which the clemency
> of Heaven cannot touch or reach:
> all the sparkling constellations,
> all the sands of all the oceans,
> every atom, every mote upon
> the air, and all these joined together,
> are as nothing to the sins
> which the good Lord God can pardon.

Contempt, scorn, division, separation, hopelessness, despair — these are the goads to crime and destructiveness. And this is what Julia recognizes when the ladder leading back to the convent is withdrawn.

> Ah, but I begin to understand
> the depths of my misfortune.
> This is a sign my way is barred,
> and thus when I would strive
> to creep back, a penitent,
> I am shown my own cause is hopeless.
> Mercy is refused me.
> Now a woman doubly scorned,
> I shall perpetrate such
> desperate deeds even Heaven
> will be astounded, and the world
> will shudder at them till
> my perfidy outrages all time
> to come, and the deepest pits
> of hell shall stand agape
> with horror at my crimes.

Understood symbolically, according to the dialectic of fall and redemption, male and female principles, and the subversion of humanity by the authoritarian necessity of honor, Julia's intentions and subsequent crimes are not the ludicrous things they appear to be when viewed according to cause-and-effect realism. They are the dramatic epiphanies of closely interwoven lines of thought, feeling, and action rising from all that "devotion to the cross" can imply. It is only the misuse of symbolic meaning which is ludicrous. Calderón makes this clear immediately following Julia's speech, at the start of Act Three.

Gil enters "covered with crosses; a very large one is sewn on his breast." The situation is reversed: a man is now following a woman's "bidding," as Gil says with regard to Menga, adding,

> I go . . .
> scouring the mountainside for firewood,
> and for my own protection
> I've concocted this stratagem.
> They say Eusebio loves crosses.
> Well, here I am, armed from head to foot
> with them.

But Gil's cross is not charismatic. He sees Eusebio, hides in a bush and is immediately stuck with thorns. Eusebio at this point is brooding over the meaning of the cross inscribed on Julia's breast:

> I was driven by the impulse of a higher power
> whose cause prevailed against my will,
> forbidding me to trespass on
> the Cross — the Cross that I respect . . .
> Oh Julia, the two of us were born
> subject to that sign, and thus I fear
> the portents of a mystery
> which only God can understand.

Then the scene where he discovers Gill is oddly discordant, mixing serious and comic elements to such effect that Eusebio's cause appears ludicrous.

Gil [*aside*]. I can't stand it any longer;
I'm stung all over!

Eusebio.   There is
someone in the bushes. Who's there?

Gil [*aside*]. Well, here's where I get tangled
in my snare.

Eusebio [*aside*]. A man tied to a tree,
and wearing a cross on his breast!
I must be true to my word and kneel.

Gil. Why do you kneel, Eusebio?
Are you saying your prayers, or what?
First you tie me up, then you pray
to me. I don't understand.

Eusebio. Who are you?

Gil.   Gil. Don't you remember?
Ever since you tied me up here
with that message, I've been yelling out
my lungs but, just my luck,
nobody's yet come by to free me.

Eusebio. But this is not the place
I left you.

Gil.   That's true, sir.
The fact is, when I realized that
no one was passing by, I moved on,
still tied, from one tree to the next,
until I reached this spot.
And that's the only reason
why it seems strange to you.
                          [Eusebio *frees him.*]

Eusebio [*aside*]. This simpleton may be of use
to me in my misfortune.
— Gil, I took a liking to you
when we met the other time.
So now let us be friends.

> *Gil.*   Fair enough,
> and since we're friends I'll never
> go back home but follow you instead.
> And we'll be highwaymen together.
> They say the life's ideal — not a stitch
> of work from one year to the next.

Gil's mention of "the other time" refers to the occasion in Act Two when Eusebio found Gil and Menga in the mountains, tied them to tree trunks, and left them with a crucial message for Curcio — a message Gil failed to deliver. The message is about something Curcio does not yet know and through which Eusebio hopes for a reconciliation with Lisardo's father and to clear himself from the charge of murder. Eusebio does not know that Gil did not deliver the message, nor is it certain that if Gil had done so the course of events up to this point would have been altered. Gil's appearance immediately after Julia's speech at the end of Act Two, the absurd story he tells Eusebio about progressing "still tied, from one tree to the next," and Eusebio's curiously quixotic reaction to Gil's cross are all puzzling and disconcerting details. Gil's antics are as bathetic as Eusebio's devoutness is ludicrous, and both appear to be defects of taste and dramatic emphasis.

Considered symbolically, however, the scene is anything but bathetic or implausible; on the contrary, it comes as a sharp, immediate reminder of the opposing claims of honor and mercy, of vengeance and devotion, the very theme developed in the play's movements and countermovements which we have been tracing. In effect Calderón is reminding us that Eusebio's devotion is a cause squarely opposed to Curcio's vengeance, and that one has its provenance in a heavenly mystery symbolized by the cross as the other has in the code of honor. Troubled by the symbol on Julia's breast, Eusebio is caught off-guard when Gil's presence interrupts his thoughts. He does not know it is Gil; all he sees is the cross on Gil's breast, to which he automatically responds by kneeling respectfully, according to his vow. It is the symbol and not the man he responds to. The act immediately makes him out to be a fool — not the crazy fool Gil takes him for, but the "fool in Christ," the devoted servant of the cross. Gil, of course, has correctly guessed that wearing the cross will protect him from Eusebio, just as it saved Alberto, the priest, at the beginning of Act Two. What Gil does not understand is the objective power and principle of the cross; and we may see in his being entangled in the briers until Eusebio frees him an exemplum of this mistaken view. The absurd story he tells about moving, tied, from tree to tree, is an extension of his mistaken view because it supposes that Eusebio, though dangerous, is merely simpleminded. But the effect of Gil's story is to identify him and to bring Eusebio's attention away from the symbol in order to recognize the simpleton who is wearing it. Eusebio awakes to his own situation, his self-defensive strife against Curcio's pursuit of vengeance, in which Gil "may be of use" to him as one who knows the mountain passes. On the other hand, all Gil can conclude from Eusebio's offer of friendship is that the other's addiction to crosses somehow involves the charmed life of brigandage — "not a stitch / of work from one year to the next." The fact is, however, that Eusebio's situation is narrowing and, as later events show, he is ridden by anxiety and by the burden of his cause. He is fast approaching his own end, which will entail the complete revelation of heaven's secret symbolized by the cross. But while waiting for the mystery to unfold, he must contend with Curcio's vengeance. So he acts feverishly, half terrified, half audacious, as a man aware of some impending catastrophe would act.

This is notable in his response to Julia, who has reappeared dressed as a man, and who after attempting to kill him has told the story of her crimes. He says:

> I listen to you fascinated,
> enchanted by your voice,

> bewitched by everything you say,
> although the sight of you
> fills me with dread . . .
>   I fear Heaven's
> retribution looming over me . . .
> I live in such horror of that Cross,
> I must avoid you.

His anxiety is also apparent in the orders he gives his men, and later in his hand-to-hand encounter with his father.

> I do not know what reverence
> the sight of you instills in me.
> But I know your suffering awes me
> more than your sword . . .
> and truth to tell, the only
> victory I seek is to fall
> upon my knees and beg you
> to forgive me.

And so it is almost with relief that he receives the mortal wound at the hands of Curcio's men. He can at last yield to his father and die; but also — and this he does not know — he is to be resurrected in order to receive absolution at the foot of the cross where he was born. In this way his destiny is fulfilled, his secret cause revealed, his life career run full cycle. But there is also the posthumous miracle of his heavenly ascent which includes the sanction of Julia. Besides proving Julia's earlier declaration about the clemency of Heaven, this last miracle reclaims her from the perversely male-dominated role of revenger ("the symbol / of terrifying vengeance") in which the honor machine has cast her. There is perhaps a conclusive irony in this last turn: that the monolithic, all-pervasive engine of the honor machine on earth can only be transcended by the more powerful, absolutist machine of heavenly mercy.

6 Honor Humanized:

The Mayor of Zalamea

The events in *El alcalde de Zalamea*, 1640–1644 (The Mayor of Zalamea) have a historical setting. They derive from an episode in Philip II's campaign to annex the Portuguese throne left vacant in 1578 by the sudden death of King Sebastian (the monarch in *Secret Vengeance*) in a battle against the Moors in Africa. Philip's campaign succeeded, resulting in a Spanish-Portuguese union which lasted sixty years, 1580–1640. There is an earlier play of the same title, based on the same episode, and Lope de Vega was for a long time cited as its author. (Calderón's original title was significantly different: *El garrote bien dado* — The Best Garroting Ever Executed.) The pseudo-Lope play, dealing with similar characters and events, is crude and diffuse when compared with Calderón's masterful construction.[1]

Often celebrated in ballads and in other plays of the period, Don Lope de Figueroa, the field commander and *comendador* of the district was a historical personage, famous for his exploits in Flanders, Italy, Africa, the Azores, and Portugal. He commanded the *Tercio de Flandes* (the Flanders Regiment), the best-known military group of the period. It is with a company in this regiment, more especially its captain, that Calderón is concerned in the action of his play. The captain who seduces the daughter of the wealthy farmer, Pedro Crespo, and is executed by her father when Crespo becomes mayor of the town, provides the main plot interest. But equally pertinent is the concurrently developed view of the social impingements of a caste system on the lives of ordinary provincial people.

Violations of peasants' rights by the military caste and the nobility is a frequent subject of Golden Age drama, particularly in Lope's *Fuenteovejuna* and *Peribañez*. By contrast with the violent wife-murder plays, such a subject invites a more humane view of social relationships. Provincial life is less austere than life in the capital; also, provincial customs are associated with the ancient spirit of independence going back to the *municipalia*, the enduring unit of town organization and social identification brought to Spain by the Romans. Lope and Calderón emphasize pastoral virtues in country towns where the immediate concerns are expressed in terms of living by the land and a natural reverence for life and creation. In *The Mayor* Calderón shows greater interest in details of human character and idiosyncracy than he does in plays dealing with the autocratic vengeance principle. And he is now able to criticize the offenses committed by the military caste against the peasantry. The historical situation and the abuses depicted in the play are set forth in a note by Norman Maccoll:

. . . the Spanish army was largely recruited from the dregs of the population, and to trail a pike in Flanders was the last resource of needy and desperate adventurers. Irregularly paid and often starved, the soldier indemnified himself by plundering and ill-treating the inhabitants of the country in which he was quartered, and looked upon them as beings without rights and wholly subject to his will; nor when he returned to Spain was he by any means inclined to change his habits, especially as he was exempt from the jurisdiction of the magistrates, and he had always a chance of escaping the not very strict surveillance of the military tribunals. Even in the great days of Spain discipline was lax, and such outrages as that at Zalamea must have been not uncommon. In Calderón's time matters had gone from bad to worse, and the Spanish troops had become a terror even to the inhabitants of the capital. In May 1639 Pellicer remarks that not a morning dawns without people being found in the streets killed or wounded by soldiers or robbers; without young girls having been maltreated and plundered. In July of the same year he declares that, within a fortnight, seventy men had been killed in Madrid by the soldiers, and forty women were lying in the hospitals who had been wounded by them.[2]

The pastoral condition in *The Mayor of Zalamea,* sharpened by the criticism of military abuses, gives Calderón the chance to realign the concept of vengeance in the honor code. Its severity is not so much mitigated as dialectically reoriented. In the course of events top dog and bottom dog appear to exchange positions: the nobleman is punished by the peasant, but without revolutionary implications. Implicit here is the standard irony of comedy (though the author calls it "a true history," not a comedy), working out its purpose on a serious theme. The irony is conveyed by the freedom-of-the-soul principle which breaks the impasse of determinism framed by the autocratic honor play (*Secret Vengeance* and *The Surgeon of His Honor*) and the theocratic mercy play (*Devotion to the Cross*). The old law of an eye for an eye remains the same, but there is a different resolution in personal terms. For now the victim who becomes the victor at the end has gained a real instead of an illusory satisfaction because the claims of justice have been reapportioned. To say this in another way: the victor is freed from the punishing machine of the code so that his victory no longer entails the sacrifice or extermination of his personality. In becoming more humane, the victory of honor grows real and not merely Pyrrhic.

Only a glimmering of the same possibility is seen in *Devotion to the Cross.* In the first act Julia stands up to her father on conscientious grounds that are justified in principle, even under an autocratic or patriarchal dispensation.

> Sire, a father's authority
> precedes all others; it dominates
> one's life, but not one's liberty
> of conscience.
>
> .   .   .
>
> The only freedom proper to a child
> is the freedom to determine
> for himself his state of life.
> In this his free will should not be forced
> by the dictates of an impious fate.

She is within her rights to state the principle of the freedom of her conscience against her father's decision that she take the veil. She provokes his anger and is accused of rebellion only when she suggests that he apply his own will to himself and not to her. "Since you're determined to live my life, / take the very vows you'd have me take." If he were not himself a victim of the honor code, and if the play were not tragic, her remarks might be taken differently, as in a comedy where the rule of irony may dominate and range freely as a critical weapon. This is what happens in varying degrees in *The Mayor of Zalamea* and *The Phantom Lady*. Not only does free will range more widely in these plays than in *Devotion* and *Secret Vengeance*, but the effect of allowing the principle such range is to achieve greater character individuation and to quicken, increase, even multiply the elements of peripeteia and catharsis. But we must remember that these are matters which an audience rather than the characters themselves are meant to feel.

The ambiance of *The Mayor of Zalamea* is free-flowing and quick-changing. Though many scenes take place in Crespo's house, the impression is that the out-of-doors predominates, that things are literally and figuratively out in the open. From the soldier Rebolledo's raucous expostulations against marching orders in the opening scene, to the crowds of farmers, soldiers, and officials listening to the banter of Don Lope and Crespo, Chispa and Rebolledo in the closing scenes, the play abounds with jaunty speech, the excited intermingling of classes, and rapid scene shifts which follow the intrigue and the conflicts of interests. Characters tend to pair off and move now toward and now away from other pairs as they reflect or mark off changes of situation: Rebolledo and La Chispa, his sweetheart; the captain Don Álvaro and his sergeant; the impoverished hidalgo Don Mendo and Nuño his servant; Pedro Crespo the mayor and Don Lope the commander; Crespo and his son Juan; Crespo and his daughter Isabel; and finally, Isabel and her cousin Inés. Crowding around these pairs are the farmers and clerk-citizens of Zalamea, representing a fixed, fruitful way of country life as against the soldiers and their transitory, rapacious existence. The meeting, clash, and reconciliation of such characters and groups, with their different interests, accompany the development and resolution of the play.

The opposition between military and civilian interests is announced at the start. The soldiers marching toward Zalamea are listening to the braggart veteran Rebolledo's complaints. Soldiers, he says, are forced to follow their banner aimlessly, vagrant as gypsies, the helpless victims of official chicanery which determines whether they will be permitted to rest in town or not. He swears he is going to desert. But he is reminded of their severe commander, Don Lope de Figueroa, who punishes desertion with death. The ameliorative note is sounded by La Chispa, a camp-follower, who prefers the hazards and rewards of military campaigns with Rebolledo to the dull security of town life with the magistrate she has recently left behind. Her mercurial disposition defines the picaresque woman who has abandoned society to live according to her wits and inclinations. Then Don Álvaro announces that the company will be billeted in Zalamea, a small provincial town, until Don Lope arrives with orders to resume the march.

The next scene, between the captain and his sergeant, presents the military attitude toward the peasantry, and in particular, Crespo's family where the captain is to be quartered. Though a peasant, Crespo, "the richest man in town," "proud as a peacock . . . and full of pomp and circumstance, / like the royal prince of Leon," is "entitled to be vain" because of his wealth. But his daughter, the loveliest girl in Zalamea, could not interest the captain romantically; for, despite her pride and beauty, she would "still be / nothing more to me than a peasant / with her dirty hands and feet." Class rivalry, satirically treated, is deepened when the impoverished squire Don Mendo and his servant Nuño appear. Mendo is explicitly identified with Don Quixote:

> some chap
> just dismounted at the corner
> from a scrawny nag that looks
> like Rosinante. The chap himself's
> so stiff and spare you'd think
> he were another Don Quixote—
> the one Cervantes wrote about.

Besides supplying a standard comic interlude, the exchanges between the squire and his servant mock the denatured aristocratic idealism of the honor code, which is being reconstituted in the play according to Crespo's democratic code of honor. Mendo, who fancies himself a suitor of Crespo's daughter Isabel, is thus made to reveal the baser motives behind his suit.

> *Nuño.* If you're so wrapped up in devotion,
> why not ask her father
> for her hand in marriage?
> That way you'd kill two birds with one stone:
> you'd get three meals a day
> and he'd have noblemen for grandsons.

> *Don Mendo.* Nuño, let's have no more of that.
> Am I to get down on my hands
> and knees for a bit of cash and let
> a man of common stock
> become my father-in-law?

> *Nuño.* Well, I used to think it was
> important to have a simple
> commoner for one's father-in-law,
> though it's often said such men are traps
> to gobble up a son-in-law.
> But if you do not mean to marry her,
> why go through the motions of
> professing your undying love?

> *Don Mendo.* Aren't there nunneries enough
> where I can drop her if she bores me,
> without my marrying the girl?

His boast anticipates the actions of the other nobleman, Don Álvaro, which force Isabel into a convent at the end of the play.

Another parodic foreshadowing occurs when the captain schemes to get into Isabel's room. By prearrangement he provokes Rebolledo's insubordination so that the soldier will seem to be escaping the captain's fury by seeking refuge in the upstairs room where Isabel is staying. The ruse anticipates the climactic insubordination when the peasant Crespo arrests and executes the nobleman, Don Álvaro. When Crespo, instead of being punished, is vindicated and rewarded by the highest authority, the king, his action becomes a triumph for the reconstituted freedom-of-conscience principle, which is the theme of the play.

Another foreshadowing is the metaphoric build-up occurring in the first act when Crespo gives an oddly lyrical account of a visit to his farm.

> I went to see the fields all richly
> heaped in piles with sheaves of grain.
> They looked like mounds of purest gold
> as I approached them, and the grain
> so precious it could only be
> assayed in heaven. The breeze
> flows gently over them, the fork lifts
> grain to one side while chaff falls

> to the other; even here it seems
> the meek make way before the strong.
> I pray God grant me leave
> to bring it safely to the granary
> before a squall flings it far away
> or a whirlwind lays it all to waste.

In the timely gathering of the harvest we sense inherent analogies to the precariousness of honor, the distinction between social classes, and the safeguarding of Isabel. The whirlwind will soon come and lay waste to Crespo's harvest when the captain seduces Isabel. And the captain's passion will shortly be excited, like a sudden squall, when he hears that Crespo has taken pains to hide her in an upstairs room. When he does break into the room, Isabel checks the captain by appealing to his sense of duty as a gentleman. But there is more than self-defense in her statement; she is also criticizing a courtly ideal which venerates woman without respecting her as an individual. And this sort of criticism is at the core of pastoral: its ethical standard habitually deflates false ideals that have become social weapons to oppress individuals. Crespo and his son Juan view the captain's ruse as a violation of the nobleman's prerogatives. Crespo says, "Expecting in my fear / to find you killing a man, / I find you're . . . simply flirting with a woman. / You're a nobleman, no doubt of that: / you quickly forget your anger." Earlier, Crespo had insisted on his honor as a peasant against his son's suggestion that he buy a patent of nobility to protect himself from the indignity of having to quarter the military.

> Tell me,
> but truly now, is there anyone
> who doesn't know, however pure
> my ancestry, that I'm a simple
> commoner? No, of course not!
> Well then, what use is there
> in purchasing a patent from the King
> if I cannot buy the noble blood

to go with it? Would I be taken
for a better man than I am now?
That's ridiculous. Then what would
they say of me? That I've become
a gentleman by virtue of five
or six thousand silver pieces.
Well, that's money for you, not honor.
No one can ever purchase honor.
Here's the plainest little story
to illustrate my point.
Suppose a man's been bald for ages,
then finally gets himself a wig.
According to his neighbors,
has he stopped being bald?
Not at all. When they see it they say,
"The old so-and-so looks good
in that new wig!" But what's he gained?
Though they cannot see his bald spot,
everyone knows he still has it.
       . . .
I can do without such wiggish
honor which only calls attention
to what I lack by hiding it.
My parents and theirs before them
all were peasants; I trust my children
accept their lot.

That honor is not reserved for the nobility, and that
"pure ancestry" is possible to a commoner, are further
points in criticism of an authoritarian principle which no
longer fits the facts of life. Of course, the argument here
can be put so forcefully because Crespo's wealth entitles
him to a choice in the matter. But a higher moral is also involved, which is that Crespo's innate sense of proportion,
self-respect, and free conscience are virtues he can live by
precisely because they are nourished by his surroundings.
One might say they are natural and nowhere better seen as
such than when contrasted with the fitful, rationalized,
and arbitrary standard of honor Don Álvaro exemplifies.

Just as such innate virtues come to blows with the sham
and exigent nobility of the captain, the fight is interrupted
by the appearance of Don Lope, the commander. Told
what has happened, Don Lope upholds the law of the military, which says that any civilian assault against a member of the King's army may be immediately punished by the
razing of the town where the act occurred. This is the
letter of the law, modified now by Don Lope's realism, as it
will be again, at the end of the play, by the king's charity.
Pedro Crespo is allowed to vindicate himself now, at the
end of the first act, by standing on his rights, the divinely
ordained patrimony-of-the-soul principle.

> *Crespo.* Sir, I thank you heartily
> for your gracious intervention.
> It has saved me from the consequence
> of suffering a fatal loss.

> *Don Lope.* How do you mean — suffering
> a fatal loss?

> *Crespo.* The result
> of killing a man against whom
> I bore no grudge at all.

> *Don Lope.* In God's name, you know that
> he's a captain, don't you?

> *Crespo.* In God's name, yes, and even if
> he were a general, I'd kill
> the man who sullied my good name.

> *Don Lope.* Sullied or not, should anyone
> so much as touch the cuff
> of the lowest soldier here,
> I'd hang him, as Heaven is my judge!

> *Crespo.* Should anyone so much as breathe
> a syllable against my honor,
> I'd hang him too, as Heaven
> is my judge!

> *Don Lope*. Don't you know
> you're duty-bound, because of who
> you are, to lend your services?

> *Crespo*. Of my estate, but not my honor.
> My life and property I render
> to the King; but honor is
> the heritage of my soul,
> and my soul belongs to God alone.

> *Don Lope*. By Heaven, there seems to be
> some truth in what you're saying!

> *Crespo*. Yes, by Heaven, and I've always
> said so.

Although, perhaps because, this view of honor is humane, it comes close to being a punishable heresy when it is unexpectedly pitted against the autocratic rule of the military caste. Such a view of honor is just tolerable in the name of the spirit, not the letter, of the law — and only in spirit, perhaps, while it is being expressed self-defensively. As Crespo proclaims it in the environment of pastoral society, at a time when the military caste, intent on a war mission, is momentarily juxtaposed to it, he cannot be said to stand in open defiance of the law. Yet the dramatic interest of the play surely depends on how long he can continue to hold his convictions without running afoul of autocratic law.

The lines between the two views of honor are sharpened in the second act. Don Álvaro, a typical Calderonian nobleman, ignites with the passion of unreciprocated love, like a missile about to haul itself off into outer space.

> This fire and passion which I feel
> are not the pangs of love alone
> but a fixed idea, a madness,
> a raging inner fury.

Part of his fury comes from knowing he has been spurned by a peasant girl.

Not even the slightest word
of recognition from her!
To stand upon her virtue
as though she were a lady!

His sergeant's reply emphasizes the conventional split in manners between the two classes.

Such girls aren't smitten, sir,
with gentlemen like you.
It would take some bumpkin
of her own class, wooing her
accordingly, to make her
turn her head. Besides, your courtship's
not very opportune. Since you leave
tomorrow, how can you expect
a woman to respond and give herself
to you within a single day?

The question gives Don Álvaro an opportunity to explain the force that drives him, the feeling for necessity, the seething compulsion to snatch glory in the face of death and the natural attritions of time.

Within a day the sun sheds light
and fades away; kingdoms fall and rise
within a day. In one day,
the proudest building lies in ruin;
in a day a losing battle's won.
An ocean storms and stills within a day;
in a day man is born and dies.
And so within a day my love,
like a planet, may come to know
both dark and light, and like an empire,
pain and joy; like a forest,
men and beasts; like an ocean,
peace and storm; as in a battle,
victory and defeat; and as
master of all my faculties
and senses, know life and death.
And so, having come to know within
one day an age of love's torment,

why may it not still grant me time
to know its bliss? Is joy so much
more sluggish to be born than pain?

Sergeant. But you've seen her only once.
Is this the pass it's brought you to?

Captain. Having seen her once, what better
reason is there for seeing her
again? The slightest spark will
all at once burst into flame;
a sulphurous abyss will all at once
heave up a furious volcano.
All at once a bolt of lightning
consumes whatever's in its way;
and all at once the sleeping cannon
spews forth its deadly horrors.
Is it any wonder then that love,
a fire four times more intense,
containing flame and cannon shot,
volcano and the lightning bolt,
should terrify and scorch,
wound and lay one low, all at once?

The military must fan patriotic ardor and encourage
foolhardy acts and vainglory in pursuing the collective
goal of victory. When these passions and acts are mis-
applied to such nonmilitary objects as a woman's "perfect
beauty," their destructive fatality soon becomes apparent.
It is against this concentrated, obsessed, annihilating drive
in Don Álvaro that the discreet and self-conserving force
in Crespo gradually asserts itself.

Sir, I always answer as I'm
spoken to; yesterday I was
compelled to use the tone
which you applied to me. I take it
as a prudent policy
to pray with him who prays,
and swear at him who swears at me.
I am all things to all men.

Crespo's status and reputation are backed by good will and by wealth, the rewards of his husbandry and his amicable relations with other men. These assets give him substantial reasons to believe in his own honor, supporting as they do his personal and social identity in civil life. Don Álvaro's identity is enforced by birthright, by military rank, and by the combative, egocentric idealism of his class. These same conspicuous attributes cause his undoing in a civil society dominated by Crespo's pastoral virtues. But the outcome of the conflict between military and civil standards must be held in doubt until the end. For until that point, Don Álvaro's more precipitous actions cannot be properly evaluated since they are dramatically expedient — that is, they are needed to provoke Crespo's astute counteractions. Meanwhile the two equal forces are sustained in uneasy balance: one disruptive and centrifugal, directed away from the civil status quo, and the other conservative, retaliatory, and centripetal, directed toward the fixed pastoral center.

Before Don Álvaro succeeds in abducting Isabel, the mitigating circumstances which will permit Crespo later to take the sternest countermeasures are carefully built up. Don Lope, who has been Crespo's house guest, has by now become close friends with him. For his part, Crespo has offered his son Juan as Don Lope's orderly in the military campaign. It is as if, in giving a hostage to the opposition, Crespo were disarming its inevitable assault against his own standard. His parting advice to Juan, sometimes compared to Polonius's speech on a similar occasion, abounds with the cautions of an ascendant middle-class morality. In self-defense, it emphasizes not the classical virtues of heroism but the virtues of social propriety: service, sacrifice, sentiment, and expedience.

> By the grace of God, my son,
> your lineage is as pure
> as golden sunlight, though

you come of peasant stock.
Remember both these things:
the first, so that you won't
allow your natural pride,
through lack of confidence,
to stifle prudent judgment
by which you may aspire
to make something more of yourself;
nor forget the second, so that
you won't be so puffed up
you become something less
than what you are. Be equally
aware of both endowments:
employ them with all humility.
Being humble, you'll be more likely
to conform with right opinion,
whereby you'll find yourself forgiven
where prouder men are soon accused.
Think how many men succeed
in erasing some personal
defect through humility;
then think how many, having
no defects whatever, acquire
them because they lack humility.
Be courteous in every way,
be generous and goodnatured.
A hand that's quick to doff a cap
and offer cash makes many friends,
but all the gold the sun observes
heaped up in the Indies
and wafted hither overseas
is less precious than the general
esteem a man is held in by
his fellows. Don't speak ill of women;
even the most abject of them
is worthy, I assure you,
of all possible respect.
Were we not all born of women?
Fight only when you have just cause.
Now when I see those in our towns

> who teach the use of foils, I often
> tell myself: "Their schools leave
> something wanting, it seems to me.
> The chap they teach to duel with so much
> fervor, skill and gallantry
> should be instructed first
> as to why not how he fights.
> And I believe if there were only
> one fencing master prepared
> to teach the why and wherefore
> of the duel, we'd all entrust
> our sons to such a man."
> To this advice I add the money
> to defray expenses for your journey
> and to buy your several uniforms
> when you reach your quarters.
> Now with Don Lope's benefactions
> and my blessings, I pray God
> I shall see you soon again.
> Farewell, my son. Words fail me.

("Words fail me" must surely be the play's most unconsciously ironic sentence; Crespo is the play's most articulate verbalist.) Shrewd, obsequious, opportunistic, the
speech grates on modern ears; yet the advice is intended
as genuine, and must be taken as such. Moreover, it is truly
earned, reflecting Crespo's own practice, personality, and
tempered ideals. Crespo, after all, is a self-made man, and
it is clear that his middle-class code is meant to stand
firmly against the captain's disruptive usurpations when,
at the close of Act Two, phrases from this speech crop up
in Juan's cautionary response to the fading cries of the
abducted Isabel resounding across an open field.

Act Three begins with Isabel, alone, weeping in the
forest, after Don Álvaro has raped and abandoned her.
Her lengthy soliloquy is curiously magnified in tone and
diction, echoing the centrifugal consciousness of her seducer. It is as though the violence of his attack had made
a true heroine of her. Certainly she is more interesting as a

victim of assault than she was as an overprotected daughter. We notice especially that the captain's action by necessity, aimed at overcoming the attritions of time and circumstance, now permeates Isabel's plea to the sun to hold back the dawn. (Ironically, if the circumstances of the affair had been happier, this might pass for a traditional love lament.)

> Oh, never let the glorious day
> touch my eyes again nor waken me
> to know my shame beneath its shade!
> Oh morning star, harbinger of so
> many fleeting planets, stay and give
> no quarter to the dawn which now
> invades thy bluest canopy.
> Let it not erase thy quiet face
> with dewy smiles and tears.
> But as I fear this must come to pass,
> admit no smile at all, dissolve
> in tears. Now, sun, thou greatest star
> of all, delay, hold back,
> and linger yet awhile below,
> in the ocean of cold foam.
> Let night for once protract
> its hushed and trembling empery,
> and thus, attentive to my prayer,
> assert thy majesty by will
> and not by sheer necessity.

Apparently "will" opposes "necessity" just as restraint, prudence, husbandry, and foresight — the pastoral virtues — oppose the passion, rashness, destructiveness, and blind fury embodied in the autocratic honor principle. Or, as Isabel puts it more sharply a little later, the opposition is between her father's "reverend love" and the captain's villainy, "Whose only law is that honor / must succumb to force." Again the pastoral emphasis emerges in a clinching smile concerning the captain and his military marauders.

> I think
> of them only as ravenous wolves
> who steal inside the fold
> and snatch away the suckling lamb.

The personification is not merely rhetorical; for Isabel, at this point, the captain actually loses human outline and seems to merge into an abstract image of discord:

> the wretched
> ingrate, who on the very day
> he came to lodge with us
> brought with him such unheard of,
> such unspeakable discord
> (full of guile and treachery,
> outbursts and violence)...

The discordant force, the antagonist-by-necessity, is also the perverter of love and sex.

> Beware of him, I say beware
> the man who seeks forcibly
> to win a woman's heart:
> he cannot see nor understand
> that love's victory is not
> in snatching up the spoils
> but in securing the affection
> of the loveliness that's treasured.
> When desire seeks to gain
> such loveliness dishonorably,
> by force, it then becomes
> a lust for beauty that is dead.

In response to this view, and because he represents the conservative, noncombative principle, Crespo does not accede to that part of the honor convention which demands that a father kill his dishonored daughter. This is why his reaction is so gentle and benign, even forthrightly Christian.

> Stand up, Isabel, my child. No,
> do not kneel before me on the ground.
> If it were not for such torments

and afflictions, all our sufferings
would go unrewarded, and all
our joys quickly turn to ashes.
This is the lot of man,
and we must gird ourselves
to bear it deep within our hearts.

Isabel has been so taken up by the terror and fascination of her downfall that she momentarily doubts Crespo's motives. She cannot see that she has been wrenched out of the captain's destructive world of necessity to be sheltered in her father's conservative world of free will.

Above all now, Crespo must act circumspectly. To aid the countervailing movement he now initiates, fortune suddenly bestows official power on him. He learns that Zalamea has selected him its mayor, and he recognizes that this new power may complicate his task.

Just when my honor was to be
avenged, the staff of magistrate
is thrust into my hands!
How can I exceed the law myself
when I am committed to the role
of keeping others within its bounds?
But such matters need further
mulling over.

Yet how he proceeds to resolve the problem as mayor-magistrate is not mulled over but rapidly demonstrated in a chain of dramatic actions. Meanwhile, to forestall the inevitable, the captain on learning he has been apprehended is quite sanguine about his immunity.

Good, I could wish for nothing better.
Since they've found me out, there's no need
to worry now about the townsfolk.
The law obliges them
to turn me over to
a military court, and there,
although the case is awkward,
I'll be perfectly safe.

The scene which follows between Crespo and the captain is a masterly dramatization of the offended father's character and principles. Laying aside his staff of office, he asks Don Álvaro to speak "simply as one man to / another, unburdening his heart." He offers the captain all his wealth and his children's as well, if Don Álvaro will marry Isabel. This is no mere driving of a bargain on the part of a shrewd peasant. Crespo's anguish, pride, and sincerity, expressed in rhythms of impassioned pleading and restraint, are never in doubt — incredibly enough, even when as a last resort he offers to sell himself and his son into slavery and add the proceeds to Don Álvaro's dowry. He places all his resources, the most tangible evidence of his husbandry, at the captain's disposal. When the offer is shunned, he pleads on the grounds of simple humanity.

> *Crespo.* You mean my misery does not
> affect you?
>
> *Captain.* An old man's like
> a woman or a child: his fears
> are easily dissolved in tears.
>
> *Crespo.* For all my wretchedness, you've not
> a single word of sympathy?
>
> *Captain.* What more sympathy do you need?
> I have spared your life.
>
> *Crespo.* Look, sir:
> I am down upon my knees.
> I beg you to restore my honor.
>
> *Captain.* How tiresome can you be?
>
> *Crespo.* Look, sir:
> I am mayor of this town.
>
> *Captain.* I am not subject to
> your jurisdiction—only
> to a military court's.
>
> *Crespo.* Is that all you have to say?

Captain. That's it, you tedious old babbler!

Crespo. Is there no remedy at all?

Captain. Yes, indeed. The best remedy
for you is silence.

Crespo. Nothing else?

Captain.   No.

Crespo. Then, by God, I swear you'll pay
for all this dearly. Ho, there, come in!

> [*He rises, picking up his staff.*]

Crespo has carried his pleas to the sticking point; he has left no possibility of self-sacrifice unmentioned. Reciprocally, the captain's obstinacy, if his rape of Isabel were not already enough to antagonize an audience, rises to its own sticking point. It is as though Crespo's desperate humility were forcing Álvaro to be cruel automatically, out of some corresponding sense of extreme disgust. Álvaro's mistake is overconfidence, weaned on false pride and the security of his rank. It is the very defect which by his own admission in Act Two Don Álvaro recognized as the cause of his mistaken impression of Isabel.

> Overconfidence was precisely
> my undoing. The man aware
> of danger finds protection
> in forewarning; the man who runs
> a risk is the man who's all cocksure:
> danger takes him by surprise.
> The girl I thought would be another
> peasant wench turned out to be
> a goddess. Does it not follow then
> that danger overcame me
> through my very inadvertency?

Crespo and the captain have acted strictly according to character, facing each other as equals in terms of the opposing principles they represent.

A humorous sidelight to this incident is provided by Chispa, the camp follower, who, disguised as a groom, was the captain's accomplice, together with Rebolledo and the sergeant, in Isabel's abduction. When the Mayor cross-examines her, her alibi apes the captain's in seeking exemption from the law.

> *La Chispa.* You can't torture me.
>
> *Crespo.* Why not, may I ask?
>
> *La Chispa.*   It's a
> pretty well accepted thing.
> And there's no law against it.
>
> *Crespo.* What alibi have you?
>
> *La Chispa.* A great big one.
>
> *Crespo.*   What is it? Speak up.
>
> *La Chispa.* I'm pregnant.
>
> *Crespo.*   And bold as brass, I see!
> This is the last straw! Aren't you
> the captain's groom?
>
> *La Chispa.* Not at all, sir:
> I'm nearer to another's bridle.

The same condition affecting such intense disruptions of life and self-esteem with regard to Isabel's rape is here passed off lightly as a pun.

But though the captain is patently guilty, his case must still be legally processed and judged. And this is what the rest of the play is about. Slow to assert itself against Don Álvaro's precipitous assault, Crespo's cause cannot be vindicated until he has worked it out by himself and on his own terms. We note this as soon as the captain surrenders his sword. It is as though Crespo had thereby captured the autocratic principle which it symbolizes.

> *Captain.* Now treat it with due respect . . .

Crespo. Right you are! I heartily agree.
Take him to his cell, with due respect.
Then, with due respect, shackle him.
With due respect, see to it
he does not communicate
with any of the soldiers.
Then put the other two in jail
as well, and, as it befits their case,
keep them duly separated
so that afterward, with due respect,
they may each of them submit
their sworn depositions,
whereupon if any two of them
evidence their culpability,
by God, I'll hang them one and all
at once—with due respect.

Captain. Oh, these peasants drunk with power!

[*The* Captain *is led away by the Farmers.*]

This is the last view of Don Álvaro alive. Next, Crespo arrests his son Juan for having wounded the captain in the forest. As a benign man of power, he can now play the game of tyrant with some bravura. The Mayor exclaims:

I wouldn't hesitate to treat
my father this way, if I had to.
[*aside*] I do it to save his life,
but it will probably be taken
as the oddest piece of justice
ever wrought!

His next move, equally unconventional, is to make Isabel sign a complaint against the captain. She is rightly surprised, since by doing so, according to the honor code, the insult is made public and thereby compounded.

Crespo's conscientious scruples, nurtured by years of husbandry, remain unmodified now that he must act as an official dispenser of justice. His self-abasement before the captain has only hardened his purpose to act according to the law. And this purpose is next tried by the appearance of Don Lope, who does not yet know that Crespo is the offending mayor. When he discovers this, Don Lope drives his own purpose more sharply, knowing that the other's obstinacy equals his own. Calderón again dramatizes the opposing principles as a precariously balanced struggle between well-equipped antagonists.

> *Don Lope.* I've come to take the prisoner
> away and punish his keeper.
>
> *Crespo.* And I'll keep the prisoner right
> here for all the wrongs he's done us.
>
> *Don Lope.* Don't you understand he is
> an officer of the King
> and I'm his judge?
>
> *Crespo.* Don't you understand
> he broke into this house
> and snatched my daughter from me?
>
> *Don Lope.* Don't you know I'm sole arbiter
> in any case?
>
> *Crespo.* Don't you know
> he ravished my daughter in the woods?
>
> *Don Lope.* Do you know how much greater
> my authority is than yours?
>
> *Crespo.* Do you know how much I pleaded
> with him first and he refused me,
> which left no other course than this?
>
> *Don Lope.* No matter how you argue it,
> you've trespassed on my authority.
>
> *Crespo.* He's trespassed on my good name,
> which is beyond your authority.
>
> *Don Lope.* I assure you I'll settle that account;
> he'll be made to pay for it in full.
>
> *Crespo.* I've never left to someone else
> what I can do myself.

> *Don Lope.* I tell you once for all:
> the prisoner is mine.

> *Crespo.* I am drawing up the evidence
> of this trial right here.

> *Don Lope.* What evidence?

> *Crespo.* Certain papers I am gathering
> from witnesses to support the case.

> *Don Lope.* I am going straight to your jail
> now and take him away.

> *Crespo.* I cannot
> prevent your going there,
> but remember this: my orders are—
> shoot anyone who's caught approaching.

Their points of view are irreconcilable. The issue is not that one law or authority surpasses the other, as Don Lope argues, but that behind civilian law stands Pedro Crespo and the pastoral ethic which must triumph in this play. This it cannot do until a further, and indeed the highest possible, defense of it is made before the king himself, who arrives providentially just as Don Lope's soldiers move to storm the jail and raze the town.

The pastoral ethic is favored by the tradition of autonomous local rule, going back to the ancient *municipalia,* in deciding cases concerning the town's own welfare, as well as the humane principles Crespo displays in his plea before the captain. As the injured father, rather than the judge, Crespo offered to accede to the autocratic honor code if the captain would marry his daughter. In the higher court of Don Lope's jurisdiction, Crespo not only bears the authority of civilian law, but also the power of the injured man to whom personal satisfaction has been refused. Still, from the military point of view, Crespo is guilty of insubordination, for which not only he but the whole town may be punished. "Death to the peasants!" the soldiers shout. Now only the king can vindicate Crespo in what Don Lope calls "the most insolent piece / of peas-

ant villainy / that has ever been reported." But even here
we are made to feel that Crespo's unprecedented actions
have wrested justice out of an inflexible machine by force
of sheer conviction and audacious strategy.

In explaining the case to the king, Crespo defines the
terms of right action which justify him.

> ... if any stranger
> brought the same complaint, would he not
> deserve to have like justice done him?
> Of course he would; then why
> should I not treat my daughter's case
> as I would any stranger's?
> Besides, I've put my own son
> in prison, which should show
> I'm impartial to the issue
> where the family tie's concerned.
> Here, let Your Majesty himself
> decide if the trial was fair,
> or if anyone can say that
> malice has misled me,
> if I have suborned a witness,
> or if there is any evidence
> beyond the facts I have given you.
> And if so, I shall pay for it
> with my life.

Once the king admits the death sentence is justified, Crespo
presents the astonished company with a *fait accompli:*
Don Álvaro "revealed garroted in a chair." When the king
takes exception to the manner of the execution, Crespo reminds him of the traditional concept of paternalistic law
as a many-armed body.

> *Crespo.* All royal justice, Sire, is contained
> in one body with many hands.
> What difference can it make then,
> if one arm of justice perform
> the job intended for some other
> arm? What harm's been done

if some detail is slighted
in accomplishing the broader
purpose which justice must serve?

King. Well, suppose I grant you that.
But how is it you did not behead
the prisoner as he deserved,
being a captain and a nobleman?

Crespo. I am sorry you should doubt me
on that score, Your Majesty.
In these parts the noblemen
are so well behaved, it happens
our executioner never learned
how to go about beheading
anyone. In any case,
that scruple should properly concern
the dead man—it's within
his jurisdiction, one might say;
but since he's not complained yet,
I trust others need not be concerned.

King. Don Lope, the deed is done.
The execution was fully
justified; to deviate
in some particular
is unimportant so long as
justice is upheld in principle.
Let no soldier stay behind now;
order all to march away at once.
We must reach Portugal without
another moment of delay.
[*to Crespo*] And you are hereby appointed
permanent Mayor of this town.

Crespo. Sire, only you would know how to
honor justice so completely.

And here the matter is concluded.

If one complains that the argument for royal justice
has been wrenched a bit by Crespo's levity, the answer is
that the spirit and not the letter of the law has been allowed

to triumph. Moreover, as the spirit partakes of the ameliorative principle of the freedom of conscience, the victory is immense, considering the repressive autocratic law against which it was gained. The sop thrown to the Cerberus of paternalistic justice has been promptly accepted. A seventeenth-century Spanish audience, knowing that Philip II's imminent campaign in Portugal would succeed, might have been reminded that history rewarded the king's generosity on this occasion—just as, perhaps, in the final situation of Calderón's *Secret Vengeance* (where the monarch who sanctions wife-murder departs for a campaign in which history left him dead and his cause defeated), the audience would see an equally appropriate sort of poetic justice beyond the play.

Still another sop is provided when Isabel, the seduced daughter, goes to end her days in a convent. The triumphant pastoral ethic cannot rescue her as its does Pedro Crespo or his son Juan, who is released from jail to join Lope and make his fortune on a successful military mission. Isabel's fate is to suffer the full penalty of a woman victimized by the autocratic honor code, except that Crespo's concluding pronouncement seems to mitigate her fate, in view of the caste principle he has been at such pains to vindicate.

> She has chosen
> to enter a convent now
> where she will be the bride of One
> who cares nothing for the difference
> in social origin among us.

While it is only rationalized in this play as a criticism of class differences, the question of woman's fate is directly confronted, reproved, and to some degree reversed under the license of comedy in such a play as *The Phantom Lady*. Meanwhile it remains true that if religion is for women, honor (the personal and social code) is for men. In the name of that honor a peasant has outfaced the king and has proved himself a match for the king's highest military officer. These are no small rewards to the pride of a self-made man. In the larger view, they are considerable attainments where honor must become humane before it can be thought worth fighting for. And in the scheme of the traditional honor play this new sort of victory is most significant.

7 Flickers of Incest on the Face of Honor: *The Phantom Lady*

The pastoral ethic is represented by that set of ameliorative principles in *Devotion to the Cross* and *The Mayor of Zalamea* working to assuage the intolerable burden of fear and vengeance exacted by the autocratic honor code. These principles receive maximum dramatic range, with the happiest consequences, in *La dama duende*, 1629 (The Phantom Lady). The issue is not so much the honor of a woman in danger of losing it, though this hazard is real and accounts for much of the play's dramatic interest. It is rather the clandestine yet clearly approved means by which a lady of rank asserts her rights as a woman in love. Without knowing the otherwise fatal role of honor in Calderonian drama, a casual reader would miss these positive implications of the theme; to him the play would seem little more than an auspicious forerunner of Restoration comedy, which indeed it influenced.[1]

Seen in line with the other honor plays, *The Phantom Lady* presents a woman's rebellion against the code's autocratic male principles as she seeks to achieve the liberty to love whom she pleases. Like the rebellious Crespo, who accommodates the spirit to the letter of the law in order to assert his liberty of conscience, Doña Angela works out her assault on constituted authority within the framework of that authority. She finds freedom in a state of bondage by using stratagems to such effect that actual bondage becomes illusory and illusory freedom becomes real. In gain-

ing her ends she is more advantageously cast than Pedro
Crespo because *The Phantom Lady* is a true comedy, where
ironic reversal is the rule, and also a romance, where the
psychology of love is dominant and must triumph at the
end. Angela's license to act freely is essentially poetic. Her
daring ruses are not only poetically determined, they are
also imaginatively enforced in their variety and versatility.
This is especially notable because the tenor and chief
setting of the play are immured, claustrophobic and dark,
being limited to the adjoining apartments of the two
lovers, Angela and Manuel.

One effect of Doña Angela's strategy is to reduce the
formalism of courtly love to absurdity. Don Manuel, the
gallant friend of her brother Don Juan, who invites him to
stay in their house in Madrid, has just arrived from Burgos with his servant Cosme. Don Manuel's presence in the
household is the occasion Angela uses to devise her libera-
tion from the imprisonment forced upon her by her brother
since her recent widowhood. Cosme's unsophisticated credulity regarding the supernatural gradually infects and
disarms Manuel's skepticism to the same degree that Angela's aggressive ruses as the victimized lady in need of
his help turn his bewildered courtship into something
anachronistic and quixotic. Similarly, by an extension of
her cousin Beatriz's instigative role, Don Luis (Angela's
second brother, who is vainly courting Beatriz), the potential honor-struck hero wracked by jealousy, is made to look
absurd. It is the most virulent way imaginable of criticizing his type. The multiple objects of attack dramatized by
such reversals are: the insincerities of court life and
courtly love; the credulity of superstitious attitudes toward
the supernatural; the sequestration of women by male
members of their family; and the rash behavior of the
egotistic swain, the autocrat in love — the type who initiates the honor quandary, such as Don Luis in *Secret
Vengeance* and Don Álvaro in *The Mayor of Zalamea*.
These criticisms run their course in an atmosphere of misrule, the topsy-turvy world of romantic intrigue, swarm-

ing with veiled ladies, mistaken identities, false assumptions, and characters who are always "in the dark" concerning one another's intentions.

The romantic theme is signalized immediately in the play's induction in Cosme's long speech answering Don Manuel's "We've come an hour late and missed / the grand festivities." Cosme recalls that "things often / went awry before because / someone lost an hour more or less," and provides allusions to the classical lovers, Pyramus and Thisbe, Tarquin and Lucretia, Hero and Leander, as well as a certain "Moorish hero of romance." He likens the entry of his master and himself into the home of Don Juan to "two / knights errant being feted / for the tournaments." With these anachronistic allusions prominently established, we are prepared for the various romantic situations which the play proceeds to treat with such comic profusion.

When Manuel and Cosme are interrupted by the veiled Angela and her maid Isabel, Cosme's first response — "Was that a lady or a whirlwind?" — introduces the leading countertheme of superstition swathed in mystery. Typical of the beseiged romantic lady, Doña Angela's plea comes so suddenly and forcefully it seems more a challenge than a request.

> Sir, if you are the gentleman
> your manner and attire indicate,
> defend a woman urgently
> in need of your protection.
> My very life and honor are
> at stake if I am overtaken
> by that hidalgo at my heels.
> By all that's sacred, I implore you:
> save a noblewoman from
> coming to grief; then some day, perhaps,
> she will . . . Farewell. Alas,
> I must run or I am lost.
> [*Exit* Doña Angela *and* Isabel *in great haste.*]

To Cosme's question, "What will you do?" Don Manuel, visibly caught up by the lady's histrionics, responds with an ultra-romantic assumption regarding the lady's pursuer.

> What a question! As a man
> of honor, what else can I do
> but defend the lady
> from misfortune and disgrace?
> No doubt the chap in question
> is her husband.

The bizarrely histrionic note is further developed in the formalistic encounter between Don Manuel and Don Luis, the lady's pursuer who, as it turns out, is also her brother. But here as elsewhere this note is set against Cosme's comic realism. Cosme succeeds in creating a delaying action which allows Angela to escape while at the same time engaging his master in a duel with Don Luis.

> *Don Manuel, aside.* I must intervene,
> throw caution to the winds,
> and face up to him. — Sir,
> that's my servant you're knocking about.
> I should like to know how
> he has offended you to warrant
> such ill treatment.

The alacrity with which gentlemen fall to fighting is mocked by Cosme when Don Luis's servant invites him to duel at the same time.

> *Rodrigo.*   Come now,
> let's see your sword.

> *Cosme.*   Since mine
> is still a blushing virgin
> whom no one's spoken for as yet,
> I cannot expose her
> to public view.

Cosme's role is to provoke and instigate others, like the old *eiron* of Greek drama; hence his is a critical voice, although he shows himself to be excessively credulous where his own interests are concerned.

Don Juan's adventitious appearance stops the duel and provides for a recognition scene with his friend Don Manuel. It also occasions their departure homeward when he learns that Don Manuel has been wounded. This leaves the stage free for Don Luis to woo Doña Beatriz, his brother's fiancée, hastily left in Don Luis's protection. But first we are treated to Cosme's ripe comment on his master's behavior: "How / appropriate! It serves my master / right for playing Don Quixote / to every passing Dulcinea!" The remark serves to deflate the courtly formalism of the preceding encounter as well as Don Luis's address to Doña Beatriz, which follows. The lady herself enforces this criticism in replying to her suitor.

> Don Luis, I am of course obliged
> to you for these compliments,
> granting that they mean to show
> your heart, and are all your own.
> But you should know I cannot
> otherwise respond to them:
> they address the stars, which may comply,
> but no mortal woman surely.
> If I seem to take your words
> so lightly, that's because the Court
> commonly regards nothing else
> so highly. Therefore, be grateful
> for my frankness, which is, at least,
> as rare a thing as you will find
> these days at Court. Good day, sir.

The inclination to duel at the drop of a hat and the expression of exaggerated courtesies lead to absurdities in action. Similarly, the formulas of stylized address in courtship disguise a vacuous or ill-intentioned heart. Don Luis, a thwarted libidinous force, twice thrown off in his passionate quest, now seeks refuge in a prurient complaint against his brother, in the course of which Doña Angela's situation at home is revealed.

> What pains me most of all
> is my brother's heedlessness.
> Consider it, Rodrigo:
> he brings a gay young gentleman
> to stay with us at home where,
> as you know, my lovely sister lives,
> who though she is a recent widow
> still is under age. Scarcely a soul
> knows of her presence there, she lives
> in such seclusion. At that
> the only visitor she sees
> is Beatriz, whom we allow
> because she is our cousin.

To this Rodrigo replies that her safety from assault at home is assured because "A panelling of glass mirrors / has been installed" between her apartment and the adjoining one where Don Manuel is to stay, "So that no one would suspect / there'd ever been another door there." Rationalizing his frustrations, Don Luis resorts to the formula of honor and the indignation of an imminently dishonored brother.

> Such precautions
> only double my uneasiness,
> for what you tell me, in effect,
> is that the only thing now standing
> as bulwark to my sister's honor
> is a frame of glass a single blow
> will shatter in a thousand pieces.

His hypocrisy is soon magnified by the revelation that the veiled lady he had been pursuing was his own sister.

The next scene opens in Don Juan's house, where the rest of the play is set, except for a brief interlude in a nearby street. Thus, the ensuing actions take place indoors, either in Doña Angela's or Don Manuel's apartment, and

often in darkness where even the intervening glass panel
seems to give way to the fluid movements back and forth
of Doña Angela's yearning for her lover. One might say
that she creates the freedom she seeks within the very
walls of her imprisonment, the physical restraints imposed
by her honor-bound brothers. The sense of the difference
between outside and inside is immediately made apparent
in Angela's first words on entering her own apartment
from the street.

> Here, Isabel, give me back
> my widow's hood, worse luck!
> And wrap me up again
> in that black shroud; as cruel fate
> will have it, I must be buried
> in this way, alive.

The house represents the will of her brothers who guard
her honor, although she has already shown the spirit to
rebel.

> Heaven help me!
> The two of them will be
> the death of me. They have cooped me up
> behind these walls where I can scarcely
> see the light of day, and when night falls
> my aching heart is fit to burst
> this dungeon — here where the fickle moon
> herself, imitating me,
> can never boast she saw me mourn
> my turn of fortune. Imprisoned here,
> what freedom have I gained in
> widowhood when my husband's death
> releases me simply
> to be wedlocked to a brace
> of brothers? And then, if I happen
> to go out, in perfect innocence,
> to see the plays which everyone
> in town's been flocking to,
> authority decrees that though

> I go there veiled, it's as if
> I'd just committed murder. My luck's
> so miserable and so unfair!

Her rebellion against authority and social conventions is
not surprising. But her insistence on freedom and the evidence that she has already acted on it by leaving the house
begin to appear as conscientious moves aimed at creating
some new or alternative situation for herself. Moreover
she has additional justification of another sort. "Wedlocked
to a brace / of brothers," and pursued by Don Luis, Angela
wishes to cast off the impending threat of incest, however
unconscious it may be, which makes the rationale of the
honor code seem not only absurd but also something fright-
ening. For these reasons, Isabel's retort is needed in order
to soften the asperity of her mistress's rebellion and to
draw Doña Angela's attention to Don Manuel.

> But madam, it should not seem so strange
> to you. After all, your brothers,
> considering your youth, your charm,
> and your vivacity, must take
> precautions to protect you.
> For such attractions are just
> calculated to arouse some crime
> of passion, especially here
> at Court. For don't I cross myself
> a thousand times a day in passing
> those blossoming young widows?
> There they go, flouncing down the street,
> pretending they're so prim and chaste,
> so holier-than-thou, you know,
> when all they really care about
> is showing off their latest gown.
> Yet let them once take off their toques
> and those airs of being so devout,
> and they'll go bouncing off agog,
> from one young fellow to another,
> like a football. But madam, let's drop
> this subject for awhile; instead,

> let's discuss the gallant stranger
> whom you begged to be your champion
> and in whose keeping you recently
> deposited your honor.

Isabel's speech suggests there is a difference between license and licentiousness. The insincerity of courtly behavior which Beatriz has already criticized is matched by the hypocrisy of the prurient young widows which Isabel notes here and which Don Luis himself enacts in his headlong pursuit of his sister. After her ostensibly innocent stroll outdoors, Angela now senses how closely her behavior approached licentiousness; this is revealed in her remark, half serious and half coy, regarding Don Manuel.

> I was mad
> to urge him on so; but then, how can
> a woman, scared to death, ever stop
> to weigh the consequences?

Isabel, in turn, pins down the serious implications of the statement when she replies, "I do not know if you / incited him, but I do know / that afterward your brother stopped pursuing us." Precisely at this point Don Luis bursts in with his curious brooding remarks about his sister's honor. We observe that he is still distracted and that his insistence now, as before, upon this scruple is a thin excuse for his own frustrated passion. The ambiguity of his remarks, complicated in this exchange by the ambiguity of Angela's fears, reveals his disoriented libidinous quest.

> *Doña Angela.* Why, brother,
> you seem so upset. What's happened?
> Is anything the matter?

> *Don Luis.* Everything's the matter
> When one's honor is at stake.

> *Doña Angela, aside.* Good Lord, now it's out — he saw me!

> *Don Luis.* I am concerned because
> your honor is so lightly treated
> in this house.

Doña Angela. Is there reason
for you to think so? What troubles you?

Don Luis. The worst of it, Angela, is
that when I come to see you, I am
no less vexed than I was
before I came.

Isabel, aside. This is it now!

Doña Angela. But brother, how can I possibly
have offended you? Consider . . .

Don Luis. You are the cause, and when I look
at you . . .

Doña Angela. Oh, dear me!

Don Luis.   . . . Angela
I realize how little
my brother thinks of you.

Doña Angela.   That is true.

Don Luis. For see how he now adds new sorrows
to those which brought you to Madrid.
And so I was not so wrong
in turning my annoyance with
Don Juan against his guest and friend
whom, out of some presentiment,
I wounded in a duel today.

The would-be rake who salves his conscience by blaming
his brother for neglecting his sister's honor is addressing
the sister he pursued; and she, in her turn, admits to
having spuriously attracted a stranger, Don Manuel. The
double ambiguity in their speeches hangs on the unconscious guilt each feels with regard to actions aimed at
freeing their libidos. The hypocrisy of motive is deeper
where Don Luis is concerned; for he shifts the blame to
his brother and to Don Manuel, whom he imagines he
has wounded "out of some presentiment." He unconsciously views both of them as rivals for Angela's favors.
This point crops up again in Don Luis' excited retelling of

the event precipitating his chase of "the veiled lady" from the palace grounds.

> To determine who she was,
> I followed her. And as she ran,
> she turned continually to glance
> behind at me, as if in utter
> terror; yet her dismay
> simply spurred my curiosity.

Being basically immoral, Don Luis's pursuit of women is tinged by sadism; he feels pleasure in provoking and prolonging their distress. This feeling underlies another ambiguity in his speech when, half recognizing the disastrous consequences that might have been in store, he concludes, "That's all there was, although / it might have been much worse."

For her part, Angela's relief at having escaped unrecognized allows her to identify vicariously with the alluring hussies whom her brother pursues and whom Isabel has complained of.

> I declare! To think that wicked
> woman led you into such a trap!
> Why, of all the shameless, conniving
> wenches who . . . I'll wager
> she did not even know you,
> and only ran away
> to make you follow her.
> Now this is why I've often warned you,
> as you recall, not to lose
> your head over hussies whose
> only thought is how to wreck men's lives.

But Don Luis is still distraught and, as if jealous of his brother, repeats his question that reveals a vicarious involvement in his sister's honor.

> *Don Luis.* Did our brother come to see you?

> *Doña Angela.* He has not been here since morning.

Don Luis. I cannot tolerate his neglect
of you.

Doña Angela. Well, you had better not
be vexed, and finally accept
the situation. Remember,
he is our elder brother
whom we count on for our keep.

Don Luis. If you can reconcile yourself,
I shall have to do the same,
since it is only on your account
that I've been vexed. And now
that you've advised me of your feelings
in the matter, I shall go
to see him, and even pay
my compliments to his friend.

[*Exit.*]

When Don Luis departs one feels that he has unwittingly confessed his incestuous complicity with his sister from which she, because his admission relieves her of a similar sense of guilt, hastens to absolve him.

As Doña Angela continues to speak her mind to Isabel, she indicates her charmed astonishment at Don Manuel's mysterious advent, almost as if the stranger had come to counteract the brothers' erotic designs on her.

I can scarcely bring myself
to believe the story. It seems
so incredible that a stranger
just arriving in Madrid
should instantly find himself
enjoined to save a lady's life,
then be wounded by her brother,
only to become her other
brother's house guest. Strange, though
not impossible — and yet
I shan't believe it's happened
till I see it with these eyes.

Clearly Don Luis has fired her wishful imagination with
the possibility of asserting her desire for an affair. Isabel's
role is to steer her mistress away for Luis's mere licentiousness so that she can achieve something more gratifying
with Don Manuel. Isabel proceeds to do this by focussing
Angela's imagination on the possibility of opening a passage between her apartment and Manuel's by means of
the removable glass panel. As soon as this possibility is
indicated, Angela's alacrity in undertaking the adventure
surprises even her maid.

> *Isabel.* Gracious, madam, do you really
> mean to go inside?
>
> *Doña Angela.* I have
> the foolish notion that
> I must discover if this man
> is indeed the one who saved my life.
> For if he spilt his blood on my behalf,
> as his wound would testify,
> I shall do everything I can
> to show my gratitude — provided
> I may do so without the fear
> of being apprehended.
> Come, Isabel, I must inspect
> the panel; and if I can really
> get into his room without
> his knowing I am there at all,
> I shall repay him for his kindness.
>
> *Isabel.* Indeed, that would be a tale to tell.
> But what if he should tell it?
>
> *Doña Angela.* That he will not do, Isabel.
> He has proved himself a gentleman,
> a man whose courage is only equaled
> by his sense of honor
> and discretion. From the very first,
> his noble qualities touched my heart.
> Bold and chivalrous, gallant, prudent—
> why, I do not for a moment doubt

> that a man so liberally endowed
> could possibly expose me.
> So many fine qualities
> would never have been wasted
> on a man who babbles all he knows.

Obviously Doña Angela's gratitude is of mixed quality. Don Manuel has indeed saved her life by thwarting the incestuous drive of Don Luis; in doing so he has actually saved her passional life and redirected it toward a new sense of freedom and a new possibility of finding legitimate gratification beyond the erotic threats of her brothers. As the liberator of her imagination, Don Manuel becomes the object of her wakened curiosity: the erotic prince charming (not the bestial male aggressor she fled from in Don Luis) who came to rouse her sleeping womanhood. Against the defects of her brother's erotic anarchy are the clearly enumerated virtues in Don Manuel: self-sacrifice, discretion, courage, sense of honor, and so forth. Because she believes he possesses these virtues, Angela can feel safe with him, safe from rude assault; she can also feel free to perform her womanly role in courtship, which is to reciprocate with her will and imagination by endowing him with the instinctive gifts of love.

These are the very gifts which Calderón's honor victims, subdued by rape (Isabel in *The Mayor of Zalamea*), incestuous assault (Julia in *Devotion to the Cross*), and sterile jealousy (Doña Leonor in *Secret Vengeance*), are unnaturally prevented from bestowing. They are the gifts of a woman's realistic love for a man, framed by the pastoral virtues and unhampered by the paternalistic strictures of the honor code.

What follows next is Don Luis's disingenuous gesture toward Don Manuel: the surrender of the sword with which he fought over Angela.

> You must take this
> from me; I can no longer bear
> this instrument which wounded you.

It cannot please me nor be
of further service to me, and so
I must discharge it as a master
would some tiresome unruly servant.
Therefore I place this miscreant sword
Here at your feet to beg forgiveness
for itself and for its master.
Take it, and if your cause requires
vengeance, turn it on its master.

Intended as an extraordinary courtesy, the gesture augurs
something much more meaningful if we consider Don
Luis's fitful nature and unconscious motivations. The
sword, of course, symbolizes a gentleman's aggressive
and self-defensive instrument, the prime implement of his
courage and manhood as well as the honor weapon he
uses in order to assert these attributes. As we discover
later, Don Luis is disarmed of these attributes again and
loses another sword to Don Manuel. At the moment, the
free surrender of his weapon smacks of an admission that
he is yielding up his potency and his libidinous designs
on Angela to a rival. He appears thereby to be transferring
incestuous blame to "this miscreant sword," from whose
aggressive thrusts he wishes to disassociate himself. He
also wants to be forgiven and, as though sensing he had
committed an unpardonable crime, even asks to be punished. Far from dissuading Don Manuel, the speech and
gesture redouble his suspicion that Don Luis is his rival
— if not the lady's husband, then surely her lover. Don
Luis's unconscious self-deception is analogous to a larger
self-deception to which Don Manuel is subjected by
Cosme's bizarre credulity and Angela's love rites.

As the guileless reader of romances whose report on
ill-fated lovers initiates the action, Cosme is now shown
to be a confirmed wine-bibber as well as a believer in
magic.

Once I read a book
about a thousand flowing fountains,
and the water had the power to change

> itself into every sort of shape
> and form. So I wouldn't be surprised
> if the water I was soaked in
> had suddenly been changed to wine.

But his credulity and buffoonery, like his drinking, are boastful and matter-of-fact, to be enjoyed and demonstrated for their own sake. As soon as he is alone, Cosme extracts his purse and triumphantly descants upon his skill as a pickpocket.

> There you are, my dear, my precious joy:
> you've come into your own!
> You started out this morning
> thin as any untried maiden;
> now you swell and bulge like a wench
> that's nine months gone. Should I
> count the money? No, that would be
> a waste of time . . .

He rationalizes not unpacking his master's bags in order to leave the house and get a drink:

> pleasure
> before business, you know —
> especially where the first's your own
> and the other is your master's.

When Cosme leaves, Angela accompanied by Isabel makes her first visit to Don Manuel's apartment through the removable paneling. There her inquisitive examination of his belongings is incited not by possessiveness but by her awakening love and the lure of his physical proximity.

Doña Angela. What's that?

Isabel. A bundle of papers.

Doña Angela. Are they love letters?

Isabel. No, madam.
I think they're legal briefs of some sort.
They're sewn together and quite heavy.

Doña Angela. They'd be light enough if some woman had written them. Discard them.

Isabel. Here is some of his linen.

Doña Angela. Is it scented?

Isabel.   It has the smell
of being clean.

Doña Angela. That's the sweetest
scent of all.

Isabel.   It also has
three other qualities: it's white
and soft and very fine. But madam,
what do you make of all
the instruments inside this case?

Doña Angela. Let me see. Ah, this one seems to be
a tooth-puller; these are tweezers;
and that's a curling iron
for his forelocks, and another
for his mustache.

Isabel.   Item:
hair-brush and comb. Gracious,
but this guest of ours has come
so well equipped he hasn't left
a shoe-last out.

Doña Angela. How's that?

Isabel. I'm holding it in my hand.

Doña Angela's contact with Don Manuel's intimate possessions will be followed by the gifts of clothing and sweets she subsequently sends him — gifts of her dawning love. By contrast, Cosme's acquisitiveness is repaid by Isabel when she substitutes charcoal clinkers for the pilfered coppers in his purse. Cosme's discovery of the substitution and the presence of clothing strewn around the room leads him to believe the house is haunted. And when

his outcries bring his master and Angela's brothers in,
Don Luis's ironic and spiteful remark to Don Manuel —

> It is fortunate you are
> valiant, sir, since everywhere you go
> you are forced to draw your sword
> to settle every quarrel
> this fool must get you into.

— calls attention to Cosme's instigative role in the love-
quest that now begins in earnest.

Don Manuel's discovery of a strange lady's note under
his coverlet seems to support Cosme's inference regarding
a supernatural intrusion. But Don Manuel will suppose
nothing further than that the sender is the veiled lady he
protected, probably Don Luis's mistress. Cosme, insisting
on a supernatural explanation, presses the case against
his master's principled but somewhat shaken rational view.

> *Cosme.*   So far, so good;
> that's neatly reasoned out,
> but my fears go much further.
> Suppose she is his mistress
> (and incidentally, sir,
> congratulations, since now
> she smiles at you), how could she
> possibly have known beforehand
> what was to happen on the street
> so that she'd have the letter written
> and waiting for you here?

> *Don Manuel.* She could have had it written later,
> after seeing me, then had
> her servant bring it here.

> *Cosme.* Yes, the servant might have brought it,
> but how could he have got it here
> if nobody has stepped inside
> this room all the while that I've been here?

> *Don Manuel.* There was time enough for doing that
> before we came.

Cosme.   Very well.
Writing the letter's only one thing,
but how do you account for
the scattering around of all
our traveling bags and clothes?

Don Manuel. Go see if the windows are closed.

Cosme. Barred and bolted, sir.

Don Manuel.   It's puzzling.
Now I'm flooded with new suspicions.

Cosme. About what?

Don Manuel.   I can't say exactly.

Cosme. Well, what do you intend to do?

Don Manuel. Oh, I shall answer her, of course,
but in such a manner that
there'll be no question of
her having pierced my armor
with apprehension or surprise.
For as long as we engage
in correspondence, I am sure
some occasion will arise
when we discover who the person
is who brings and takes the letters.

Cosme. And we're not to breathe a word of this
to either of our hosts?

Don Manuel.   Of course not.
How could I possibly betray
the woman who confides in me?

Cosme. Then you'd rather betray the man
you think's her lover?

Don Manuel.   No indeed;
all I know is this : I can
proceed honorably
only if I do not betray her.

Pressed by Cosme's close questioning, Don Manuel gives way occasionally to rationalization as well as to the blandishments of being courted by a rival's lover; yet he accepts the responsibility of being the thorough gentleman that Angela takes him for. But he must continue to contend with a double threat: the veiled lady's designs on his libido — "There'll be no question of / her having pierced my armor / with apprehension or surprise" — and Cosme's attack on his rationality. For the moment, however, it is easier to put off his servant's supernatural explanation than provide an explanation of his own on convincingly rational grounds.

> *Cosme.* No, sir; there's more to this
> than you believe. I'm convinced of that
> in spite of everything you say.

> *Don Manuel.* Exactly what convinces you?

> *Cosme.* Letters and things going in and out
> of this place, and still, you,
> with all your brains, cannot explain
> how such things happen. What
> would you believe?

> *Don Manuel.*   Simply
> that someone with wit and skill
> has found an entrance and an exit
> to this room, and some way
> of opening and concealing it,
> which we as yet have not discovered.
> and I'd rather lose all my brains
> at once, Cosme, than believe
> some supernatural thing
> had had a hand in this.

Cosme's demonology and Don Manuel's rationality become the horns of dilemma on which the matter is left hanging at the end of Act One.

> *Cosme.* All right, but what will you do?

> *Don Manuel.* Stay up day and night and never
> bat an eye until I solve
> this mystery, in spite of every
> ghost and goblin in the universe.

> *Cosme.* As for me, I still maintain
> some sort of devil's at the bottom
> of it all; and he can fetch
> and carry letters, among
> other things, as quick as
> anyone would puff tobacco smoke.

Though we are not in the dark as Don Manuel and Cosme are, and though our interest in what follows will be conditioned by the complications which finally bring enlightenment to these characters, how much of the mystery do we clearly understand? Is there any mystery at all, and if so, what is it and how are we to view it?

The answer to these questions relates to the thematic center of the play. If we assume that *The Phantom Lady* is more than a romantic comedy, that it deals chiefly with the assertion of a woman's right to love, and that Calderón is thereby setting up a positive and humane alternative to the homicidal rigors of the honor code with its incestuous implications, then the mystery we have at hand is one patterned on a mythotypical ritual allied to the initiation and fertility rites out of which the oldest comedy sprang. Such a ritual prescribes the sacredness of human life, the resurrection of a paradisal image of mankind living in a golden age, an encounter between the forces of good and evil, and a sacred marriage between the earth goddess and the sky god in a culminating marriage feast or festival. The sacred marriage at the end symbolizes the powers of natural fertility induced through sympathetic magic into the planting of crops. In old comedy the initiates wore artificial phalluses to symbolize their roles. They also wore masks, and certain stages of the initiation were marked by changes of garment, the symbolic discarding of old for new clothing. These rites, variously incorporated into the state religions and the dramas of the ancient world, appear most prominently in Aristophanes' plays. As Frances Cornford has written,

The reign of Zeus stood in the Greek mind for the existing moral and social order; its overthrow, which is the theme of so many comedies, might be taken to symbolise, as in the *Clouds*, the breaking up of all ordinary restraints, or again, as in the *Birds* and the *Plutus*, the restoration of the Golden Age of Justice and Lovingkindness, that Age of Kronos which lingered in the imagination of poets, like the after-glow of a sun that had set below the horizon of the Age of Iron. The seasonal festival of Saturnalian character celebrated the return, for a brief interregnum, of a primitive innocence that knew not shame, and a liberty that at any other time would have been licentious. Social ranks were inverted, the slave exercising authority over the master. At Rome each household became a miniature republic, the slaves being invested with the dignities of office. A mock king was chosen to bear rule during the festival, likc the mediaeval Abbot of Unreason or the Lord of Misrule.[2]

And of course we recognize in the Mardi Gras a survival of the same festival — the Lenten festival mentioned, incidentally, in Cosme's first speech in Act One.

It is not as though Calderón were deliberately patterning the action of *The Phantom Lady* on old Attic comedy or any prehistorical Greek mystery. It is more likely that the pressure of his moral and imaginative concerns with regard to his theme led him to the use of symbols and devices appropriate to its expression and employed by writers since the beginnings of drama and religion in the Western world. What Colin Still hypothesizes concerning Shakespeare's creation of a mystery in *The Tempest* may be applied to Calderón's imaginative uses in *The Phantom Lady*.

The earliest versions of the theme are found, of course, in the myths of antiquity. Observe that it is important to distinguish between the genuine myth and mere legend. The genuine myth is a kind of mystery play dealing in the form of dramatic narrative with truths that are valid, actually or potentially, for all sorts and conditions of men. It is an allegory which expresses some aspect of human experience so truthfully, and by means of figures that appeal so irresistibly to our instinctive sense of fitness that it lives unchanged from age to age. It may or may not form part of the body of religious dogma professed by those who cherish and perpetuate it; but in either case it has a permanent value which the evolution of theologico-philosophical thought cannot impair. It cannot die, because it is true for all men; nor can it suffer radical change in the course of transmission from generation to generation, because the aesthetic instinct, individual or collective, of those by whom and to whom it is passed on recognises, consciously or unconsciously, the appropriateness of its imagery and neither desires nor permits any essential deviation in this respect. Hence, in presenting allegorically any given aspect of universal experience, the artist inevitably reproduces to some extent, intentionally or otherwise, not only the substance, but also the form of such genuine myths as deal with the same subject; and the degree of resemblance is directly proportionate to the aesthetic merits of his work.[3]

As we find them at the end of Act One, Don Manuel and Cosme are being inducted into a mystery, created by the phantom lady, whose purpose is to convert the rule of honor into the rule of love. She is the sometimes veiled and hidden priestess of the new rule, accompanied by her servants and by Beatriz. Manuel is the initiate whose faith must be tested by various trials which will indicate his fitness to serve and, eventually, marry the lady. Cosme, whose faith is being challenged on a lower level, is also involved, and such involvement is deepened by his close relationship to a master whom he typically serves as an alter-ego — that is, as an instigator and guide through the mystery, but also as a threat and a challenge to his rational mind. Don Luis and Don Juan, as the representatives of the rule of honor, the old principle, are the antagonists and Doña Angela's keepers within the walls of the house. But Juan is distinguished from Luis on several counts, the most notable being that, as Doña Beatriz's favored lover, Juan's autocratic rule is tempered and conditioned by Angela's cause of love. On the other hand, as the unconscious assailant of his sister's honor, the marauder and homicidal force perpetuating the old rule, Luis must continually seek to disrupt Angela's love rites. In such a situation, the fear of dishonor and the enticements of incest spring up together in the same breast. But one must remember that Juan, when his suspicions are aroused, acts no differently from his brother, and in this sense with regard to Angela — "wedlocked to a brace of brothers" — he is also an antagonist to the new rule. The developments of the ensuing mystery are not only mythotypical, they are also the standard devices in Calderón's vengeance plays of sequestering the man-with-a-cause inside his own consciousness, of swaddling his movements and strategies with the utmost secrecy, and of isolating him in his growing knowledge and sense of purpose from all possible antagonists until he is ready to strike. But because Angela is the principal actor, a woman-with-a-cause, and because the ethos she acts in is the social ethos of comedy instead of tragedy, she shares her knowledge and purposes with female accomplices who help her penetrate her isolation, go through walls, and light up the darkness.

Indeed, her penetration into Don Manuel's apartment, her ruses by candlelight in the darkness, are attempts to free instinctive forces in herself and in her lover so that the cause of erotic love will triumph. Against these designs stands Don Manuel's rationality, which is the predominant possession of an honorable man. Rationality serves him in somewhat the same manner that rashness and irrationality serve Don Luis. One might say that Doña Angela's imaginative view of Don Manuel will become a reality only when she disarms him of rationality long enough for him to succumb to the suppressed forces of his libido. Her incursions into his apartment and his later induction into hers are all carried out with this intention. The way he

responds to these rites tests his fitness for the role she has
chosen for him. If he is a true gentleman, and really prizes
the mystery of courtship, he will be worthy of her love.

Dramatizing Don Manuel's situation in their contrary
roles are Cosme and Don Luis. Cosme with his facile
superstitions and materialistic concerns is an enemy of the
mystery; his misguided interpretations lead to fear and
confusion instead of joy and enlightenment. But in this
role, his irrationality closely accompanies Don Manuel's
rationality. Don Luis is a more objective antagonist: a
libertine whose unsuppressed irrationality constantly
threatens to disrupt the rites of love. If Don Manuel is to
triumph he must conclusively put down the threat which
Don Luis represents; but he will not be able to do so until
he himself has been initiated by Doña Angela and enlightened by her cause.

A shift from the dubious tone with which the mystery
is greeted at the end of Act One is noted immediately at
the outset of the next act. Doña Angela's apartment is now
filled with an excited glow of wonder. Don Manuel's reply
to her letter is taken up as an auspicious and "remarkable"
sign, and he is praised for accepting the challenge of "the
adventure." Don Manuel's style, broadly imitative of traditional courtly rhetoric, is called "gallantly expressed," "gay
and highflown," "Much as the knights of old would write
/ on similar occasions." These signs and sentiments, over
the signature of the "Knight of the Phantom Lady," are
just the kind of dedication Doña Angela requires.

The rites of love are further celebrated when Don Juan
enters and his colloquy with Beatriz on the effects of love
ensues. We learn that Beatriz has been sent to stay with
Angela because of her father's displeasure.

> *Don Juan.* Though I should be sorry
> to discover happiness
> in the very circumstance
> which pains you, the pleasure
> of your present company

> has silenced all compunctions.
> The effects of love, you see,
> are so subtly various
> that the reason for your sorrow
> becomes the substance of my joy,
> and in this is like the asp
> whose bite discharges both the venom
> and the antidote to cure it.

But Beatriz's reply is a good deal more realistic than Don Juan's conventional play on the pleasure-pain metaphor. She points out that he himself has been the direct cause for her father's displeasure.

> It's true I've come because my father
> is displeased with me. But you
> must take the blame for that.
> When he learned I'd spoken
> at my balcony last night
> to some gentleman (not knowing
> the gentleman was you), he promptly
> sent me here, while he cools his rage,
> to stay with my cousin
> in whose virtue my father has
> the highest confidence.

Then she frankly indicates that this circumstance does not make her sorrowful but joyful. For it appears that her father's rage and mistaken confidence have ironically given her the license to act as an outlaw from paternal authority. Sharing Angela's cause, she is thus allowed to exploit the virtue, not of obedience, but of freedom in the rites of love. "It seems," as Doña Angela puts it, "a profitable day / for lovers"; and when she adds, as Don Juan departs,

> the good Lord only knows
> what troubles Don Juan's guest has caused me,
> troubles enough to last me
> all my life,

her irony points to the hopeful conclusion of these rites in marriage. Angela's realistic perceptions continue to support her cause. She likens the mystery of being conducted through the secret entrance to the simple but, until discovered, impenetrable problem posed in the story of Columbus and the egg.

> Well, the wisest men alive
> had exhausted all their wits
> endeavoring to set the egg
> upright on a jasper table when
> Columbus came along, gave the egg
> a simple tap, and solved the problem
> once for all. The greatest
> difficulties solve themselves
> once you know the simple answer.

As long as Don Manuel exhausts his wits — his confirmed rationality — upon the mystery, he will not come upon "the simple answer," the "simple tap" of sensibility and enlightenment that must resolve it. In addition, however, Angela is counting on Don Manuel's credulity, the other side of his rational bias, to keep her secret. And in this we see her craftily using Don Luis's apparent rivalry as a weapon. The evidence she goes by is indicated in her astute remark regarding Don Manuel's real motive for adopting the anachronistic style in his correspondence.

> I'm sure the very thought
> that I may be the mistress
> of Don Luis has already
> made him fearful and uneasy,
> and explains the reason why
> he writes me in so guarded
> and overwrought a manner.

Such perceptions reassure her that she can establish a free interchange between Don Manuel and herself and still sustain the mystery.

> Now listen, this will be the most
> remarkable device of all:
> I shall walk straight into his room,
> with no danger of his seeing me;
> then he'll walk into mine,
> but not know where he is.

The insistence on Don Luis, however, as an antagonistic and menacing presence continues to be enforced. Isabel's jocular remark to the audience at this point emphasizes not only his threatening nature but also the curiously evanescent manner in which the two brothers, "wedlocked" to Doña Angela, fade in and out of the scene, as though they were a single presence.

> *Isabel.* According to the script, insert
> the other brother's name at this point
> in the margin, for here comes
> Don Luis.

In fact, the difference between the two can only be established by Beatriz, whose love for Don Juan has enlightened her.

> *Doña Beatriz.* How differently the stars
> influence our character! For in
> two men of equal gifts and merits
> exist such inequalities of
> disposition that what pleases us
> in one annoys us in the other.
> Come now, Angela, I want
> no words with Don Luis.

But Don Luis enters and forcibly detains her; stung by her scorn, he asks, "Am I then the lowering night?" His subsequent discourse is full of the affectations of pathos of the unrequited lover using rhetoric to force the issue. Doña Beatriz recognizes his skill but spurns him.

> *Doña Beatriz.* You manage to complain
> so eloquently, I feel
> I should requite you for your pains.

But I cannot bring myself
to do so, simply because
it happens to be you.

    Don Luis. I warn you, if you persist
in treating me so coldly,
I too know something of the language
of disdain.

    Doña Beatriz. Very well, then: use it.
Perhaps your eloquent disdain
will cure your ill-bred disposition.

        [Don Luis *stops her as she is about to leave.*]

    Don Luis. Listen to me: if this is your
revenge, you must suffer it with me.

    Doña Beatriz. I've no intention to. Good Heavens,
Cousin, can't you stop him?
                          [*Exit.*]

    Doña Angela. What little self-respect you have
to ask for such humiliation!

    Don Luis. Oh, sister! What am I to do?

    Doña Angela. Forget your foolish passion.
To love someone who hates you
is an ordeal worse than death.
                  [*Exit with* Isabel.]

    Don Luis, *addressing the absent* Doña Angela.
Forget her when my heart is choked
with rage? Impossible! Who could?
First let her be kind to me,
then I'll forget her, gladly.
But after she insults me? Never!
The wisest man alive, no less
than I, would tell you this:
kindness is easily forgotten,
since it never sticks or sinks
so deeply as an insult.

The insult-vengeance formula of the honor code, appropriate to Don Luis's temperament and situation, is clearly in retreat. Rejected in this way, its agent is made to look more ridiculous than pathetic. Angela, to whom he appeals and expostulates, has already left the stage as he continues to grind his teeth in rage. Then, to emphasize the duplicity of Don Luis's gallantry, Calderón focuses on an exchange between him and Don Manuel.

> *Don Luis.* If I may be of service, sir,
> in whatever way at all, you need
> only say the word, you know.
>
> *Don Manuel.* I am much obliged to you.
>
> *Don Luis.* It is no mere courtesy,
> I assure you.
>
> *Don Manuel.* I am certain
> you have my interests at heart.
>
> *Don Luis, aside.* Yes, indeed, — and the sooner I am
> rid of you the better.

We see that if Don Luis is the guest's unconscious rival for the favors of Angela, he is also his brother's manifest rival for the hand of Beatriz. And because Beatriz scorns him, his suit is intensified at the same time that his increasing sense of betrayal and victimization by women leads to frustration. As for Don Manuel, the discovery that Angela is not Don Luis's mistress leads to an intensification of rational detection, involving him more deeply in the mystery and increasing his perplexity until he descends to Cosme's commonly held view of women's impenetrable wiles.

> If it's true she is that lady,
> then she cannot be his fiancée:
> he would not have her living
> in his house if she detested him.
> but here's an even crueler doubt:
> if she is not his mistress

> and does not live here in the house,
> how can she correspond with me?
> Ah, so one deception ends
> only to give way to another.
> What am I to do or think?
> I am more confused than ever. God
> help me, for there's a woman in it!

The fear of women's impenetrability is related to the fear of the supernatural, which Cosme also voices; and Don Manuel must contend against this fear, too, the more Cosme infects him with it.

> *Don Manuel.* Well, what's the matter?
>
> *Cosme.*   I'm frightened.
>
> *Don Manuel.* Is it becoming in a man
> to be afraid?
>
> *Cosme.* No indeed, sir;
> it's not at all becoming!
> but here's a man afraid because
> it's warranted.
>
> *Don Manuel.* No more nonsense now.
> Go and fetch a light. I've several
> things to write and papers to arrange
> before we leave Madrid tonight.
>
> *Cosme.* Yes, I'm sure, and the reason why
> you change the subject is that
> you're every bit as scared of spooks
> as I am.

"Fear plucks me like an instrument," Cosme murmurs just before Isabel, having entered through the panel on a mission for Angela, strikes him over the head and blows out his candle. In the confusion she escapes and leaves Don Manuel holding the basket of linen she has brought. Cosme protests that he has seen the ghostly visitor: "He looked like a huge friar, / and he had on an enormous cowl . . ."; to this Don Manuel replies, more to reassure himself than

Cosme, "Fear can make you see anything!" Then he reads
the note enclosed in the basket and is thereby officially
enlightened regarding his further involvement with the
phantom lady: "Concerning what you have said about Don
Luis and myself, your notion that I am his mistress is, I
assure you, not only untrue but can never ever be true."
The phrase "can never ever be true" would suggest that
her brother's unconscious incestuous aggression is not only
illegitimate in motive but also cannot be tolerated as a
possibility. Subsequently, in the course of a long comic
speech, Cosme specifies the punishment he has received
at the hands of the mysterious forces in the house, whereas
the same forces treat his master favorably: "It's just as if
that spook / were treating you with silken gloves / and
me with iron claws." Don Manuel, it would appear, has
been "elected" to approach the center of the mystery.

Meanwhile, Angela continues her assault on Don Manuel's rationality, as if she would exhaust his wits until he is
prepared to receive enlightenment, the boon of love.

> *Doña Angela.* And after all this, if I can
> manage that interview with him
> in the way I've indicated,
> he'll surely go out of his mind.

> *Doña Beatriz.* At this rate, Angela, the sanest
> man alive would be completely stumped.
> Imagine his wanting to find you
> and not knowing where, and then
> meeting a beautiful woman
> who's rich and elegant besides,
> and not knowing who she is or where
> she comes from (all of this
> according to your little plan),
> and finally, being led
> blindfolded in and out of the room
> so that he isn't sure where he is!

Yet as Doña Angela rightly foresees, the ceremony of love
cannot be enacted while the antagonistic brothers are in
the house.

> Your presence here keeps my brothers
> in the house; they're so in love with you,
> they burn with starry-eyed devotion,
> and while they do, they're in my way
> and I can't risk doing anything.

When Don Luis appears behind the arras to spy on them, the conversation he overhears drives him into a frenzy of jealousy, on his brother's account no less than on his sister's and Beatriz'.

> *Doña Beatriz.* But then what could we say
> if they saw you here again?
>
> *Doña Angela.* Well, why should that surprise you?
> Don't we have brains enough to think
> of some other little stratagem?
>
> *Don Luis, aside.* I'm sure you have. The more I hear
> of this, the more I feel old griefs
> and torments welling up within me.
>
> *Doña Beatriz.* And that is how, my dear,
> unknown to anyone,
> I shall secretly await the end
> of your remarkable affair.
> For when I'm out of sight
> and everyone has gone to bed,
> I am sure that he can safely slip
> into your room from his,
> and not give rise to any scandal.

As he stands there overhearing their plan, he "grovels in humiliation," like any honor-bound marauder in the vengeance plays. And like such a figure, whose sense of insult is self-inflicted, he rebounds automatically. The jealousy involving sexual possession is too infuriating to bear, for it corresponds to the sexual exaltation of which it imagines itself deprived.

> This passion
> burning in my heart must break out.
> I have no other choice; the last

> resort of jealousy is to ruin
> the happiness of others.
> Saints alive, support me now!
> Since I am torn apart by love,
> I must die of jealousy.

Don Juan's reappearance is the occasion for reaffirming his attachment to Beatriz, a digression which leaves the stage clear for Angela while it magnifies Don Luis's jealousy.

Meanwhile, however, Cosme's neglect of certain important documents has caused him and his master to return in order to retrieve them in the darkened house. Under cover of night, Don Manuel's refusal to rouse his host puts him in the position of confronting the mystery in his apartment, which Doña Angela has just entered. Darkness and sleep are also subjects which Angela thinks of: "Isabel, everyone's retired / and sunk in sleep that steals / half their lives away." This is the environment of the erotic unconscious, and yet before Don Manuel can gain a glimpse of beauty, he recoils in fear, his rationality slips, and he is brought crashing down to Cosme's level of credulity. Perhaps because his master's fear vindicates him, Cosme himself seems less alarmed.

> *Don Manuel.*   God help me, but this
> is really supernatural!
> Suddenly a light appears —
> it's just not human!
>
> *Cosme.*   Aha,
> and so you finally admit
> that I was right.
>
> *Don Manuel.* I'm petrified!
> I'm for getting out of here.
>
> *Cosme.* So, you're only human after all.
> You're scared.

The collapse of his rationality prepares Don Manuel for a revelation, and as he watches Doña Angela sitting at his table in the light of a single candle, his rapt exclamations are counterposed to Cosme's stubbornly literal demonology.

> *Don Manuel.* Hold on! Everything comes clear now
> in the candlelight. I have
> never seen such perfect beauty
> in all my life. God in Heaven,
> what am I to make of this?
> Wonders seem to spring up
> hydra-headed all about me.
> What in the world shall I do?

> *Cosme.* She surely takes her own sweet time.
> Now she's moved the chair.

> *Don Manuel.*   The hand of God
> has never drawn a creature
> half so beautiful before.

> *Cosme.* True enough: there's nothing earthly
> to her.

> *Don Manuel.* Her lustrous eyes
> outshine the candlelight.

> *Cosme.* I'd say her eyes are lamps
> like Lucifer's that fell from Heaven.

> *Don Manuel.* Her radiant hair glints like sunlight.

> *Cosme.* Also stolen from above, no doubt.

> *Don Manuel.* Her curls, a diadem of stars.

> *Cosme.* She very likely swooped them up
> and brought them here as well,
> from paradise, limbo or hell.

> *Don Manuel.* I never saw such utter loveliness!

> *Cosme.* I'll wager you wouldn't say so
> if you could see her feet;
> the likes of her are always sure
> to have a pair of cloven hooves.

Don Manuel. Wondrous beauty, angel fair!

Cosme. Yes, it's as I say: an infernal
Angel, cursed in the hoof.

Don Manuel. I wonder what she means to do
with all my papers.

Cosme.   I would guess
she simply wants to go through them
and find the things you're looking for,
just to be saving you the trouble.
Oh, she's a helpful little devil.

Don Manuel. God only knows what I should do.
I've never thought myself a coward
till this moment.

Cosme.   Unlike me,
who always have.

Don Manuel.   I feel as though
my feet were bound in icy chains,
my hair, standing on its ends,
and every breath I draw,
like a dagger thrust straight
to the heart, or like a rope
tightened around my throat.
Must I go on like this, a prey
to my own fears? No, by Heaven,
I'll break this spell, I will!

To regain his senses, he seizes Angela's arm but does not
recognize her; in order to subdue him and escape, she
adopts the speech of an enchantress. But Don Manuel's
rationality keeps wrestling with his fear; vexed and angry
with himself, he draws his sword. At this, Doña Angela's
only recourse is to admit her love as simply as possible.

> How can you kill a poor unhappy
> woman? I confess that's all I am.
> If it is a crime to love someone,
> it is surely not so heinous
> as to deserve such punishment.

Asked to identify herself, Doña Angela replies,

> It seems at last I'm forced to do so,
> and thereby call a halt to all
> my fancies' fond designs,
> the purity of my desire,
> the sweet and earnest pledge of love.

As Cosme goes off to bring another candle and Don Manuel turns to bolt the door, she manages to slip back into her rooms through the panel, leaving her lover to entertain his "doubts a little longer." Against Cosme's renewed claim that she is a devil, Don Manuel, with tactile evidence in mind, tries to convince himself she is a particular woman.

> There was something ghostly in the way
> she suddenly appeared
> in that fantastic light,
> but there was also something human
> in the way that she avoided
> being seen and touched—
> something mortal in her fear,
> something feminine in her distrust.
> Yet she simply came apart
> like an illusion, and
> like a spirit vanished in the air.
> By God, if I gave this matter
> any further thought, who knows,
> who knows if I could any longer
> separate credulity from doubt.

In this state of mind, Don Manuel is prepared to be inducted into Doña Angela's presence, and as Act Three opens he is standing outside her door, believing that he has been led to it through obscure streets and a graveyard out of doors. He has succumbed to the challenge of love.

> In pitch darkness I found a woman
> (or so she seemed) waiting there alone.
> And without a word she led me
> from one room to another.

I said nothing, heard nothing,
saw nothing. I only groped my way
behind her till I came here.
Ah, now I see a light glimmering
through the keyhole.
> [*Looking through the keyhole.*]
> Love,
you've conquered me; there's the lady now.
The risks were all worth taking.
What a magnificent house!
What an exquisite table!
And what lovely women! Look,
how elegant they are!
How they glitter as they walk!
Such complete magnificence!

He is conducted into her rooms and finds her sitting "elegantly dressed," surrounded by curtseying ladies as though she were a queen. Awed, he delivers an extravagantly hyperbolic speech to which Doña Angela replies with disparaging directness.

Although I'm grateful to you, sir,
for such a pretty speech, I am
afraid your flattery's excessive
and rather questionable.
We do not dwell in Heaven's mansion
where the noblest passion
is so stormily expressed it would
reduce a tempest to exhaustion.
We live in this poor humble house
where such exaggerations
as you offer sound suspicious.
Do not compare me to the dawn
whose fixed smile I do not share,
for I am not frequently so blissful.
Nor am I like the early morning
light in shedding pearly tears;
I hope you have not found me weeping.
nor can I like the sun divide
the light of truth I love

into so many parts.
And so, although I cannot say
exactly what I'm like,
I only know I'm not the dawn,
the morning, or the sun of day.
At least I cannot think I am
the sunlight all aglow,
or weeping like a stream.
In sum, my dear Don Manuel,
the only thing I'd have you say
of me is that I've always been
and am a woman, and you are
the only man I have ever asked
to visit me in private.

Disarming though her confession of love has been, Don
Manuel insists on learning who she is. Doña Angela offers
to visit him and be visited by him again, but only on condition that he does not ask her name.

Accept me as something enigmatic,
for I am not what I appear
to be nor does my appearance now
belie the person that I am.
So long as I remain in hiding,
you may see me, and I see you;
but once you satisfy
your curiosity and learn my name,
you shan't be fond of me again,
though I continue fond of you.
When death has limned the features
what one sees is not a portrait.
The life descried in one light
is transfigured when it appears
in any other. The same is true
of love, the painter, for whom I sit
portrayed in double light,
which is why I fear that what you
delight to see in me at present
is but one aspect of me, and that
perhaps you will detest me when

> you come to see me in the other.
> All that I can tell you now
> which matters to me is that
> your notion about my being
> the mistress of Don Luis
> was utterly mistaken.
> You have my word, there is no ground
> for any such suspicion.

In this glittering setting, love's apotheosis takes place; yet in spite of the secrecy and expense of her imaginative efforts, and against her own wish to be taken "as something enigmatic," Doña Angela's plea is surprisingly forthright. To sustain the reality of appearances is to feed the image of love; to strip reality of its appearances, to emerge into the light of day, to become a name instead of a presence is to transfigure the image of love and kill it in the eyes of the beholder. To be a woman in love is hopefully to sustain its rites in anonymity, like a precious candle in the dark which lights up only what it touches. To be named and identified is to defeat the imagination and to introduce a "double light" which, like death, falsifies the living light, the light of single truth. In double or divided light where things are named, actions revealed and judged, and insidious motives attributed to the imagination of love, one is forced to cope with incest, jealousy, and vengeance — all the spurious claims of patriarchal authority typical of Don Luis's passion-torn world. The world of divided light is also the egotistic world of pretty speeches, vain compliments, love's power-politics, and the urgent force of rationality with its restless "curiosity" to identify and seize the object.

These consequences of "seeing double" immediately become apparent when Beatriz, according to plan, calls Angela "Your Excellency," and Don Manuel jumps to the conclusion that she is a wealthy, highborn lady.

Don Manuel, aside. There, that was a slip, enough to lift the irksome veil on all my doubts.

> Now I know she is a noblewoman,
> which is why she's so intent
> on cloaking her identity;
> and so, it was her money
> that devised and kept her secret
> plan in motion all this while.

The false rationalization automatically separates him from Doña Angela: *"The voice of* Don Juan *is heard; general consternation ensues."* And Don Manuel is thrust into the dark again — appropriately so, since it is his suspicion that lets in the outside world and breaks Angela's spell. "So help me," Don Manuel says, "there goes my life, / and my honor too, in one fell swoop." Doña Angela manages to divert her brother's suspicions but not before he has assailed her for the liberties she has taken in putting on her fineries and jewels.

Confusions multiply. Thinking he is still groping his way in some strange house instead of his apartment, Don Manuel stumbles on his servant without recognizing him, is insulted by him, and is vexed into declaring, when he discovers it is Cosme after all, "You'll drive me out of my mind." He is brought down to the level of Cosme's credulity again, and this abasement brings about further confusion when Cosme, mistaken for Don Manuel, is conducted into Doña Angela's apartment. At this point, with Cosme taking his master's place, there is an ironic repetition of the former scene's revelation. Cosme's addiction to folklore and romances causes him to exclaim: "Am I really Cosme, or am I / Amadis of Gaul? Just little / Cosme, or Belianis of Greece?" Like an impostor out of *Don Quixote,* he believes himself bewitched, and when the ladies ask him to come closer to the light, he delivers himself of an obscene anecdote about a shepherd having intercourse with the devil disguised as a woman. In effect, it is like an actor in ancient comedy beating his phallus and hurling invectives fearfully against the forces of evil. At such a moment Cosme seems entirely mad in his fixation on the devil. To

bring him out of it, Doña Angela remarks, "Collect yourself. / Here, take a sweetmeat and some water. / Fright
sometimes brings on thirst." He refuses the balm, and his
desecrating disbelief brings in the jealously fixated Don
Luis, whom Cosme guesses "must be the honest-to-good-
ness / phantom."

Like a flaming arrow flying toward its mark, Don Luis
rushes through Angela's apartment and the secret opening
into the darkness of Don Manuel's rooms, giving himself
time to snatch a lit candle after remarking, "I only hope
it's not my brother / hiding from me in this fashion," and
adding,

> Merciful Heavens! The foolish
> jealousy love planted in my heart
> which drove me here to interfere
> now gives way to insult.
> Yet I must take this candle,
> however rashly, and if light
> uncovers everything,
> light my way to honor lost.

Meanwhile, the ladies go off to seek refuge in the house of
Beatriz's father.

The encounter in the next apartment climaxes the conflict between antagonistic principles. Don Manuel is forced
to assert his partisanship in Doña Angela's cause, not accidentally but in recognition of his own commitment. He
is piqued by Don Luis' imputation that he has taken advantage of the brothers' hospitality in order to violate their
sister — an accusation which the circumstantial evidence
only too clearly supports. On this ground, Don Manuel's
rationality and Don Luis's irrationality become indistinguishable. In fighting now, they will "Share this light between us, equally" — in the darkness. To enforce equality
between them, Cosme, discovered hiding under a table, is
removed from the room. Then in the brief duel which follows, Don Luis's sword is knocked out of his hand — the

second time he has lost a sword. But Don Manuel will not press his advantage; as an honorable man enrolled in love's cause, he asks Don Luis to get another sword, and the latter departs, disarmed in more ways than one.

> One way or the other,
> I must find some excuse
> to resolve this question and
> determine what it is I owe him.

It is at this point that Don Juan, having found his sister "in stockinged feet" wandering in the street outside, and thinking that his guest is still absent, thrusts her into Don Manuel's apartment to wait until he satisfies himself concerning her activities by speaking privately with her maid. Still unrecognized by Don Manuel, she is ordered to reveal herself when he finds her there.

> *Don Manuel.* What are you, woman, a shade
> or some illusion sent here
> to destroy me? Tell me,
> how did you get in?
>
> *Doña Angela.* Don Manuel . . .
>
> *Don Manuel.*   Tell me.

And what she reveals is much more than either Don Manuel or the ironically enlightened audience has reason to suspect. It is the story of a misadventure in the darkness outside where she was apprehended by Don Juan, who in his jealousy came dangerously close to assaulting her. Having fled the mad rage of Don Luis indoors, she wandered through the streets, looking for Doña Beatriz's house,

> all my sluggish senses
> muffled in the silken prison
> of my clothes. Confused, alone,
> and terrified, my errant steps
> led me roundabout to some dim

> familiar threshold, to the haven,
> as it turned out later,
> of my former cell, and not
> the refuge of the sanctuary
> which I sought.

Disarmed of the protective devices her imagination had forged into love's mystery indoors, she stood, a helpless prey, to Don Juan's honor-masked unconscious.

> At first, I forebore,
> then vainly I delayed, to tell him
> who I was, though knowing that
> by refraining I put us both
> in certain jeopardy. Still,
> who would think silence in a woman
> could be dangerous? Yet it was
> precisely this, my being silent
> and a woman, which nearly
> finished me. For, as I say,
> there he stood—good God! waiting in
> the doorway just as I arrived—
> like a frozen volcano
> or an alp on fire. There,
> in the dim moonlight he caught
> the sudden gleam and flash of jewels
> around my neck—not, by any means,
> the first time that such baubles
> have betrayed a woman. And there
> he heard the rustle of my skirts—
> nor, there again, was it the first time
> a woman's dress gave her away.
> He mistook me for his mistress,
> to whom he flew directly
> as a moth would toward the flame
> it would be consumed by,
> the mere ghost of his lustrous star.

As the flame is to the star, so lust — the undisciplined libido — is to love. And now we understand why Don Juan condemned the elegance of jewelry and dress in Doña

Angela's apartment earlier: they inflamed his suppressed sexual passion. It is this passion which greeted Doña Angela on the threshold when he presumably mistook her for Beatriz just as Don Luis, on a former occasion, mistook her for an anonymous young widow at the palace. The unleashing of his passion puts Don Juan in the same obsessed state as Don Luis, so that there is no differentiating one brother from the other.

> Who would suppose a gallant, wracked
> by jealousy, should so utterly
> mistake his own adverse destiny
> as not to know that jealousy
> would be his fixed and awful fate?
> He tried in vain to speak,
> but deepest feeling's always mute.
> At last his quaking voice,
> which quickly blurred the words
> his tongue would utter just
> as they reached his lips, inquired
> why he had been made to suffer
> such an insult. I tried to answer,
> but, as I've said, deep emotion
> silenced me. I could not say a word.
> Perhaps it was because I sought
> to color the guilt I felt
> that fears came surging up
> to cloak my reason. It always
> follows that when one must seek
> excuses for one's innocence,
> they never come, or if they do,
> arrive too late, so that
> the very crime one would deny
> asserts itself more flagrantly.

The psychological principle with regard to innocence and guilt, reason and fear, is of course perfectly applicable to the incest-drive which both brothers have been guilty of. Since they would resort to the honor code as a means of disguising their own misdirected passions, Doña Angela, the proponent of love's rites, is now in danger of being sacrificed as a victim of the honor code.

> "Get inside," he said. "My sister
> is a wanton, and the first to stain
> the honor of our ancient name.
> I shall leave you under lock and key,
> and while you're safely hidden,
> I'll deliberate upon
> the wisest course to follow
> in redressing this insult."

Doña Angela's only recourse is to identify herself and declare her love for Don Manuel.

> To love you
> I became a phantom in my own house.
> To honor you, I became
> the living tomb of my own secret.
> Indeed, I could not tell you that
> I loved you nor how much
> I respected you for fear
> that any open declaration
> would jeopardize your presence
> as our guest, compelling you
> to quit the house at once.
> I only sought your favor
> because I loved you and because
> I feared to lose you. My only thought
> was keeping you, to cherish
> and obey you all my life, to wed
> My soul with yours, and so all
> my desire was to serve you,
> as now my plea is but
> to urge you to support me
> in my pressing need: in effect,
> to save me, comfort and protect me.

A gentleman and a rational man, Don Manuel must abide by the honor code at the same time that he is obliged to defend womankind, following the humane interests of

the love principle. As such, he is now involved in a fundamental conflict of allegiances, calling on the deepest part
of himself to resolve.

> *Don Manuel, aside.* All my troubles seem to rise up
> hydra-headed from dead ashes.
> What am I to do, sunk in this deep
> abyss, this human labyrinth
> of myself?
>
> .   .   .
>
>   if I try
> to free her and defend her
> with my blood, or let my sword
> underscore her innocence,
> I thereby compound my guilt,
> for that's to say that I've betrayed
> him as a guest in his own house.
> If I plead my innocence
> by implicating her, then that's
> to say she was the guilty one,
> which my sense of honor won't allow.
> Then what am I supposed to do?
> If I reject her, I'm a villain.
> If I defend her, a thankless guest:
> and fiendishly inhuman,
> if I yield her to her brother.
> Say I decide to protect her;
> that makes me a false friend;
> and if I free her, I violate
> a noble trust; if I don't free her,
> I violate the noblest love.
> Whichever way I turn, I'm in
> the wrong. So I'll die fighting.
> [*To Doña Angela.*] Madam, have no fear. I am a
> gentleman; you shall be protected.

We have come full circle from Don Manuel's initial defense of Angela in the first act. Now, however, his response
is far from being the automatic reflex it was in the beginning. For what seems his insufferable delay and caution

in answering Doña Angela's hope and need is actually a clearing of the ground before the principles of love and gentility can be fully vindicated. The audience, having all the evidence summed up in this fashion, can now fully appreciate the mystery of love's rites and understand it. Don Manuel has retrieved the pastoral ethic at the last moment from out of the jaws of the honor-incest complex. Yet in order to do so, he must seem to be acting in accord with the face-saving formula regarding the preservation of family honor. This he accomplishes when Don Luis returns, shortly followed by Don Juan, and vows to marry Doña Angela before taking her from the house. Don Juan will now marry Beatriz. Love triumphs, though honor is not overthrown. Cosme is restored from madness, though when refusing the offer of Isabel's hand, he shows himself to be the confirmed bachelor cynic, fearful of women and devil worshipper to the end. And with this, *The Phantom Lady* is concluded.

When the play ends we feel that the irrational, in the double form of phantom lady and imaginary devil, has been given its due. The incest threat flickering across the anxious face of honor has been put down, and for once in Calderón the rites of love have superseded the bleak honor formula with its insult-vengeance complex.

8 The Magnanimous Prince and the Price of Consciousness:

Life Is a Dream

The appeal of *Life Is a Dream* can never be wholly accounted for. From one point of view it seems incomplete, even fragmentary, like Marlowe's *Doctor Faustus*. From another, the play powerfully condenses in its enacted metaphor of living-and-dreaming an overwhelming perception about life's worth together with man's failure to make much if it. The play is many-faceted: it keeps changing as one holds it up to scrutiny so that its real theme seems impossible to pin down. It has the appeal of a mystery, but one in which the living energy that makes up the mystery is withheld, and while being withheld gets transformed into something different from the rigid terms and structure meant to contain it. Though following a straightforward dramatic pattern and the clearly stated and often repeated idea framed in the title, the play's meanings are not reducible, as they are often made to seem, to a few neat exempla about the turnings of fate and religious belief. The meanings grow, they shift their ground, they multiply with each reading. It is what happens in all great literary works: for a moment we behold the full and clear design only to note immediately beneath it the baffling multiplicity of effects raying out beyond into so many intimately related ideas we cannot even begin to name them.[1]

In this play honor is seen in its broadest possible sense as related to the whole of life, interwoven with the very substance and meaning of life. The title implies the question, Is life worth living? By a further implication, if honor is an illusion, so is life, and if this is true, how does one cope with such a vast and fearful discovery?

Another related and basic problem is the question of how to deal with the violent and secret crimes of the older generation. Since Rosaura as well as Segismundo have been dishonored by their fathers, how can they redress their personal grievances without rupturing the relationship of one generation with the next, the succession of life itself? The old myths stir beneath the surface: Zeus dethroned Cronus, as Calderón fully showed in another play, *La estatua de Prometeo* 1669 (Prometheus's Statue); Zeus raped Leda as a swan and Europa as a bull; Aeneas abandoned Dido. All the actions pertain here to the sexual crimes of worldly men as fathers and lovers. Clotaldo raped and abandoned Violante, Rosaura's mother, and the rapist duke Astolfo abandoned Rosaura. In political terms, Segismundo will swear to overcome his father and trample on his beard.

Rosaura and Segismundo both have good cause to seek vengeance. They have been brutalized. Rosaura has been raped, deprived of her sexual honor, and rejected as a woman, without explanation. And, as far as he knows, also without explanation, Segismundo has been spiritually assaulted, deprived of his liberty, his free will, his honor as a man, and left since birth in a prison tower, like his father's guilty rotting dream. Deprived of his power as a man and as a prince, Segismundo has also been left ignorant of the existence of women, of love, of social communion.

To regain her honor (since there is no one to act for her), Rosaura must pretend to be a man — dress and act like one — so that she may have the sexual and political freedom needed to force the issue. To redress his grievances, Segismundo must seek power by revolution, imitate a tyrant in order to dethrone one, so that when he triumphs he can accomplish three things: rectify the misuse of power and dispense justice; restore his own freedom and gain the power proper to him as a man and as a prince; destroy the opposing vision: his father's self-rotting dream.

No other course is possible since, as the situation of the play proposes, even if *la vida es sueño, vida infame no es vida* — a life disgraced is no life at all.

Segismundo must be twice awakened and have Rosaura's help before he attains to consciousness. So, too, Rosaura, in order to restore her honor as a woman, cannot finally act as a man; when her father fails her she can only seek Segismundo's help. He in turn is thus forced to confront her as a libidinous object and then to recognize that if he were to overmaster and take her as a woman, the act would be a violation of the sort she is now doubly seeking to redress: her father's rape and abandonment of her mother, and Astolfo's rape and abandonment of her. She must serve Segismundo as a benign influence, a test and a guide, not as his sexual partner.

Theirs is a strange relationship. It seems that the similarity and common urgency of their grievances have set up something like an incest barrier between them. Perhaps it is not so much a relationship as a brief series of crucial confrontations. She arrives to bring him a new sense of the world of which he has been deprived since birth. Her beauty and her light are essentialized in her name: the spirit of the rose (*rosa aura*) and a series of dawns (*auroras*, her name anagrammed). Beholding her beauty and person as the gifts they are, Segismundo instinctively wishes to possess them. He must learn that he can have her only as one who identifies his life's struggle for him and as someone who then must share a mission with him. In the darkness of the prison tower, in the open doorway waiting to emit him, Rosaura sees the womb and tomb of life:

> The front door
> stands open to . . . what is it,
> a mausoleum? And pitch darkness
> like the night itself comes
> crawling out as from a womb.

It is life, unaware of itself as yet, for it has been buried in death, a light in the darkness at first, followed by the clanking of chains as the prisoner, man himself, emerges in animal pelts. Can it be that Rosaura is privileged to witness this birth scene because she is Segismundo's "twin" — that at this moment she, too, is being born into consciousness through her recognition of his birth?

We know that Calderón was coauthor, with Antonio Coello, of a *Vida*-like play, *Yerros de naturaleza y aciertos de fortuna,* 1634 (Nature's Errors Redeemed by Fortune), written presumably the year before *La vida es sueño.* The two plays have a good deal in common.[2] The plots are similar, and the names of the two characters, Segismundo and Rosaura, identical, though these do not happen to be principal characters in *Yerros.* The leading figures in *Yerros* are an attractive but fatally disrupted set of twins, Matilde and Polidoro, heirs to the throne left vacant by their recently deceased father, King Conrado. Matilde, the daughter, is more aggressive than her brother. In order to gain the throne she plans to kill him (first giving out that she herself has been drowned) and take over his identity and dress and rule in his place. She is aided in this plot by the support of an older (and Clotaldo-like) character, Filipo, who has found Polidoro compromising his daughter Rosaura by entering her room. But instead of doing away with Polidoro, as he has promised, Filipo shuts him up in a tower. Then Segismundo, Filipo's son (Segismundo and Rosaura are indeed brother and sister in *Yerros*), arrives, seeking vengeance on Polidoro, gets into the palace, and kills someone who looks like his intended victim. (The someone, of course, turns out to be Matilde.) Subsequently Polidoro is brought from the tower and proclaimed king, whereupon he pardons all his enemies and takes Rosaura as his wife.

The unconscious vibrations of attraction and repulsion marking Segismundo's encounters with Rosaura in *Life Is a Dream* seem to have a start in the two sets of sibling relationships (Matilde-Polidoro and Segismundo-Rosaura) in the *Yerros* play. It is almost as if Calderón had not yet brushed out of his mind certain aspects of these relationships — the twins, the masculine sister, the names of other characters who are related as brother and sister, the incest threat, the accession of the imprisoned man to the kingship at the end — before he began to write the *Vida* play. Vibrations of attraction and repulsion based on the incest taboo are actually featured in other Calderón plays — *Devotion to the Cross* and *Los cabellos de Absalón*, 1634 (The Hair of Absalom) — in which the incest barrier is dramatically knocked over. There is some precedent, for magnifying such sexual affinities in Calderón. In any case, one reason to stress the unconscious motif here is that the strong cause which Segismundo shares with Rosaura against brutalization is usually scanted in favor of discussions about techniques and metaphysics in the play. It is not often seen that the mysterious interdependence between Rosaura and Segismundo has directly to do with the moral realism of their claims in a male-dominated, autocratic society. They need each other not only to regain their womanhood and manhood, respectively, but also because what they have to face is an extremely adverse and unpromising set of circumstances, not least because they are going against the rule of custom and law as represented by guilty, well-meaning, and unjust men: Basilio, the King; Clotaldo, his chief counsellor and Rosaura's father; and the duke, Astolfo. And so the act of restoring the human integer of magnanimity in the face of its thorough brutalization by well-intentioned, civilized men is nothing short of saintly. And this is what Segismundo proceeds to do.

If the life of consciousness is the only life worth living, then Segismundo is clearly the only character in the play who succeeds in attaining it. He emerges from the dream of life, which is the condition of all the other characters, to triumph over the sleep of death, the anonymity in which he is seen at the beginning. The other characters are there to aid, block, and test him along the way, as in a dream vision. Their special counsel is against action, for they use the formula of life-is-a-dream in the narrowest sense, as a palliative, in order to civilize, taunt, even torment (read *tame*) the prince. But Segismundo's only chance to achieve his own identity is by recognizing that the formula refers to his unborn condition. This he must discover before he can be regenerated.

The stages of his regeneration are marked off by certain of his speeches and soliloquies which other characters overhear and by actions which they then witness. But these characters, often like figures in a dream, do little or nothing to show that they have been personally affected by his behavior in the narrative sequence of the play. Through his soliloquies and what he says to others, Segismundo seems constantly to be setting up rationales for acting the way he does as he goes along. The other characters, Rosaura especially, are there to feed him with the possibilities of experience which will turn out, when he understands it, to confirm his own gradual acquisition of moral consciousness. This sort of procedure, involving both being-there and not-being-there at the same time, resembles what happens in dreams and in dream allegories. There is an unalterable line to be followed which only the consciousness of a single actor may pursue, since it is essentially from his actions leading to his awareness that the real business of the play takes its meanings.

The ambiguous creature wearing animal pelts and lying chained in the tower is the prince of mankind. This is how Segismundo begins. Thereafter we are obliged to judge the moral and psychological distance he traverses in the course of the play in order to become consciously human. He must go from the lowest form of human life, the equivalent of the cave man, to the highest — the human being who learns to be civilized by responding to everything around him while doubting it all and believing in nothing. (How could someone who has scarcely even been born believe in anything?) Others may say life is a dream; Segismundo must find out whether this is true or not by living his own life. He must fight for the power he has been denied, but once it is achieved he must also wear it lightly, pardoning his enemies and renouncing his love. Shakespeare thought of magnanimity in this way too: "They that have the power to hurt and will do none / . . . They are the lords and owners of their faces, / Others but stewards of their excellence (Sonnet XCIV). And Donne, of course, too, in lines just as familiar:

> Because such fingers need to knit
> That subtile knot, which makes us man:
> So must pure lovers soules descend
> T'affections, and to faculties,
> Which sense may reach and apprehend,
> Else a great Prince in prison lies.
> ("The Extasie," ll.63–68.)

The precise virtue, then, which Segismundo will attain is magnanimity, the quality of the highest civilized behavior. Battle in a just cause, the pursuit of one's honor, the achievement of knowledge and intellectual pride, and the unswerving course of loyalty are other virtues embodied by characters in the play. But none of these saves them from suffering desperation, an unresolved moral dilemma. Only Segismundo's attainment frees the others; or — since they frequently seem to be little more than figures revolving in Segismundo's orbit — enables the lesser virtues they represent to be seen against his fundamental moral evolution.

Like honor, of which it is part, his magnanimity means

nothing in itself; it must be won by experience, past which, as he himself says,

> If my valor is destined
> for great victories, the greatest
> must be the one I now achieve
> by conquering myself.

This is no mere rephrasing of the familiar Greek adage; coming nearly at the end of the play, the sentence rings out as a momentous renunciation of power politics, the life of tooth and claw, the deceptions of intellectual and sexual pride, the blandishments of romantic appetite, and even the ambiguities of filial piety. We see that to achieve magnanimity Segismundo has had fully to recognize who and what he is, through a series of acts which includes one murder and several attempts at murder as well as threats of parricide and rape. He has had to learn to love and then to undo his love, to overcome himself, and to vanguish his father. It is not an easy formula at all. His career is a paradigm of several millennia of human history.

For magnanimity to arise it must contend with the brute in man as well as the brute in society. Half man and half beast as Segismundo recognizes himself to be at the beginning, his first understanding is that though he has an intellect which makes him superior to animals, he lacks the freedom to use it, a freedom which even the animals have.

> A brute is born, its hide all covered
> in brightly painted motley,
> which, thanks to nature's brush, is lovely
> as the sky in star-strewn panoply,
> till learning man's cruel need
> to lunge and pounce on prey
> when it becomes a monster
> in a labyrinth. Then why should I,
> with instincts higher than a brute's,
> enjoy less liberty?

Included in his recognition here are the labyrinth myth of Theseus and the Minotaur (of which his own present state of being is another version), the interiorized beast in man, and "man's cruel need" to hunt and to imprison a being as natural as himself. His first impulse on having been overheard by Rosaura is to want to kill her for thus learning about his defects: "so you won't know that I know / you already know my weaknesses." The effect of her plea for compassion — "I throw myself at your feet. / If you were born human, / my doing so would free me." — is to becalm him: "it is you, and you / alone, who douse the fire of my wrath, / fill my sight with wonder / and my hearing with admiration." Apparently the humane virtue is even more powerful than the beast in him. Moreover, in his delight at seeing her and recognizing something about the nature of his needs, he makes a complicated compliment contain a deep psychological truth; for, as he puts it, the prospect of not looking at her now.

> would be worse
> than fiercest death, madness,
> rage, and overwhelming grief.
> It would be life — for, as
> I've had so bitterly to learn,
> bringing life to one who's desperate
> is the same as taking life away
> from one who swims in happiness.

Having just entered Poland, dressed as a man, to revenge herself on Astolfo, Rosaura, a stranger in misery, is momentarily encouraged by Segismundo's view of her. It stimulates the educating role she is to play from that moment on. Much later, toward the end of the play, Rosaura is to face Segismundo and remind him of the three disguises she has worn in confronting him. Each appearance in a different guise has affected him strongly and unaccountably. He himself tells her that she has brought him the gift of life, he who is perhaps dead, perhaps not yet born. She serves to soften his annihilating rage, fill him with a sense of wonder, the first stirrings of love, and the need for communion with a fellow creature; and she gives him his first taste of inner freedom, intimations of the conscious life, a sense of self. Even later, when Segismundo is thrown off by the doubts and delusions of others, and he wants to take her as a woman in order to escape his fear, we recognize that she also proves herself a taboo object — someone with whom he has identified himself too closely, almost incestuously. Much as Julia, Eusebio's actual twin sister, serves the hero of *Devotion to the Cross,* Rosaura serves Segismundo as an inner temptation and check, a surrogate sister whom he attempts to violate, as if to challenge or escape the delusion that if life is merely a dream, he may have no identity or potency as a man.

In her own right, of course, Rosaura is also a victim of passion. Her arrival in the first scene of the play echoes with the wild animal sounds of the horse which has just thrown her:

> mad horse
> ... You rage like a storm,
> then flicker like lightning
> outspeeding light ...
>   to hurl
> and drag yourself through
> this labyrinth of tangled rocks!

She is a refugee from passion, which partly explains why she is there, dressed as a man. In the last act, when she appears on the battlefield to join Segismundo and plead for his aid in her own cause, she enters dressed "in the loose blouse and wide skirts of a peasant woman, and wearing a sword and a dagger." She is both hunter and hunted — the hysterical state of many a wronged victim of the honor plays. And it is clear that she suffers from the ambivalences of her successively alternating roles, sug-

gesting that until she is fully met and honored as a woman
she may be mistaken as a hermaphrodite; the very am-
bivalence is a factor here with which Calderón plays:

> As a woman I come hoping to win you
> over to my honor's cause;
> but also as a man would, I come
> to swell your heart, battling for your crown.
> The woman yearning for your sympathy
> kneels down here at your feet;
> the man who comes offering his service
> lends you both his person and his sword.
> But should you turn to take
> the woman in me as all woman,
> the man in me would kill you,
> in strict defense of my good name;
> for, to triumph in the war of love,
> I must be both the humbled woman
> who appeals to you and the man
> who's out for honor and for glory.

Segismundo turns aside but when he finally replies, it is
with the full passion of a man who has recognized her as
a woman he cannot have:

> I do not even look at you because
> as someone sworn to look after
> your honor, I have all I can do
> to keep from looking at your beauty.

And Segismundo leaves to join the wild mobs that have
put themselves in his hands so that he may seize the
kingship.

But we do not leave Rosaura without recalling how
much she has served, both consciously and unconsciously,
in the play as an educating agent. When she needs to
appear in court in order to contact Astolfo, she disguises
herself as a maid in the service of Estrella, and calls herself
Astrea. Then we recognize that the names of mistress and
maid here are homonymic and that both names are syn-

onyms for *star*. Estrella is associated more with the idea
of fate and destiny (which is what she serves when she
becomes Segismundo's wife at the end); Astrea suggests
the generic term for *star*. This difference is perhaps con-
tained in another distinction, one which Rosaura herself
makes when addressing Astolfo while still disguised as
Astrea

> Es que Estrella — que lo puede
> ser de Venus — me mandó

"[I can only tell you] that Estrella, bright and beautiful /
as Venus, has asked me." There follows the business of
the return of the true portrait, which Astolfo is wearing
around his neck, demanded by Estrella, and the confusion
over two portraits, when there is only one, brought on by
Rosaura-Astrea's ruse to get her own back. One wonders
if by this interchange Calderón means that Astrea (Rosaura), as the true intended for Astolfo, must first merge
with another "star" (Estrella) in disguise before she can
claim him, and hence the confusion over (fusion with)
the identity of the woman in the disputed portrait. Rosaura, at any rate, succeeds so well with her ruse that she
not only recovers her own portrait but also manages to
get from Estrella the admission that it — because it looks
like Rosaura — is the true one. Incidental to all this, but
by no means unimportant, Rosaura has begun to regain
her honor.

The analogue to Rosaura's retrieval of her portrait is
Segismundo's recognition, almost coincidentally at the end
of Act Two, that the relationship between dream and
reality, illusion and life, sleeping and waking, might be
the same as the imposition of one's free will upon the
stream of life, which we call experience:

> for the world
> we live in is so curious
> that to live is but to dream.
> And all that's happened to me tells me

that while he lives man dreams
what he is until he wakens.

. . .

I dream that I am here
manacled in this cell,
and I dreamed I saw myself
before, much better off.
What is life? A frenzy.
What is life? An illusion,
fiction, passing shadow,
and the greatest good the merest dot,
for all of life's a dream, and dreams
themselves are only part of dreaming.

What we do, what we become through what we do, is the
substance of our dream which is our life. Moreover, he
has also come to sense that the rational factors of one's
consciousness are quite separate from one's irrational and
unconscious life, which is the area of experience most in
need of self-education, control, experiment, and the imposition of will, the life force. (Of course he has been
formally tutored all along by Clotaldo in the tower; he has
had instruction in politics, natural history, and the Catholic faith before being let out of the tower. In fact, his
"formal education" is one of the sources of the delusion
Clotaldo practices on him when he awakens in the tower
at the end of Act Two.) It is at this point that one sees
something of his self-educative process: from having been
"wakened" by Rosaura in the tower, at the beginning, from
the "dream" of life into the more advanced stage now of
his consciousness of its reality as "experience" — what a
man does is what he is. It is only disillusionment (*desengaño*), the wakening dream of death-in-life, the condition of being immured, stillborn, in the tower, that he has
come to detest. Having accepted the dream of life, Segismundo is ready to act; he is ready to deal as a prince with
the chance and irrational events of experience. He has
begun to control his impulses.

As for King Basilio, his father, the life of impulse is more overwrought by rationalization and more protected by the majesty of his position. If Segismundo's progress toward higher consciousness is marked off by his soliloquies, Basilio's decline as a potent figure of authority is noted in his long, self-justifying speeches and by his fitful behavior in the presence of his son. We see him at first as a savant, a conscientious ruler eager to assure the peaceful transference of power on resigning the throne so that he may pursue his extraordinary studies. But then we learn that it is his intellectual pride, his boastful knowledge of the stars, which caused him to imprison his infant son as a monstrous tyrant-to-be. His uneasy curiosity to discover whether he has done the right thing initiates the action of the play, bringing the young, chained Prince Segismundo out of the tower and into the palace.

The guilt that fans these rationalizations is revealed when Basilio imputes to his son the murder of his mother in childbirth, using this excuse as the reason for accepting the adverse prophecies of the stars. There is also his over-eagerness to settle the crown on Segismundo's cousins, Astolfo and Estrella, by a gratuitous public test of Segismundo's unfitness to rule. Basilio's fears and pride allow him to deny the realistic auguries of experience, proof of which is brought to bear by Segismundo's sharp arguments. But these arguments, the strongest in the play, do not overcome Basilio; the power of arms he wishes to abjure and his own compounded fears are what overcome him. When these defeat him he is ready — as one wishing "to do something, Clotaldo, / that has long needed doing" — to give in, submit his pride and guilt to Segismundo, and kneel at his son's feet.

But if there are mythical reverberations in Segismundo's struggle toward higher consciousness, something similar subsists beneath Basilio's tremors, something that goes to the heart of the play. For it appears that what Basilio is fighting is the blind fear of the succession of life, which he has suppressed by imprisoning his son. The power he seems so eager to resign he is actually wishing to preserve by transferring it to less threatening and remoter kin. He thereby avoids the issue of its true passage and transmission to a natural heir whose identity he had kept a secret and against whom he now gathers all the other characters to conspire. He would make this conspiracy as effective as he believes he has made his boastful challenging of the auguries of heaven. The gift of life Rosaura has stirred up in Segismundo is what Basilio has all the time been zealously withholding from him. And subsequently, when Segismundo's experience teaches him how to understand the caution that "life is a dream," the prince is ready to accede to the soldiers' invitation to rebel against his father and actively wrest the power which Basilio has been hoarding.

To do so Segismundo must first break the conspiracy which prevents him from acting, surrounded as he is, like a bull, by baiters cautioning him to accept the illusion of life as self-explanatory. It would appear that he must break out of this chain — the impediment to his credulity and manhood — in order to be disillusioned and thrown back into the nullity of dreaming before he can understand the use of power necessary to subjugate his father. Then he must use renunciation to cast off the illusion of false victory — which is the enjoyment of power for its own sake — and incidentally, to reestablish the structure of society which his rebellion has so severely threatened. All these are forces and tests which Basilio's hidden fear and intellectual pride have set in motion.

To effect these transformations Calderón employs the *gracioso* Clarín and the rebellious soldier in the final act. (He has used the palace servant for a similar purpose in the second act, when needing a violent example of a substitute sacrifice. There Segismundo had to be shown as unbearably vexed by the conspiracy he had not yet been able to withstand; he could not yet strike out against any person greater than the presumptuous servant and succeed.) Another heedless and arbitrary aspect of power manipulation, especially when enforced by rebellion, is shown through Clarín. Because he babbles too much, Clarín is imprisoned in the tower and there mistaken for the prince by the rebels. Earlier, in the second act, the prince had impulsively taken Clarín as an ally: "You're the only one who pleases me / in this brave new world of moribunds." Clarín is incapable of illusion or disillusionment; he stands outside the course of events in order to comment on them from a nonmoral point of view. But now in the third act it is just such a point of view which Calderón finds especially useful: first, to underscore the folly and taint of the power drive, and second, to provide a victim for another substitute sacrifice, one that must now be made for Segismundo's taboo crime of a son overcoming a father, and worse, overcoming him as the divinely appointed king in an act of rebellion.

So Clarín's fate — to be shot to death while hiding from the battle — accomplishes two things. It shocks King Basilio into understanding his own vainglory in opposing the designs of heaven, hence preparing him to succumb to Segismundo; it also releases Segismundo from the crime of rebellion. And when the dissident soldier is sent to the tower, we recognize that the order of constituted authority has been restored by Segismundo. Chaos and anarchy have been consigned to the house of illusion, sleep, and death. The tower itself is preserved; it is not destroyed. What Segismundo suffered in it others will continue to suffer. Segismundo himself points to this condition in the closing words of the play:

> Why are you surprised? What's there
> to wonder at, if my master in this
> was a dream, and I still tremble
> at the thought that I may waken
> and find myself again locked in a cell?
> Even if this should not happen,

> it would be enough to dream it,
> since that's the way I've come to know
> that all of human happiness
> must like a dream come to an end.

This speech follows exclamations of praise for Segismundo's "judgment," "changed disposition," "prudence" and "discretion." In a sense the burden of his reply to these praise words must be taken as half-bitter, half-jocose. For he has learned, among other things, that human beings are finally not as good as they may be. Their failures are significant since it is precisely these failures which cause others trouble and suffering. And under failures one would include all the deceptive ideals, false hopes, and easy disillusionments. But despite this disquieting discovery, he has also learned that life must be lived honorably, even if it does turn out that life is a dream, something we pass through dreaming. For life is also an unbroken chain, a succession of generations tied to one another, physically and spiritually. And it is also in some sense a sacred mystery that must not be destroyed. Segismundo touches on this subject in some cautionary lines during his last long speech:

> Those who lie
> and are mistaken are such men
> who'd use them to bad purpose
> trying to penetrate the mystery
> so as to possess it totally.

Stressing the nature of the play as a waking dream vision with the leading thematic concern it expresses for the triumph of consciousness indicates how Calderón essentializes thought and action while giving both the widest possible applicability in a strict dramatic form. Though *Life Is a Dream* is Calderón's best-known play, it is not, like his *auto* of the same title, a religious but a metaphysical drama. Yet it shares with a good many of his plays a basically antiauthoritarian bias. What is more, it is aligned

with such a variety of other plays as *Devotion to the Cross,
The Wonder-Working Magician, The Mayor of Zalamea,*
and *The Phantom Lady* by its persistent exploration of
the humane virtues of clemency, love, and magnanimity,
held up against the combative principle of the strict honor
code — the power drive, vengeance, absolute law. In *Life
Is a Dream,* perhaps uniquely among Calderón's plays, a
metaphysical problem is supported not by appeals to faith
or insistence on ideality but from the proofs of experience
itself. For the virtue of magnanimity to emerge in Segismundo it must be shown to overcome the lesser virtues
breeding the brutalization of experience — false pride,
rape, murder, and perverted sexuality. By implication the
play is a criticism of inflexible rule, of self-deceptive au-
thoritarianism masquerading as benevolent justice, and of
all abuses to the individual arising from it.

Appropriate to such criticism are Calderón's disclosures
of the life of impulse which underlies the motivations of
his characters. Such disclosures often lead typically to a
formula whereby compulsive action, moral desperation,
and distraught behavior must issue from sidetracked and
guilty consciences: the pursuit of vengeance and the expression of doubt from the fear of infidelity, perverted love,
and incest. But from this and other examples of his psychological realism, we see that Calderón at his best is never
merely a preacher or an upholder of an abstract morality.
He essentializes in order to identify; he dramatizes in
order to characterize; and he particularizes experience in
order to show that relation of misguided motives to the
espousing of false ideals and the necessity of earned perception for the attainment of practicable ideals. This still
seems a lesson worth having.

9 An Ending

In these pages the honor theme has been regarded as generating certain timeless instances of the conscience battling to emerge into fuller self-awareness. Battles of this sort have been going on at least since Shakespeare and probably since Sophocles. Because they still go on, we cannot overlook such difficult particular lessons as Calderón's plays have to offer. We who have never lived in his world, but find it difficult to live in our own, feel a certain kinship with the conscience-torn, honor-bound man of Calderonian drama. Perhaps the only place where such contrasting, uninhabitable, yet real worlds may co-exist is in the poetic world. P. N. Dunn, an astute commentator on the honor plays, observes that "A dramatist makes imaginary people in order to show them to real people who, from the point of view of moral awareness, may be scarcely more real than the imaginary ones."[1] As a twentieth-century audience to seventeenth-century drama, we may be more real than Calderón's contemporaries only because we are more attentive, more sensitized to the issues and the consequences than they were.

We can read ourselves in Calderón because we pick up and appropriate what Northrop Frye calls the "illustrated meaning": "Reading all poems in terms of their presented or illustrated meaning, we come to realize that there are no dead ideas in literature. The imagination operates in a counter-historical direction — it redeems time . . . and literature exists totally in the present tense as a total form

of verbal imagination."[2] Reading in this way makes us
see that the things we imagine are unique to our own
time may very nearly duplicate the experience of an earlier
age. Even Frye's description of a conscientious impasse
peculiar to our time sounds oddly like the situation of the
Calderonian hero in the honor plays: "The center of the
anxiety of privilege, as we keep searching for it, seems to
be first a fear of the significant moment, then a fear of
pleasure itself, and then, perhaps, a fear of taking the
privilege which is ours by right and is not gained at someone else's expense."[3] More particularly this might be sum-
marizing Calderón's hunt for freedom dramatized by the
honor-bred virtues and defects: magnanimity, hospitality,
civility, self-sacrifice, protectiveness, on the one hand; suspicion, jealousy, sterility, vanity, incest, rape, and murder,
on the other. We see that however negative or ambiguous
Calderón's critical depiction of the heroic principle appears, honor somehow still remains a viable subject, a
valuable idea, and a necessary part of our lives — one of
those things we tell ourselves makes life worthwhile. To
be so estimable, Calderonian honor must obviously be
seen in twentieth-century terms, while still retaining its
own curiously persuasive, seventeenth-century expression
of the conscience. From occasionally noting this possibility in these pages to insisting that the relevance of the
anachronism be made demonstrable is an emphasis now
needing to be sustained. I do not mean to discard strictly
historical and structural emphases, which receive constant attention from the scholars, but perhaps only to
observe that they are by now less fruitful means of portraying Calderón's universal merits.

Allusions have here been made, sometimes with a de-
liberate sense of the anachronism involved, to the psychological subthemes, motifs, and resonances which arrest
attention in the plays. These concern the father-son conflict and sibling rivalry; the subjection of women and the
eruption of incestuous desires; the general unreality of

relationships in the honor-seized family; the suppressed life of impulse behind unconscious motifs; and the alternation of effects raised by allegory with its wide psychomythic identifications we call archetypal. As the reverberant centers of the drama most felt by a modern reader, they deserve further looking into.

The relationship between father and son is the crucial one in any authoritarian society. It capsulates all dependency ideas which society counts on in order to survive: leadership; obedience; ownership; the peaceful passage of power and goods to the rightful heirs; the protection of the family, particularly the female, against assault; the military protection of the state; the recognition and enforcement of laws which transcend the rights and impulses of the private individual. Calderón reworks the father-son conflict in countless plays, but especially, as we have noted, in the visceral conduct of antagonists in *Life Is a Dream* and *Devotion to the Cross*. Aristotle may have been the first literary critic to understand the basic implications of the relationship to be found in such plays when he observed that "The patriarchal family supplies the primal model for political government; the first form of government is kingship, because families are always monarchically governed."[4] The oppressions resulting from patriarchal obligations — to work, to pay homage to older men, to be ruled by authority, to fight for the fatherland — are versions of the oppressions inflicted on the son by any authoritarian father.

Franz Kafka's fiction is the grimmest contemporary presentation of this instance. *Letter to His Father* is the quintessential document revealing the personal basis of the relationship in all the fiction: "My writing was all about you; all I did there, after all, was to bemoan what I could not bemoan upon your breast." And "For me you took on the enigmatic quality that all tyrants have whose rights are based on their persons and not on reason." This surely recalls the condition of Eusebio in *Devotion to the Cross;*

even more explicitly, an almost point-for-point parallelism might be made between Segismundo complaining to Basilio and this complaint of Kafka's to his father:

Hence the world was for me divided into three parts . . . one in which I, the slave, lived under laws that had been invented only for me and which I could, I did not know why, never completely comply with; then a second world, which was infinitely remote from mine, in which you lived, concerned with government, and with the issuing of orders and with the annoyance about their not being obeyed; and finally a third world where everybody else lived happily and free from orders and from having to obey. I was continually in disgrace: either I obeyed your orders and that was a disgrace, for they applied, after all, only to me; or I was defiant, and that was a disgrace too, for how could I presume to defy you; or I could not obey because I did not, for instance, have your strength, your appetite, your skill, although you expected it of me as a matter of course . . .
. . .
Once again one had, so it seemed to the child, remained alive through your mercy and bore one's life henceforth as an undeserved gift from you . . . One was, so to speak, already punished before one even knew that one had done something bad.

Towards the end of the *Letter* (which was never sent) the words Kafka puts in his father's mouth seem to sum up Segismundo's history as framed by Basilio in the action of the play. In some measure they are also a condensation of Segismundo's long final speech in which the realization occurs that the guilty father may have been (indeed — for the whole point of the regicide to be acceptable — may have had to be) blameless: "you have proved three things: first, that you are not guilty; second, that I am the guilty one; and third, that out of sheer magnanimity you are ready not only to forgive me but (what is both more and less) also to prove and be willing to believe yourself that — contrary to the truth — I also am not guilty."[5] In preserving the myth of the king's inviolability, all evidence to the contrary notwithstanding, one preserves the inviolability of the kingship: "The King is dead; long live the King." Since by nature the son must rebel against his father, the next king will incite his son's rebellion and so insure his own — at least symbolic — downfall. Treason, though locked up in the tower, is still present in the kingdom, and will no doubt erupt again to aid the unborn sons in overcoming unjust fathers, so that the issue of succession may proceed "naturally."

Along with the passage of power from father to son goes the transference, from one caretaking hand to the other, of all the prosperity, honor, and stability in the state. Through the father-son conflict, curiously enough, the state sees itself growing stronger. The issue of the succession, accompanied by a battle involving the honor of the participants, feeds the state power and fortifies the authority of the king, through whom the inviolability of all power and authority is sustained. As Ramón Menéndez Pidal says, "the king and the fatherland honor themselves and grow in moral strength by avenging an insult. And far from being faulted as an act of egotism, vengeance in the name of honor must be regarded as an heroic deed."[6] To illustrate the point he quotes from Lope de Vega's drama *La feria de Madrid* (The Market Fair in Madrid):

> Los padres viejos romanos
> por la patria o el honor
> los hijos con mas furor
> degollabn con sus manos.

> For honor or for country
> the ancient Roman fathers
> would with special fury slaughter
> their own sons with their own hands.

Segismundo-Calderón and Kafka writing to his father knew all about such matters.

Considerable evidence exists in the plays that Calderón was especially, perhaps innately, concerned with the disruptions of life caused by an errant father. His biography says nothing directly of Calderón's relationship to his father, though it makes the elder Calderón out to be a hard, vindictive man who hid the fact that he had sired an illegitimate son yet required Pedro to take care of him. A. L. Constandse has written an intriguing though uneven monograph drawing on this evidence and on details in several lesser known plays. From these he infers that

Pedro's childhood had been troubled by emotional conflicts: fear of a tyrannical father, effaced memories of his mother, the company of a sister who must have replaced her early, and undoubtedly — one sees this in *Devotion to the Cross* — an ambiguous situation concerning the brothers who, on the one hand could have been allies against his father, but on the other hand, his dominant replacement.

Whatever psychological inferences are to be drawn from such conflicts, the overlying religious views expressed toward them in the plays is clear enough to constitute an impressive tenet of Calderón's personal belief. Believing man to be an emanation of the divine source, even though actually far removed from eternal unity, Calderón could imagine him capable of saving himself and in the end reuniting with God. But the search for communion and incarnation has the urgent character, Constandse supposes, of a personal need that transcends the religious. And this is what is being enacted in *Devotion* when Eusebio and his twin sister Julia are driven by desperation and deprivation toward a heavenly father, bereft of all human possibility on earth. The act, according to Constandse, goes to the root of the concept of transubstantiation, and is to be identified with "the real Eucharist" in which "the body of the divinity is imaginary. Whether flesh or bread, blood or wine. But the communion is real, it is an act of reconciliation, of reunion, a social act. All those who are born of the venerated ancestor nourish themselves on the divine bread, they take part in the mystic union and thereby form a society, a parentage, a family." And within this communion is lodged "the memory of the death of the primitive father, killed by his sons, who assimilate his vital powers through cannibalistic rites."[7]

A. A. Parker, the well-known Calderonian, has lately reversed an earlier position, which denied the validity of psychomythic theorizing, and now shows how doctrinal themes in certain lesser-known plays bear upon the biography of the playwright. Parker contends (what Constandse had already implied in his lengthy discussion of the subject in the *comedias*) that in the late allegories, particularly the last *autos*, written when Calderón was nearly eighty, "the allegory does not stem from theology but from Calderón's experience of his own boyhood, which offered him the conception of Man as the disowned and disinterested son of God, claiming maintenance from his father and receiving mercy from Christ, his brother, who is God's obedient son." In clear sight of such an hypothesis lies the conclusion that "The son's revolt against his father leads to the son's tragic death in *La devoción de la cruz* and *Las tres justicias en una;* but it leads to reconciliation through forgiveness in *La vida es sueño,* and this brings the theme of paternal tyranny and filial revolt to an end in the Calderonian dramas as a central theme, though it continues as a subsidiary motif."[8] Yet it should be said that the sons in *Devotion* and *Life*, even before knowing their fathers, are already in revolt. They have good cause to rebel; their fathers turn out to be the real culprits. This suggests that the son's revolt is not so much directed against an actual father as against what he stands for, the cumulative symbol of authority: the state, the kingship, the law. Calderón was allegorist enough to employ this kind of trope again and again, particularly when adapting certain of his *comedias* into *autos*. Parker indicates that in *Three Justices in One*, it is only after the young protagonist dies that we learn he was not the son of his reputed father. And while Parker admits that the thematic emphasis cannot be laid strictly on the father-son conflict, because this is part of the larger question of "identity," he criticizes Constandse for offering a simplified version of motivation (that is, seeing the theme of a play as the working out of an Oedipus complex), while his own interpretation of Calderón's belief seems equally, if not a good deal more, simplified.

If the question of identity is indivisible from the question of honor (*soy quien soy* — I am who I am) and also underlies the father-son conflict, it must be understood both religiously and psychologically. What, for example, is the rebellion against the father but a paradigm of Satan's rebellion against God — or the wish to become God, the original father, the creator, the engenderer? And what is the son's assault on his sister but a disguised attack against the absent mother Eve for having borne him in the first place? Desperate and extraordinary though these acts seem, they are also significant as attempts to break through the self-obliterating social role, the unjust because unquestionable plight, in which men are cast, whether they know their parents or not, on being born into a world they never made. Kafka understood the point only too well. In *Letter to His Father* he repeatedly sees it with pathetic irony: "it is, after all, not necessary to fly right into the middle of the sun, but it is necessary to crawl to a clean little spot on the earth where the sun sometimes shines and one can warm oneself a little." And again: "if the world consisted only of me and you . . . then this purity of the world came to an end with you and, by virtue of your advice, the filth began with me."[9]

In the same light the resolution to the problem of identity in *Devotion* is clearly symbolized in the visible triumph of the outlawed brother and sister being conveyed to Heaven by the cross which had presided over their birth. It must in fact be regarded as a happy solution; in being taken up by God, Eusebio and Julia gain a human identity for the first time by transcending the disrupted life inflicted on them by their earthly father. In a similar play, based on the St. Chrysanthus legend and alluded to by A. A. Parker, *Los dos amantes del cielo*, 1640 / 1650 (Two Lovers of Heaven), a father imprisons, then cruelly puts his son to death because the son disavowed him in favor of the fatherhood of God. A different solution, more in line with Segismundo's in *Life Is a Dream*, occurs in Calderón's Coriolanus play, *Las armas de hermosura*, 1652 (The Weapons of Beauty), where a vindictive father who sentences his son to death is himself subjugated by the same son later returning at the head of a victorious army. In this instance the father's plea for mercy is refused. In another play, *El hijo del Sol, Faëtón*, 1661 (The Son of Phaëthon, the Sun), one is reminded of the Eusebio story when the son, discovering who his real father is, steals the Sun's fiery chariot and burns up the world with it. Beyond these examples, Parker sees another resolution of the father-son conflict in the presentation of the fatherless son as hero in the later plays. Yet all seem versions of the same rebellious force in the earlier plays where sons are outlawed or held in captivity before they come to know who their father is.

The outlawed or imprisoned son is a figure for man, ejected at birth from Paradise, his natural home, who must answer for his life — and perhaps with his life — to his creator: the primal authority that preceded him on earth. In one form or another, the paternal figure is always there, to be accounted to, while the maternal figure is nearly always absent, except in the guise of forbidden sister or adulterous wife, beloved by a previous male who will return, and is even now lurking in the shadows, and must be done away with. We see that each situation involving the hero's family also involves the family of mankind, and that in any conflict where the hero's identity is questioned, the related question of his social and sexual honor is automatically brought up as well. In a patriarchal society this becomes a question of political power. The encroaching threat of the authority figure is omnipresent — in the abiding figure of the vengeful husband and the looming presence of the irate, punitive father, but also in the fatal absence of the mother: a silent victim of wayward authority, she can only instigate but never wield repressive power.

Lacking a just authority or a responsible father, the sons or brothers must battle for erotic ascendancy and political power in the family. In *Devotion* they engage in a fatal duel, equivalent to civil war on one level and sexual strife on another, because the father has abandoned his true function as a just and potent family head. And the mother? Though seldom there, she is always imminent as the wronged one having to be avenged through her son or disguised daughter, against the errant father. Must the female figure be sequestered, imprisoned in a nunnery, because she is so vulnerable to aggression, always about to be wronged again, and her wrong never really expiated? Is she to be seen only in her son's mad wanderings, his outlawed flight from his own identity and all authority, until he comes to a day of reckoning? And what is this reckoning but a truce with authority and its social contracts — the appropriate blood spilled, the bad conscience of society momentarily allayed? Like the bad conscience the white American feels about the Negro, was the bad conscience the aggressive Catholic Spaniard felt in driving out the Jews in the name of blood purity, a necessary social myth? Conscience acts up where one is most sensitive as a man (hence its relation to sexual pride, *machismo*): in imagining the attack on one's sense of self, one's potency. Annihilating the self in an act of expiation become imaginable as a process of being mysteriously drained — as the saying goes, "the blood drained from his face when he was insulted." Literally drained of her blood, the suspected wife, Doña Mencia, is cleansed of impurity by her husband, who thus dispatches her, in *El médico de su honra*, 1635 (The Surgeon of His Honor). The social and political equivalent may be the acts of the Holy Office of the Inquisition which, like Hitler in our time, was obsessed with blood purity and used the annihilation of heretics and Jews as a legal ritual to uphold that myth.

These, then, may be the deeper implications underlying the conjectures of Parker and other critics concerned with the typological recurrence of father-son conflicts in the plays. Whatever discoveries may yet be made along such lines, it seems necessary to admit psychomythic hypotheses in the visionary identifications which Kafka and Calderón appear to share, instead of dismissing archetypal criticism for being "unscientific" and hence less reliable than theories based on the "facts" of historical scholarship or Christian iconography.

Other neo-Catholic critics, like E. M. Wilson[10] and P. N. Dunn,[11] have emphasized the moral integrity of all Calderonian drama. The suggestion is that to understand a given play one must be guided by the dramatist's interest in his theme and the lesson implicit in it, following a pattern of ideal Christian behavior. In essential agreement, A. A. Parker has studied the *autos*,[12] which of course lend themselves supremely well to moral speculations. He has noted the masterful way in which Calderón's allegorical imagination, once it had cast off routine plotting and characterization necessitated by the *comedias,* constructed complex dramatic machines in the short theological plays he spent his last thirty years writing. Since theme and imagery mirror one another in allegory, it became apparent that some view of Calderón's dramatic tropes would be needed to interpret the plays. To fill this need Parker subsequently developed, along lines set down by E. M. Wilson and W. J. Entwistle, a general way of treating metaphor and symbolism reflecting the thematic-allegorical emphasis found in the *comedias*.[13]

In a parallel investigation, springing from Parker's work on the *autos*, A. E. Sloman studied the use of antecedent texts in eight different plays, concluding that Calderón's are in each case superior to their source plays in unity and completeness. Like Parker and Wilson extricating the plum of "thought" from Calderón's concept-enactments in order to explain theme and character motivation, Sloman saw in his examples a self-confirming method of working out the same dominant moral ideas. Sloman converts his approval of these ideas into praise of the thinking playwright:

Calderón's view of man's moral responsibility . . . imposed a strict causal sequence upon the different incidents. Man is shown to be responsible for his own fate. His will is free. However strongly disposition and environment may incline, they cannot force. Calderón's characters are not at the mercy of a cruel, implacable fate; they are rather at the mercy of themselves and their fellow men. They shape their own destinies. With reason and judgement to guide them, they must choose between the conflicting loyalties and embarrassing predicaments of life. Catastrophe and tragedy do not spring from some arbitrary change of fortune imposed from outside, but are the consequences of human behavior which has not measured up to the required standard, whether the motives are good or bad.[14]

The praise ventilates a tenable opinion but is too general to be useful. One distrusts making so dynamic a thing as an acting play a formula like a chess game played for moral stakes on the board of a supertheologian. Why should Calderón bother to write plays if he could more readily preach? (Being a priest he knew the difference between preaching and playwriting presumably.) Like Parker and Wilson, Sloman tends to read the plays for their message, as if they were *autos* extended into large-scale enactments. In this way he misses the shadings of characterization aimed at effecting an interesting dramatic moment on the stage rather than creating a supreme lesson which characters must confirm in the end. Calderón surely knew that the successful enactment of strife is more convincing than any ideational summary of its possible meaning. For example, in the first confrontation between Segismundo and his father one senses a visceral and fatal distinction between the characters, as in no other part of the play. In dramatic force derived from the compulsions of opposition, it equals the scene where Hamlet is observing his uncle at prayer or where Iago begins to poison Othello's faith. Is this merely a device to strengthen theme (which in some sense it contradicts), or is it the powerful discharge of a gifted dramatic imagination creating the right moment?

Sloman's praise of Calderón's thematic-dramatic integrity promotes the idea that the dramatist's consciousness of plotting and the dispensation of penalties and rewards both superseded other levels of intention. Such intention may in effect be totally theatrical, like the clash of unconscious desires between characters, the incest threat, and all the spontaneous outbursts which people come to the theater to see and which they implicitly understand as theater life. This is only to affirm what Lope de Vega and St. Augustine noted in different ways: the audience comes to see, to be enlightened, to share in a communal experience of joy and suffering. Sloman's and Parker's view of the playwright as preacher limits him to the practice of parochial drama — so often held up as a national Spanish stereotype — and undercuts the universality of his work. Even dubbing him a thinker is a way of limiting him, since it isolates him in terms of whatever thought, theory, or craftsmanship one can extract from the body of his work to praise. One does not ask if a thing is Freudian or Christian, or if it is well-made and logically balanced, but does it work? Morality always takes care of itself.

Critics looking too closely at craft, aesthetic theory, and moral doctrine tend to forget that what they find so distinctive in a playwright may be just what he shares with other dramatists of his time — and with all literate nonplaywrights as well. It may be the least distinctive thing about him. As critics we tend to overstate our case for our particular man. The politics of criticism, like most political maneuvers, are largely discountable as rhetorical gestures "for the good of the cause." Often they do not help to improve the writer's status but to diminish it.

All plays have to be moral, if only to guard against the censor or the merely prurient peepshow fact of their public existence in performance. That is, the moral lesson they are presumed to teach is not the material or most memorable thing about them. What is memorable about a play is its sense of felt life, its *moment*, in being witnessed with other people, and that is where the critic finds himself least inclined to look for his idea, perhaps because he can find only the unpredictable vagaries of public response and no ideas at all there. Put another way: the main interest of any play may be that it is written to satisfy man's craving for gossip as witnessed and illustrated entertainment; he comes not only to hear but also to see with others, to peep into and savor the lives of those like himself. Because the subjects people gossip about are generally immoral, the playwright has to force some redeemed "idea" or lesson into his work, a bone to the regnant authority, which the play is covertly attacking. Comedy as a funny story and tragedy as a sad story are aspects of daily life he likes to see lived out by others — as St. Augustine observes in Book III, Chapter 2, of *The Confessions* — and are no more to be understood morally than playfully. A play engrosses its audience through its magical capacity for capturing while embodying moments of *changed life*, as though that life were actual, real. During such moments we find ourselves overcome by a scene, a character, an exchange — as by a melody that lifts itself out to us in a song, a symphony. Its very time-presence affects us as it brushes by us — something quite different from the thought-presence, whatever the playwright may have had in mind which subsequently became a natural byproduct of the action. The play in its full dimensionality is a three-way communion between actor, playwright, and audience. The actor asks, "What is the character I enact supposed to be like so I can tell how to stand, move, talk?" The audience asks something similar: "What am I to feel about what I hear and see?" To this end — that of satisfying actor and audience — the play is converted and directed as "play," an auditory-visual embodiment of words lifted off the page onto the stage. The stage is the arena of the collective imagination. The page is where the play sleeps; our readings, or interpretations, become the dreams of the play, as we assign to it our own sense of felt life. The stage, and not the page, is where the play has its living moment, its existence as created, constantly renewable action and reality.

The intellectual appeal of drama on the page and its enactment on the stage are the Sylla and Charybdis confrontation no dramatic critic can escape. For the student of Calderón the job is particularly trying since the playwright's interest in ideas is indistinguishable from his interest in drama. Both seem to come together in full measure through rhetoric and imagery as well as the thematic implications of the *comedias*, and later to be solidified in the allegorical designs of the sacramental plays. What Calderón means by a representable idea is an action on the stage in a play: a speaking or moving picture. This, he himself describes in *Primero y Segundo Isaac,* 1659? (First and Second Isaac): "Allegory's fantastic forms / are not bounded by time or place." (*"que alegóricas fantasmas / ni tiempo ni lugar tienen"*); and even more pointedly in *El verdadero dios Pan,* 1670 (Pan, the True God):

> Allegory is no more
> than a mirror that transforms
> what is with what is not,
> and all its elegance lies
> in that the copy and the thing itself
> should seem so alike
> that he who looks at one

would think he is looking at them both;
now let the parity run
between the living thing and its image.

La alegoría no es más
que un espejo que traslada
lo que es con lo que no es,
y está toda su elegancia
en que salga parecida
tanto la copia en la tabla
que el que está mirando a una
piense que está viendo a entrambas;
corre ahora la paridad
entre lo vivo y la estampa.

One should not take such a metaphysician literally. He must be seen through his dramatic deeds, one of which is the triumphant use he makes of the honor formula. And we are now in a position to conclude what this usage signifies in Calderonian drama.

The common view that Calderón learned from Lope to exploit the honor formula as a popular device is no doubt correct. In exploiting it he developed the form of the *comedia* and found the theme particularly viable as a metaphor for tragic *hamartia*. Once an audience was oriented to where its sympathies lay, it could be made to empathize with the main victim and executor of the folly of honor. This it could do without looking down on him, as it would have to do at low characters in comedy enacting a very similar sort of folly. Rather than being an end in itself, *pundonor* becomes the starting point of a series of unfolding discoveries about the whole of life. It also opens a way, not of lessening but of increasing the dramatic impact of the *comedia* by an allegorical reduction of theme, character, and field of action. His condensation of means and effects should be understood as part of his entire artistic intention and is not to be criticized, as it often is even by Golden Age specialists, for narrowness of purpose and lack of humane feeling. It is true that no son or daughter is shown growing up and becoming a parent in his plays; and no fruitful mother appears, a fatal reminder of the dead mother's lonely agony in childbirth and the errant father's secret guilt. One must recognize that Calderón is thereby portraying the wasteland of the self which a sterile, paranoid society has created — a living condition which no other dramatic formula could frame so well.

One thing wrong with monolinear thematic analysis is that the license it allows the critic to identify "themes" also permits endless speculation on the ramification of historical ideas to the neglect of the practical problems a dramatist must face in shaping his work. The same disproportion occurs when the critic fastens on the analysis of structural problems. The point is that the work is itself an answer to all attempts to bind it. Implicit in the play is the criticism of the bounds that would hamper it. It embodies by its own example the idea of freedom as an artistic and a human possibility.

With these cautions in mind, a recent Calderón scholar, Alan K. G. Paterson, refuses to regard *The Painter of His Own Dishonor* as an honor play at all. Proposing that such an emphasis results in a serious misreading of the play, he reads it as a portrait of the artist, Juan Roca, driven from his work by unexpected demands on his person which he is not equipped to deal with. Roca thus loses both his art and his life when he is forced into killing his wife, her surprised lover, and himself. In this view Calderón is not intrinsically a moralizing writer but one who takes off from common ideas about behavior in order to plunge into the particular, unelaborated, and problematic stuff of human experience, which has no labels, neither moral nor theological. For *The Painter of His Own Dishonor* "has tormented depths that corrode the reassuring order laid down by an academic doctrine whose spirit any playgoer would find hard to respect."[15] The play presents "a complete fusion of comedy and tragedy" and "a universe drained of providence." According to Paterson, this does not constitute a crisis or a departure from faith in Calderón but an attempt to create a dramatic study of character against the mores and the formulas. For he was

primarily a dramatist, not a theologian or an autobiographer. His task was to explore, define and communicate our common experience, in all its complexity and mystery. The haunting suspicion that life is no more consequent than farce or comedy is known to most men, an elemental doubt that drives them to the consolation of beliefs and systems. Calderón's brilliance lies in his ability to present a shapeless, arbitrary world within a perfectly articulate form, one more instance of how Golden Age writers could open up new disturbing areas of experience for literature to explore and yet maintain a formal order. His compassion, powerful enough that we feel the tragedy of comedy, is joined with a relentless refusal to offer us a means of escape from his play's vision.

To this one might add that Calderón's plays bear the same relationship to the morality of their times that Cervantes's exemplary novels do to theirs. The moral is the matrix on which the uneasy characters, caught in the grips of self-love, self-doubt, and self-hate, work out their limited and, as it often seems, absurd fates. What the thematic critics are satisfied to call the "quandary" of the hero bound by principle must, in this view, have deeper roots — roots enmeshed with the impulses which Paterson identifies as some "secret desire for immaculacy" underlying "every relationship in the play." The absolutist ethic sparking off the paranoid obsessiveness with the self directly causes the problem of derangement in the principal characters of the honor plays. This becomes the spring of misfortune, the fatal *hamartia*, which a seventeenth-century audience, primed by Lope's and Tirso's absurd, nearly farcical heroes, would be prepared to accept with full sympathy in Calderón's plays.

If anything is clear at this late date it is that if one speaks of symbolism one wishes to show something of the way in which it bridges ideas and experiences rather than isolates them. In this sense all symbols, Christian and non-Christian, are archetypal, because the human events and actions lying behind them repeat themselves in all our lives as well as in all our myths. In Kafka's letter to his father, in Sophocles' reworking of the Oedipus myth, and in Calderón's *Devotion to the Cross*, we see the same fatal mechanism at work where guilt spurs the main actor on to some self-annihilating action. It is not enough to view symbolism as doctrinal or literary alone. One must assume that the lives of Calderón's characters are both personal subjects of his own experience and universal subjects of the experience of mankind. They are made out of the primitive as well as the civilized stuff of human behavior since the beginning of time. Only in this way can one begin to see that the central themes and paradoxes in his plays are not limited to his temperament, education, or times; as with Shakespeare, Sophocles, Dante, and Cervantes, they are part of the redemptive heritage of all literature having a universal vision of human possibility.

The proof of his genius lies in the fact that when properly read (or better, when properly seen on the stage) Calderón's plays can evoke the same sympathy in us, living in a time when providence and belief have also been drained out of the world. His particular vision of that condition restores us as living creatures who would still hope for what we cannot believe. His plays renew for us the possibility of experiencing that glory and folly which go to make a full human being.

One can do worse than conclude with St. Augustine, a figure Calderón admired, writing on the enigma of one's feelings when faced with the fantasies of life on the stage:

Are we to say, then, that tears and sufferings are things which we love? Undoubtedly what every man wants is to be glad. Or is it that, while no one wants to be miserable, one still does want to have compassion, and, since one cannot feel compassion without feeling suffering, this and this alone is the reason why sufferings are loved?[16]

Biographical Note, Appendix,
Notes, and Index

Biographical Note

In the crude engraving prefacing Calderón's collected works, a distracted old melancholiac stares out at the reader. The portrait almost seems to caricature an earlier one by Juan de Alfaro, in which a somewhat younger head emerges disdainfully from the dark cape and tunic of a Knight of Santiago. The same disdain softened by resignation dominates a third portrait showing a clerical gentleman, in severe habit and flowing cape, holding a copy of his own plays opened to the title page of *Bien vengas, mal, si vienes solo,* 1635 (Welcome, Evil, If You Come Alone). And still the haunted, indrawn stare prevails. For a man who lived eighty-one years (1600–1681), and more than fifty in court society, the record is sketchy, the relevant facts of his existence singularly bare. As if to emphasize that all this is due to the playwright's characteristic reserve, unmarred by legend or exploit, the commentators have coined a phrase, "the biography of silence."

Born in Madrid on January 17, 1600, Pedro Calderón de la Barca was the third child and second son of María Henao y Riaño and of Don Diego, the Secretary of the Council of the Treasury, a fairly substantial minor post at court. The family followed the king to Valladolid and back to Madrid before Calderón's matriculation at the Imperial College of the Jesuits in 1608. The college curriculum at the time would have required enough Latin to read Cicero, Virgil, Seneca, Catullus, and Propertius, and enough Greek to read St. John Chrysostom. His mother, who wanted her son to become a priest (he was belatedly ordained in 1651), died suddenly in 1610. Four years later, he enrolled at the University of Alcalá to study logic and rhetoric, and that same year his father remarried. But in 1615 his father died, leaving a will which admits the paternity of an illegitimate son, Francisco, thereafter accepted by the Calderón household as a relative and servant. As for Pedro, the will went on, "I charge and beseech [him], under no circumstances to quit his studies, but rather to continue and finish them."

For four years after 1616 the young Calderón divided his time between Madrid and the two university cities of Alcalá and Salamanca, where he had embarked on a course in canon law; but there is no record of his having completed the course, as some biographers maintain. His earliest known verses date from this period, and in 1620 he entered a poetry competition in Madrid to honor the beatification of Isidro, who became the city's patron saint. Lope de Vega, one of the judges, bestowed some general words of praise on Calderón's efforts. About this time a litigation between the Calderón brothers and their step-mother, who had remarried in 1618, was settled satisfactorily. In addition, there is a record of a suit against them for having killed a relative of the Duke of Frias; after a huge fine was levied, the case was settled out of court.

Calderón's literary career began in the early 1620s with the winning of several poetry prizes. His first play, *Amor, honor y poder* (Love, Honor, and Power), was performed at court in June 1623; another, *La selva confusa* (The Entangled Forest), in July; and a play about the Maccabees, *Judas Macabeo*, in September of the same year. There is no record of his whereabouts in the next two years, although it is believed he was soldiering in Italy and Flanders, mainly on the basis of the vivid geographical details which turn up in his play, *El sitio de Breda*, 1625 (The Siege of Breda) — the subject, incidentally, of Velázquez's celebrated painting, *The Lances*. Of the fifteen plays he had written by 1630, at least two have become world-famous: *La dama duende* (The Phantom Lady) and *El*

príncipe constante (The Constant Prince). In the latter
Calderón satirized the florid Gongoristic style of the court
preacher, Fray Hortensio Paravicino. He was presumably
provoked by the preacher's attack on him following an
escapade in which the playwright is purported to have engaged. Seeking revenge on the actor Pedro de Villegas, who
had wounded his brother in a duel, Calderón pursued him
into a nunnery where he is said to have molested the nuns.
One of them was Lope de Vega's daughter, Marcela, and
her father complained about the incident to the Duke of
Sessa. Calderón was put under house arrest for a few
days. But the incident only spurred the young playwright's
growing popularity and brought him into higher favor at
court. By 1637 he had written forty-one plays, among them
almost all the great secular dramas by which he is best
known.

When Lope de Vega died in 1635, Calderón succeeded
him as director of all theatrical functions at Court. Two
years later he was made a Knight of Santiago after a magnificent *zarzuela* which he had superintended at the opening of the new palace of the Buen Retiro. "This was a
musical play," Gerald Brenan notes in *The Literature of
the Spanish People,*

on the theme of Ulysses and Circe, which was later printed as
El mayor encanto amor. No play had ever been given under
such splendid circumstances. A floating stage was built on the
large *estanque* or oblong pond and lit with three thousand
lanterns. Cosme Lotti, an Italian stage machinist, designed the
décor, which included a shipwreck, a triumphal water-car
pulled by dolphins, and the destruction of Circe's palace to the
accompaniment of artillery and fireworks. The king and his
suite watched from gondolas.[1]

By 1637, two volumes of his plays had been brought out
under the nominal editorship of his brother José.

If his star was fixed in the 1630's, the following decade
saw it overcast by national and personal misfortunes. In
1640 Portugal successfully revolted against the Spanish
crown, and in the same year Calderón went off with the

army sent to put down a rebellion in Catalonia. The uprising had been brought on by outrages against the peasantry committed by Spanish soldiers stationed there. The disillusioning experience is strikingly portrayed in his famous play, *El alcalde de Zalamea* (The Mayor of Zalamea). The closing of the public and court theatres, his own ill health after the military campaign, and his withdrawal from the army led to his becoming a member of the Duke of Alba's household, where he stayed for four years (1646–1650). Then, within a short period, both his brothers were killed and his mistress died, leaving him a son. In 1650 he resigned his post at court and entered the priesthood.

He accepted a chaplaincy in Toledo when prevailed on by the king to return to court in 1663, where he remained until his death. The third (1664), fourth (1672), and fifth (1677) volumes of his collected plays were edited by friends, but in the latter year Calderón himself collected and published many of his *autos sacramentales* and wrote a preface to introduce them. His preface suggests that the reader may not get the full sense of their impact without having the sound of the music and the spectacle of the staging along with the words. In 1680 he answered a request to provide a list of his plays, which he determined as 110 secular dramas and 70 *autos*.

Little personal information exists about him in his later years. He was known to have been an avid collector of votive objects, with which he filled his apartment in Madrid. There are two other, very slight reports of him. In one a French diplomat relates that he had spoken with Calderón and gathered from the conversation that the playwright had little general knowledge and, despite his hoary locks, knew almost nothing about the rules of drama. In the other, which seems an answer to this, a eulogist declares that on the day of his death, May 25, 1681, Calderón was writing a new *auto*, so that "he died, as they say of the swan, singing."

Appendix: Passages in Spanish Original

CHAPTER 1. A BEGINNING

Page 3. *El pintor de su deshonra*

... aquí
no hay realidad de personas,
y lo alegórico puede
parar los siglos por horas ...

CHAPTER 3. HONOR AND THE COMIC SUBVERSION

Page 22. *El alcalde de Zalamea*, estudio, edición y glosario
por Augusto Cortina (Madrid: Espasa-Calpe, S. A., 1968)

que como de otras no ignoran
que a cada cosita lloran,
yo a cada cosita canto ...
$$\text{(I, i, 126–128)}$$

Page 23.

    Si acaso aquí la viera,
della caso no hiciera;
    y sólo porque el viejo la ha guardado
deseo, vive Dios, de entrar me ha dado
    donde está.
$$\text{(I, xii, 589–593)}$$

Page 23.

¿Pues no hay, sin que yo me case,
huelgas en Burgos, adónde
llevarla cuando me enfade?
                (I, iv, 336–338)

Page 23.

que los hombres como vos
han de amparar las mujeres,
si no por lo que ellas son,
porque son mujeres . . .
                (I, xv, 694–697)

Pages 25–26. *A secreto agravio, secreta venganza*, adición, prólogo y notas de Ángel Valbuena Briones (Madrid: Espasa-
Calpe, S. A., 1956)

   D. Lope.   ¡Felice yo si pudiera
volar hoy!
   Manrique.   Al viento igualas.
   D. Lope.   Poco aprovecha; que el viento
es perezoso elemento.
Diérame el amor sus alas,
volara abrasado y ciego;
pues quien al viento se entrega,
[olas] de viento navega,
y las de amor son de fuego.
                (I, i, 26–34)

CHAPTER 4. DEHUMANIZING HONOR: *SECRET VENGEANCE FOR SECRET INSULT*

Page 38.

Si hoy, que te vas a casar,
del mismo viento te quejas,
¿qué dejas que hacer, qué dejas
cuando vayas a enviudar?
                (I, i, 43–46)

Page 41.

    D. Leonor. Si no lo hace, ¡vive Dios!,
que podrá ser que a los dos
nos venga a costar la vida.
    Sirena. Desa suerte lo diré,
si puedo verle y hablalle.
    D. Leonor. ¿Cuándo falta de la calle?
Mas no hables en ella, ve
a buscarle a la posada.
    Sirena. Mucho, señora, te atreves.
             (II, i, 50–58)

Pages 41–42.

¡Qué castellana que estáis!
Cesen las lisonjas, cesen
las repetidas finezas.
Mirad que los portugueses
al sentimiento dejamos
la razón, porque el que quiere,
todo lo que dice quita
de valor a lo que siente.
Si en vos es ciego el amor,
en mí es mudo.
             (II, i, 85–94)

Page 42.

Quisiérale acompañar
a la jornada; y por verme
casado, no me he ofrecido
hasta que licencia lleve
de tu boca, Leonor mía.
Esta merced has de hacerme,
en este [caso] has de honrarme,
y este gusto he de deberte.
           (II, i, 131–138)

Page 44.

          Testigo
es Dios (otra vez lo digo),

que si yo me lo dijera,
a mí la muerte me diera,
y soy mi mayor amigo.
(III, i, 136–140)

Page 45.

¿Hay, honor, más sutilezas
que decirme y proponerme?
¿Más tormentos que me aflijan,
más penas que me atormenten,
más sospechas que me maten,
más temores que me cerquen,
más agravios que me ahoguen
y más celos que me afrenten?
No. Pues no podrás matarme,
si mayor poder no tienes . . .
(II, i, 325–334)
Page 45.

Honor, mucho te adelantas;
que una duda sobre tantas
bastará a volverme loco.
En otro sujeto toco
lo que ha pasado por mí.
(III, i, 102–106)

Pages 45–47.

¡Ay honor, mucho me debes!
Júntate a cuentas conmigo.
¿Qué quejas tienes de mí?
¿En qué, dime, te he ofendido?
Al heredado valor,
¿no he juntado el adquirido,
haciendo la vida en mí
desprecio al mayor peligro?
¿Yo, por no ponerte a riesgo,
toda mi vida no he sido
con el humilde, cortés,
con el caballero, amigo,
con el pobre, liberal,

con el soldado, bienquisto?
Casado, ¡ay de mí!, casado,
¿en qué he faltado?, ¿en qué he sido
culpado? ¿No hice elección
de noble sangre, de antiguo
valor? Y ahora a mi esposa,
¿no la quiero?, ¿no la estimo?
Pues si en nada no he faltado,
si en mis costumbres no ha habido
acciones que te ocasionen,
con ignorancia o con vicio,
¿por qué [me] afrentas?, ¿por qué?
¿En qué tribunal se ha visto
condenar al inocente?
¿Sentencias hay sin delito?
¿Informaciones sin cargo?
Y sin culpas ¿hay castigo?
¡Oh locas leyes del mundo!
¡Que un hombre, que por [sí] hizo
cuanto pudo para honrado,
no sepa si está ofendido!
¡Que de ajena causa [ahora]
venga el efecto a ser mío
para el mal, no para el bien,
pues nunca el mundo ha tenido
por las virtudes de aquél
a éste en más! ¿Pues por qué digo
otra vez) han de tener
a éste en menos, por los vicios
de aquella que fácilmente
rindió alcázar tan altivo
a las fáciles lisonjas
de su liviano apetito?
¿Quién puso el honor en vaso
que es tan [frágil]? ¿Y quién hizo
experiencias en redoma,
no habiendo experiencia en vidrio?
Pero acortemos discursos;
porque será un ofendido
culpar las costumbres necias,
proceder en infinito.

Yo no basto a reducirlas
(con tal condición nacimos);
yo vivo para vengarlas,
no para enmendarlas vivo.
                    (III, 229–286)

Page 48.

Cuando don Luis me amaba,
pareció que a don Luis aborrecía;
cuando sin culpa estaba,
pareció que temía;
y ya (¡qué loco extremo!)
ni amo querida, ni culpada temo;
antes amo olvidada y ofendida,
antes me atrevo, cuando estoy culpada,
y pues para mi vida
hoy sigue al Rey don Lope en la jornada,
escribo que don Luis a verme venga,
y tenga fin mi amor, porque él le tenga.
                    (III, 640–651)

Page 49.

y habiendo estado las aguas
tan dulces y lisonjeras,
que el cielo, Narciso azul,
se vió contemplando en ellas . . .

porque mirar tantas quintas,
cuyas plantas lisonjean
ninfas del mar, que obedientes
con tanta quietud las cercan,
es ver un monte portátil,
es ver una errante selva;
pues vistas dentro del mar,
parece que se menean.
Adiós, dulce patria mía,
que en él espero que vuelva
(puesto que es la causa suya) . . .
                    (III, 846–849; 862–872)

Page 49.

Aunque un consuelo me deja,
y es, que ya podré serviros;
pues libre desta manera,
en mi casa no haré falta.
Con vos iré, donde pueda
tener mi vida su fin,
si hay desdicha que fin tenga.
                    (III, 953–959)

Page 50.

¡Qué bien en un hombre luce
que callando sus agravios,
aun las venganzas sepulte!
Desta suerte ha de vengarse
quien espera, calla y sufre.
Bien habemos aplicado,
honor, con cuerda esperanza,
disimulada venganza
a agravio disimulado.
                    (III, 757–765)

Pages 50–51.

¡Bien la ocasión advertí
cuando la cuerda corté,
cuando los remos tomé
para apartarme de allí,
haciendo que pretendía
acercarme! Y ¡bien logré
mi intento, pues que maté
al que ofenderme quería
(testigo es este puñal),
al agresor de mi afrenta,
a quien di en urna violenta
monumento de cristal!
¡Bien en la tierra rompí
el barco, dando a entender
que esto pudo suceder
sin sospecharse de mí!
                    (III, 766–781)

Page 51.

Y vos, valiente don Juan, [*Ap. a él.*]
decid a quien se aconseja
con vos, cómo ha de vengarse
sin que ninguno lo sepa;
y no dirá la venganza
lo que no dijo la afrenta.
                    (III, 960–965)

CHAPTER 5. A STRANGE MERCY PLAY:
DEVOTION TO THE CROSS

Pages 58–59. *La devoción de la cruz,* prólogo y edición de Ángel
Valbuena (Madrid: Espasa-Calpe, S. A., 1953)

    Arbol, donde el cielo quiso
dar el fruto verdadero
contra el bocado primero,
flor del nuevo paraíso,
arco de luz, cuyo aviso
en piélago más profundo
la paz publicó del mundo,
planta hermosa fértil vid,
arpa del nuevo David,
tabla del Moisés segundo:
    pecador soy, tus favores
pido por justicia yo . . .
                    (III, 2281–2292)

Page 64.

Bien excusadas grandezas
de mi padre consumieron
en breve tiempo la hacienda
que los suyos le dejaron;
que no sabe cuánto yerra
quien, por excesivos gastos
pobres a sus hijos deja.
Pero la necesidad,
aunque ultraje la nobleza,

no excusa de obligaciones
a los que nacen con ellas.
                    (I, 128–138)

Pages 64–65.

porque un caballero pobre,
cuando en cosas como éstas
no puede medir iguales
la calidad y la hacienda,
por no deslucir su sangre
con una hija doncella,
hace sagrado un convento;
que es delito la pobreza.
Aqueste a Julia mi hermana
con tanta prisa la espera,
que mañana ha de ser monja,
por voluntad o por fuerza.
                    (I, 175–186)

Page 65.

Y sin decir nada (¡ ay Dios!)
buscó a mi padre, y los dos
(¿ quién duda para tratar
mi muerte?) gran rato hablaron
cerrados en su aposento . . .
                    (I, 474–478)

Page 65.

que sola mi voluntad
en lo justo, o en lo injusto,
has de tener por tu gusto.

          .   .   .

    Basta, que yo le he mirado,
    y yo por ti he dado el sí.

          .   .   .

    ¡ Calla, infame! ¡calla, loca!
Que haré de aquese cabello
un lazo para tu cuello,
o sacaré de tu boca

con mis manos la atrevida
lengua, que de oír me ofendo.
                (I, 585–587; 597–598; 601–606)

Pages 65–66.

En este punto a creer llego
lo que el alma sospechó,
    que no fué buena tu madre,
y manchó mi honor alguno;
pues hoy tu error importuno
ofende el honor de un padre,
    a quien el sol no igualó,
en resplandor y belleza,
sangre, honor, lustre y nobleza.
                (I, 615–623)

Page 67.

que aquella sangre fría,
que con tímida voz me está llamando,
algo tiene de mía;
que sangre, que no fuera
propia, ni me llamara, ni la oyera.

                .   .   .

    ¡Que llore muerto
a quien aborrecí vivo!
                (III, 2256–2260; 2387–2388)

Pages 67–68.

El cuerpo se retire lastimoso
de Eusebio, en tanto que un sepulcro honroso
a sus cenizas da mi desventura.
                (III, 2427–2429)

Page 68.

    Tirso. ¿Pues cómo piensas darle sepultura
tú en lugar sagrado
a un hombre que murió descomulgado?
    Blas. Quien desta suerte ha muerto,

digno sepulcro sea este desierto.
    Curcio. ¡Oh villana venganza!
¿tanto poder en ti la ofensa alcanza,
que pasas desta suerte,
los últimos umbrales de la muerte?
           [*Vase* Curcio, *llorando*]
        (III, 2430–2438)

Pages 68–69.

    Curcio. ¡Ay, hijo del alma mía!
no fué desdichado, no,
quien en su trágica muerte
tantas glorias mereció.
Así Julia conociera
sus culpas.
    Julia.   ¡Válgame Dios!
¿qué es lo que estoy escuchando?
¿qué prodigo es éste? ¿Yo
soy la que a Eusebio pretende,
y hermana de Eusebio soy?
Pues sepan Curcio y el mundo
y sepan ya todos hoy
mis graves culpas: yo misma,
asombrada de mi error
daré voces: sepan todos
cuantos hoy viven, que yo
soy Julia, en número infame
de las malas la peor.
Mas ya que ha sido común
mi pecado, desde hoy
lo será mi penitencia;
y pidiéndole perdón
al mundo del mal ejemplo,
de la mala vida a Dios.
        (III, 2547–2570)

Page 71.

¡Descoloridos, y al campo
de mañana! Cosa es cierta

que comen barro, o están
opilados.
                    (I, 85–88)

Page 72.

Divina Cruz, yo os prometo,
y os hago solemne voto,
con cuantas cláusulas puedo,
de en cualquier parte que os vea,
las rodillas por el suelo,
rezar un Ave María.
                    (II, 1636–1641)

Page 73.

¿No saltó Eusebio por mí
las paredes del convento?
¿No me holgué de verle yo
en tantos peligros puesto
por mi causa? ¿Pues qué dudo?
¿Qué me acobardo? ¿qué temo?
Lo mismo haré yo en salir
que él en entrar: si es lo mesmo,
también se holgará de verme
por su causa en tales riesgos.
Ya por haber consentido
la misma culpa merezco;
pues si es tan grande el pecado,
¿por qué el gusto ha de ser menos?
Si consentí, y me dejó
Dios de su mano . . .
                    (II, 1685–1700)

Page 74.

Al mundo, al honor, a Dios
hallo perdido el respeto . . .
Demonio soy que he caído
despeñado deste cielo,
pues sin tener esperanza
de subir, no me arrepiento.
                    (II, 1703–1704; 1707–1710)

Page 74.

Turbada y confusa quedo.
¿Aquestas fueron, ingrato,
las firmezas? ¿Estos fueron
los extremos de tu amor?
¿O son de mi amor extremos?
Hasta vencerme a tu gusto,
con amenazas, con ruegos,
aquí amante, allí tirano,
porfiaste; pero luego
que de tu gusto y mi pena
pudiste llamarte dueño,
antes de vencer, huiste.
¿Quién, sino tú, venció huyendo?
¡Muerta soy, cielos piadosos!
¿Por qué introdujo venenos
Naturaleza, si había,
para dar muerte desprecios?
Ellos me quitan la vida,
pues que con nuevo tormento
lo que me desprecia busco.
¿Quién, sino tú, venció huyendo?
de amor? Cuando me rogaba
con mil lágrimas Eusebio,
le dejaba; pero agora,
porque él me deja, le ruego.
Tales somos las mujeres,
que contra nuestros deseos,
aun no queremos dar gusto
con lo mismo que queremos.
                    (II, 1642–1670)

Page 75.

                    pues creo
de la clemencia divina,
que no hay luces en el cielo,
que no hay en el mar arenas,
no hay átomos en el viento,
que, sumados todos juntos,
no sean número pequeño

de los pecados, que sabe
Dios perdonar.
(II, 1740–1748)

Page 75.

Mas ya mi desdicha entiendo;
desta suerte me negáis
la entrada vuestra; pues creo
que, cuando quiera subir
arrepentida no puedo.
Pues si ya me habéis negado
vuestra clemencia, mis hechos
de mujer desesperada
darán asombros al cielo,
darán espantos al mundo,
admiración a los tiempos,
horror al mismo pecado,
y terror al mismo infierno.
(II, 1764–1776)

Page 76.

voy ...
que Menga me lo ha mandado,
y para ir seguro, he hallado
una brava invención hoy.
   De la Cruz dic[en] que es
devoto Eusebio; y así
he salido armado aquí
de la cabeza a los pies.
(III, 1777–1784)

Page 76.

   Pues teniendo mi albedrío,
superior efecto ha hecho,
que yo respete en tu pecho
la Cruz que tengo en el mío.
   Y pues con ella los dos,
¡ay Julia! habemos nacido,

secreto misterio ha sido
que lo entiende sólo Dios.
                    (III, 1813–1820)

Pages 77–78.

   Gil. [*Ap.*] Mucho pica, ya no puedo
más sufrillo.
   Eusebio. Entre estos ramos
hay gente. ¿Quién va?
   Gil. [*Ap.*]   Aquí echamos
a perder todo el enredo.
   Eusebio. [*Ap.*] Un hombre a un árbol atado,
y una Cruz al cuello tiene:
cumplir mi voto conviene
en el suelo arrodillado.
   Gil. ¿A quién, Eusebio, enderezas
la oración o de qué tratas?
si me adoras, ¿qué me atas?
si me atas, ¿qué me rezas?
   Eusebio. ¿Quién es?
   Gil.   ¿A Gil no conoces?
Desde que con el recado
aquí me dejaste atado
no han aprovechado voces
    para que alguien (¡qué rigor!)
me llegase a desatar.
   Eusebio. Pues no es aqueste el lugar
donde te dejé.
   Gil.   Señor,
es verdad; mas yo que vi
que nadie llegaba, he andado,
de árbol en árbol atado,
hasta haber llegado aquí.
  Aquesta la causa fué
de suceso tan extraño.
           [*Desátale.*]
   Eusebio. (Este es simple, y de mi daño
cualquier suceso sabré.)
  Gil, yo te tengo afición
desde que otra vez hablamos,

y así quiero que seamos
amigos.
    Gil. Tiene razón;
y quisiera, pues nos vemos
tan amigos, no ir allá,
sino andarme por acá,
pues aquí todos seremos
    buñuleros, que diz que es
holgada vida, y no andar
todo el año a trabajar.

                    (III, 1820–1859)

Pages 78–80.

Con tanto asombro te escucho,
con tanto temor te miro,
que eres al oído encanto,
si a la vista basilisco.

. . . temo los peligros
con que el cielo me amenaza,

. . . yo temeroso vivo
de esa Cruz tanto, que huyo
de ti.

                (III, 2007–2010; 2012–2013; 2016–2018)

Page 80.

Aunque no sé qué respeto
has puesto en mí, que he temido
más tu enojo que acero:
. . . .
aunque, si verdad te digo,
la victoria que deseo
es, a tus plantas rendido,
pedirte perdón; . . .

                    (III, 2157–2159; 2178–2181)

CHAPTER 6. HONOR HUMANIZED:
THE MAYOR OF ZALAMEA

Page 84. *La devoción de la Cruz,* prologo y edición de Ángel Valbuena (Madrid: Espasa-Calpe, S. A., 1953)

Bien, señor, la autoridad
de padre, que es preferida,
imperio tiene en la vida;
pero no en la libertad.

          .   .   .

Sólo tiene libertad
    un hijo para escoger
estado; que el hado impío
no fuerza el libre albedrío.
          (I, 577–580, 588–591)

Page 84.
Pues si tú vives por mí,
toma también el estado.
          (I, 599–600)

Page 86. *El Alcalde de Zalamea,* edición, estudio y glosario de Augusto Cortina (Madrid: Espasa-Calpe, S. A., 1968)

                    Un hombre,
que de un flaco rocinante
a la vuelta desa esquina
se apeó, y en rostro y talle
parece a aquel don Quijote,
de quien Miguel de Cervantes
escribió las aventuras.
          (I, iii, 213–219)

Pages 86–87.

Nuño. ¿Por qué, si de Isabel eres
tan firme y rendido amante,
a su padre no la pides?
Pues con eso tú y su padre

remediaréis de una vez
entrambas necesidades:
tú comerás, y él hará
hidalgos sus nietos.
    Don Mendo.   No hables
más, Nuño, en eso. ¿Dineros
tanto habían de postrarme,
que a un hombre llano por suegro
había de admitir?
    Nuño.   Pues antes
pensé que ser hombre llano,
para suegro, era importante;
pues de otros dicen que son
tropezones en que caen
los yernos. Y si no has
de casarte ¿por qué haces
tantos extremos de amor?
    Don Mendo. ¿Pues no hay, sin que yo me case,
huelgas en Burgos, adónde
llevarla cuando me enfade?
               (I, iv, 317–338)

Pages 87–88.

salí a mirar la labranza,
y están las parvas notables
de manojos y montones,
que parecen al mirarse
desde lejos montes de oro,
y aun oro de más quilates,
pues de los granos de aqueste
es todo el cielo el contraste.
Allí el bieldo, hiriendo a soplos
el viento en ellos suave,
deja en esta parte el grano
y la paja en la otra parte;
que aun alli lo más humilde
da el lugar a lo más grave.
¡Oh, quiera Dios que en las trojes
ya llegue a encerrarlo, antes
que algún turbión me lo lleve

o algún viento me lo tale!
                (I, v, 425–442)

Pages 88–89.

Dime, por tu vida: ¿hay alguien
que no sepa que yo soy
si bien de limpio linaje
hombre llano? No por cierto:
¿pues qué gano yo en comprarle
una ejecutoria al Rey,
si no le compro la sangre?
¿Dirán entonces que soy
mejor que ahora? Es dislate.
Pues ¿qué dirán? Que soy noble
por cinco o seis mil reales.
Y eso es dinero, y no es honra:
que honra no la compra nadie.
¿Quieres, aunque sea trivial,
un ejemplillo escucharme?
Es calvo un hombre mil años
y al cabo dellos se hace
una cabellera. Éste
en opiniones vulgares
¿deja de ser calvo? No,
pues que dicen all mirarle:
«¡Bien puesta la cabellera
trae Fulando!» Pues ¿qué hace,
si aunque no le vean la calva,
todos que la tiene saben?

                • • •

Yo no quiero honor postizo,
que el defecto ha de dejarme
en casa. Villanos fueron
mis abuelos y mis padres;
sean villanos mis hijos.
                (I, ix, 488–512; 517–521)

Pages 90–91.

   Crespo. Mil gracias, señor, os doy
por la merced que me hicisteis

de excusarme la ocasión
de perderme.
    Don Lope. ¿Cómo habíais,
decid, de perderos vos?
    Crespos. Dando muerte a quien pensara
ni aun el agravio menor . . .
    Don Lope. ¿Sabéis, vive Dios, que es
Capitán?
    Crespo. Sí, vive Dios;
y aunque fuera el general,
en tocando a mi opinión,
le matara.
    Don Lope. A quien tocara,
ni aun al soldado menor,
sólo un pelo de la ropa,
viven los cielos, que yo
le ahorcara.
    Crespo. A quien se atreviera
a un átomo de mi honor,
viven los cielos también,
que también le ahorcara yo.
    Don Lope. ¿Sabéis que estáis obligado
a sufrir, por ser quien sois,
estas cargas?
    Crespo. Con mi hacienda;
pero con mi fama no.
Al Rey la hacienda y la vida
se ha de dar; pero el honor
es patrimonio del alma,
y el alma sólo es de Dios.
    Don Lope. ¡Vive Cristo, que parece
que vais teniendo razón!
    Crespo. Sí, vive Cristo, por que
siempre la he tenido yo.
               (I, xviii, 850–880)

Page 91.

Este fuego, esta pasión,
no es amor sólo, que es tema,
es ira, es rabia, es furor.
             (II, ii, 41–43)

Page 92.

¡Qué en una villana haya
tan hidalga resistencia,
que no me haya respondido
una palabra siquiera
apacible!
                    (II, iii, 61–64)

Page 92.

                    Estas, señor,
no de los hombres se prendan
como tú : si otro villano
la festejara y sirviera,
hiciera más caso dél :
fuera de que son tus quejas
sin tiempo. Si te has de ir
mañana ¿para qué intentas
que una mujer en un día
te escuche y te favorezca?
                    (II, iv, 65–74)

Pages 92–93.

    Capitán. En un día el sol alumbra
y falta; en un día se trueca
un reino todo; en un día
es edificio una peña;
en un día una batalla
pérdida y victoria ostenta;
en un día tiene el mar
tranquilidad y tormenta;
en un día nace un hombre
y muere : luego pudiera
en un día ver mi amor
sombra y luz como planeta,
pena y dicha como imperio,
gente y brutos como selva,
paz e inquietud como mar,
triunfo y ruina como guerra,
vida y muerte como dueño
de sentidos y potencias :

y habiendo tenido edad
es un día su violencia
de hacerme tan desdichado
¿por qué, por qué no pudiera
tener edad en un día
de hacerme dischoso? ¿Es fuerza
que se engendren más despacio
las glorias que las ofensas?
    Sargento. Verla una vez solamente
¿a tanto extremo te fuerza?
    Capitán. ¿Qué más causa había de haber,
llegando a verla, que verla?
De sola una vez a incendio
crece una breve pavesa;
de una vez sola un abismo
sulfúreo volcán revienta;
de una vez se enciende el rayo,
que destruye cuanto encuentra,
de una vez escupe horror
las más reformada pieza.
¿De una vez amor, qué mucho,
fuego de cuatro maneras,
mina, incendio, pieza y rayo,
postre, abrase, asombre y hiera?
        (II, iii, 75–116)

Page 93.

Yo, señor, respondo siempre
en el tono y en la letra
que me hablan : ayer vos
así hablabais, y era fuerza
que fueran de un mismo tono
la pregunta y la respuesta.
Demás de que yo he tomado
por política discreta
jurar con aquel que jura,
rezar con aquel que reza.
A todo hago compañía . . .
        (II, v, 235–245)

Pages 94–96.

Por la gracia de Dios, Juan,
eres de linaje limpio
más que el sol, pero villano:
lo uno y lo otro te digo,
aquello, por que no humilles
tanto tu orgullo y tu brío,
que dejes, desconfiado,
de aspirar con cuerdo arbitrio
a ser más; lo otro, por que
no vengas, desvanecido,
a ser menos: igualmente
usa de entrambos designios
con humildad; porque siendo
humilde, con recto juicio
acordarás lo mejor;
y como tal, en olvido
pondrás cosas que suceden
al revés en los altivos.
¡Cuántos, teniendo en el mundo
algún defecto consigo,
le han borrado por humildes!
Y ¡a cuántos, que no han tenido
defecto, se le han hallado
por estar ellos mal vistos!
Sé cortés sobremanera,
sé liberal y esparcido;
que el sombrero y el dinero
son los que hacen los amigos;
y no vale tanto el oro
que el sol engendra en el indio
suelo y que conduce el mar,
como ser uno bienquisto.
No hables mal de las mujeres:
la más humilde, te digo
que es digna de estimación,
porque, al fin, dellas nacimos.
No riñas por cualquier cosa:
que cuando en los pueblos miro
muchos que a reñir enseñan,

mil veces entre mi digo:
«Aquesta escuela no es
la que ha de ser, pues colijo
que no ha de enseñarse a un hombre
con destreza, gala y brío
a reñir, sino a por qué
ha de reñir; que yo afirmo
que si hubiera un maestro solo
que enseñara prevenido,
no el cómo, el por qué se riña,
todos le dieran sus hijos.»
Con esto, y con el dinero
que llevas para el camino,
y para hacer, en llegando
de asiento, un par de vestidos,
el amparo de don Lope
y mi bendición, yo fío
en Dios que tengo de verte
en otro puesto. Adiós, hijo,
que me enternezco en hablarte.
                    (II, xxi, 686–744)

Page 96.

    Nunca amanezca a mis ojos
la luz hermosa del día,
por que a su sombra no tenga
vergüenza yo de mí misma.
¡Oh tú, de tantas estrellas
Primavera fugitiva,
no des lugar a la aurora,
que tu azul campaña pisa,
para que con risa y llanto
borre tu apacible vista,
o ya que ha de ser, que sea
con llanto, mas no con risa!
Deténte, oh mayor planeta,
más tiempo en la espuma fría
del mar: deja que una vez
dilate la noche esquiva
su trémulo imperio: deja
que de tu deidad se diga,

atenta a mis ruegos, que es
voluntaria y no precisa.
>(III, i, 1–20)

Page 98.

>bien así
como de los pechos quita
carnicero hambriento lobo
a la simple corderilla.
>(III, ii, 119–122)

Page 98.

>aquel
huésped ingrato, que el día
primero introdujo en casa
tan nunca esperada cisma
de traiciones y cautelas,
de pendencias y rencillas . . .
>(III, ii, 123–128)

Page 98.

¡Mal haya el hombre, mal haya
el hombre que solicita
por fuerza ganar un alma,
pues no advierte, pues no mira
que las victorias de amor
no hay trofeo en que consistan,
sino en granjear el cariño
de la hermosura que estiman!
Porque querer sin el alma
una hermosura ofendida
es querer a una mujer
hermosa, pero no viva.
>(III, ii, 169–180)

Pages 98–99.

Alzate, Isabel, del suelo;
no, no estés más de rodillas;
que a no haber estos sucesos

que atormenten y que aflijan,
ociosas fueran las penas,
sin estimación las dichas.
Para los hombres se hicieron,
y es menester que se impriman
con valor dentro del pecho.
(III, ii, 281–289)

Page 99.

¡Cuando vengarse imagina,
me hace dueño de mi honor
la vara de la justicia!
¿Cómo podré delinquir
yo, si en esta hora misma
me ponen a mí por juez
para que otros no delincan?
Pero cosas como aquestas
no se ven con tanta prisa.
(III, iv, 328–336)

Page 99.

Nada me puede a mí estar
mejor: llegando a saber
que estoy aquí, no hay temer
a la gente del lugar;
que la justicia, es forzoso
remitirme en esta tierra
a mi consejo de guerra:
con que, aunque el lance es penoso,
tengo mi seguridad.
(III, vi, 374–381)

Pages 100–101.

Crespo. ¿Qué en fin no os mueve mi llanto?
Capitán. Llanto no se ha de creer
de viejo, niño y mujer.
Crespo. ¡Qué no pueda dolor tanto
mereceros un consuelo!
Capitán. ¿Qué más consuelo queréis,
pues con la vida volvéis?

Crespo. Mirad que echado en el suelo
mi honor a voces os pido.
    Capitán. ¡Qué enfado!
    Crespo.   Mirad que soy
Alcalde en Zalamea hoy.
    Capitán. Sobre mí no habéis tenido
jurisdicción: el consejo
de guerra enviará por mí.
    Crespo. ¿En eso os resolvéis?
    Capitán.   Sí,
caduco y cansado viejo.
    Crespo. ¿No hay remedio?
    Capitán.   Sí, el callar
es el mejor para vos.
    Crespo. ¿No otro?
    Capitán.   No.
    Crespo.   Pues juro a Dios
que me lo habéis de pagar. —
¡Hola!   [*Levántase y toma la vara.*]
           (III, viii, 530–549)

Page 101.

Y aun aquesa confianza
me mató, porque el que piensa
que va a un peligro ya va
prevenido a la defensa;
quien va a una seguridad
es el que más riesgo lleva,
por la novedad que halla,
si acaso un peligro encuentra.
Pensé hallar una villana;
si hallé una deidad ¿no era
preciso que peligrase
en mi misma inadvertencia?
          (II, iii, 119–130)

Page 102.

    Chispa. A mí no me pueden dar
tormento.
    Crespo. Sepamos, pues,

¿por qué?
   Chispa. Eso es cosa asentada,
y que no hay ley que tal mande.
   Crespo. ¿Qué causa tenéis?
   Chispa.   Bien grande.
   Crespo. Decid ¿cuál?
   Chispa.   Estoy preñada.
   Crespo. ¿Hay cosa más atrevida?
Mas la cólera me inquieta.
¿No sois paje de jineta?
   Chispa. No, señor, sino de brida.
               (III, x, 612–621)

Pages 102–103.

   Capitán. Tratad con respeto . . .
   Crespo.   Eso
está muy puesto en razón :
  con respeto le llevad
a las casas, en efeto,
del concejo; y con respeto
un par de grillos le echad
  y una cadena; y tened,
con respeto, gran cuidado
que no hable a ningún soldado;
y a esos dos también poned
  en la cárcel, que es razón,
y aparte, por que después,
con respeto, a todos tres
les tomen la confesión.
  Y aquí, para entre los dos,
si hallo harto paño, en efeto,
con muchísimo respeto
os he de ahorcar, juro a Dios.
   Capitán. ¡Ah villanos con poder!
            [*Vanse los labradores con el Capitán.*]
       (III, ix, 572–590)

Page 103.

Y aun a mi padre también
  con tal rigor le tratara.

(*Ap.* Aquesto es asegurar
su vida, y han de pensar
que es la justicia más rara
  del mundo.)
                    (III, xiii, 677–681)

Pages 104–105.

Don Lope. Yo por el preso he venido
y a castigar este exceso.
Crespo. Pues yo acá le tengo preso
por lo que acá ha sucedido.
Don Lope. ¿Vos sabéis que a servir pasa
al Rey, y soy su juez yo?
Crespo. ¿Vos sabéis que me robó
a mi hija de mi casa?
Don Lope. ¿Vos sabéis que mi valor
dueño desta causa ha sido?
Crespo. ¿Vos sabéis cómo atrevido
robó en un monte mi honor?
Don Lope. ¿Vos sabéis cuánto os prefiere
el cargo que he gobernado?
Crespo. ¿Vos sabéis que le he rogado
con la paz, y no la quiere?
Don Lope. Que os entráis, es bien se arguya,
en otra jurisdicción.
Crespo. El se me entró en mi opinión,
sin ser jurisdicción suya.
Don Lope. Yo sabré satisfacer,
obligándome a la paga.
Crespo. Jamás pedí a nadie que haga
lo que yo me puedo hacer.
Don Lope. Yo me he de llevar al preso.
Ya estoy en ello empeñado.
Crespo. Yo por acá he sustanciado
el proceso.
Don Lope. ¿Qué es proceso?
Crespo.   Unos pliegos de papel
que voy juntando, en razón
de hacer la averiguación
de la causa.

Don Lope. Iré por él
a la cárcel.
    Crespo.   No embarazo
que vais: sólo se repare
que hay orden que al que llegare
le den un arcabuzazo.

(III, xv, 783–817)

Page 106.

... si un extraño

se viniera a querellar
¿no había de hacer justicia?
Sí; ¿pues que más se me da
hacer por mi hija lo mismo
que hiciera por los demás?
Fuera de que, como he preso
un hijo mío, es verdad
que no escuchara a mi hija,
pues era la sangre igual ...
Mírese si está bien hecha
la causa, miren si hay
quien diga que yo haya hecho
en ella alguna maldad,
si he inducido algún testigo,
si está escrito algo de más
de lo que yo he dicho, y entonces
me den muerte.

(III, xvii, 876–893)

Pages 106–107.

    Crespo. Toda la justicia vuestra
es sólo un cuerpo no más;
si éste tiene muchas manos,
decid ¿qué más se me da
matar con aquesta un hombre
que estotra había de matar?
Y¿qué importa errar lo menos
quien ha acertado lo más?
    Rey. Pues ya que aquesto es así,

¿por qué, como a capitán
y caballero, no hicisteis
degollarle?
    Crespo. ¿Eso dudáis?
Señor, como los hidalgos
viven tan bien por acá,
el verdugo que tenemos
no ha aprendido a degollar.
Y esa es querella del muerto,
que toca a su autoridad,
y hasta que él mismo se queje
no les toca a los demás.
    Rey. Don Lope, aquesto ya es hecho.
Bien dada la muerte está;
que errar lo menos no importa
si acertó lo principal.
Aquí no quede soldado
alguno, y haced marchar
con brevedad, que me importa
llegar presto a Portugal. —
Vos, por alcalde perpetuo
de aquesta villa os quedad.
    Crespo. Sólo vos a la justicia
tanto supierais honrar.
               (III, xvii, 916–947)

Page 108.

En un convento entrará;
que ha elegido y tiene Esposo
que no mira en calidad.
               (III, xvii, 955–957)

CHAPTER 7. FLICKERS OF INCEST ON THE FACE OF HONOR: *THE PHANTOM LADY*

Page 112. *La dama duende,* edición prólogo y notas de Ángel Valbuena Briones (Madrid: Espasa-Calpe, S. A., 1954)

Si, como lo muestra
el traje, sois caballero
de obligaciones y prendas,
amparad a una mujer
que a valerse de vos llega.
Honor y vida me importa
que aquel hidalgo no sepa
quien soy, y que no me siga:
estorbad, por vida vuestra,
a una mujer principal
una desdicha, una afrenta,
que podrá ser que algún día . . .
A Dios, a Dios, que voy muerta.
                    [*Vanse las dos muy aprisa.*]
            (I, 100–112)

Page 113.

        ¿Eso me preguntas?
¿Cómo puede mi nobleza
excusarse de *estorbar*
una desdicha, una afrenta?
Que, según muestra, sin duda
es su marido.
            (I, 115–119)

Page 113.

    Don Manuel. [*Aparte.*]   Ya es fuerza
llegar: acabe el valor
lo que empezó la cautela. [*Llega.*]
Caballero, este criado
es mío, y no sé que pueda
haberos hoy ofendido,
para que de esa manera
le atropelléis.
            (I, 150–157)

Page 113.

    Rodrigo.   Sacad
la espada vos.

Cosme.   Es doncella,
y sin cédula o palabra,
no puedo sacarla.
                (I, 177–179)

Page 114.

Señor Don Luis, ya sabéis
que estimo vuestras finezas,
supuesto que lo merecen
por amorosas y vuestras;
pero no puedo pagarlas,
que eso han de hacer las estrellas.
y no hay de lo que no hacen
quien las tome residencia.
Si lo que menos se halla
es hoy lo que más se precia
en la Corte, agradeced
el desengaño, siquiera
por ser cosa que se halla
con dificultad en ella.
Quedad con Dios.
                (I, 279–293)

Page 115.

lo que más siento es que sea
mi hermano tan poco atento
que llevar a casa quiera
un hombre mozo, teniendo,
Rodrigo, una hermana bella,
viuda y moza, y, como sabes,
tan de secreto, que apenas
sabe el Sol que vive en casa;
porque, Beatriz, por ser deuda,
solamente la visita.
                (I, 320–330)

Page 115.

Pues con eso mismo intentas
darme muerte; pues ya dices

que no ha puesto por defensa
de su honor más que unos vidrios,
que al primer golpe se quiebran.
                (I, 364–368)

Pages 116–117.

Vuélveme a dar, Isabel,
esas tocas (¡pena esquiva!).
Vuelve a amortajarme viva,
ya que mi suerte crüel
lo quiere así.
                . . .
¡Válgame el Cielo! Que yo
entre dos paredes muera,
donde apenas el Sol sabe
quién soy, pues la pena mía
en el término del día
ni se contiene ni cabe.
Donde inconstante la luna,
que aprende influjos de mí,
no puede decir: ya vi
que lloraba su fortuna.
Donde, en efecto, encerrada
sin libertad he vivido,
porque enviudé de un marido,
con dos hermanos casada.
Y luego delito sea,
sin que toque en liviandad,
depuesta la autoridad
ir donde tapada vea
un teatro en quien la fama
para su aplauso inmortal,
con acentos de metal,
a voces de bronce llama.
¡Suerte injusta, dura estrella!
                (I, 369–373; 379–401)

Pages 117–118.

Señora, no tiene duda
de que mirándote viuda,

tan moza, bizarra y bella,
tus hermanos cuidadosos
te celen; porque este estado
es el más ocasionado
a delitos amorosos;
y más en la Corte, hoy,
donde se han dado en usar
unas viuditas de azahar,
que al Cielo mil gracias doy
cuando en la calle las veo
tan honestas, tan fruncidas,
tan beatas y aturdidas;
y en quedándose en manteo
es el mirarlas contento;
pues sin toca y devoción,
saltan más a cualquier son
que una pelota de viento.
Y este discurso doblado
para otro tiempo, señora,
¿cómo no habemos ahora
en el forastero hablado,
a quien tu honor encargaste,
y tu galán hoy hiciste?
                (I, 402–426)

Page 118.

                Yo fuí
necia en empeñarle así;
mas una mujer turbada
¿qué mira o qué considera?
                (I, 438–441)

Pages 118–119.

   Doña Ángela. [Aparte.]
¡Ay de mí! Sin duda es
que Don Luis me conoció.
   Don Luis. Y así siento mucho yo
que te estime en poco.
   Doña Ángela.   Pues

¿has tenido algún disgusto?
   Don Luis. Lo peor es que cuando vengo
a verte, el disgusto tengo
que tuve, Ángela.
   Isabel. [*Aparte.*] ¿Otro susto?
   Doña Ángela. Pues yo, ¿en qué te puedo dar,
hermano, disgusto? Advierte . . .
   Don Luis. Tú eres la causa; y el verte . . .
   Doña Ángela. ¡Ay de mí!
   Don Luis.   Ángela, estimar
tan poco de nuestro hermano.
   Doña Ángela. Eso sí.
   Don Luis.   Pues cuando vienes
con los disgustos que tienes
cuidados te dé. No en vano
el enojo que tenía
con él, el huésped pagó;
pues sin conocerlo yo,
hoy le he herido en profecía.
             (I, 449–468)

Page 120.

Viendo que no pude vella,
seguirle determiné :
ella siempre atrás volvía
a ver si yo la seguía
cuyo gran cuidado fué
espuela de mi cuidado.
             (I, 492–497)

Page 120.

Miren la mala mujer
en que ocasión te había puesto :
que hay mujeres tramoyeras . . .
Pondré que no concocía
quién eras, y que lo hacía
sólo porque la siguieras.
Por eso estoy harta yo
de decir (si bien te acuerdas)

que mires que no te pierdas
por mujercillas, que no
saben más que aventurar
los hombres.
                    (I, 515–526)

Pages 120–121.

    Don Luis. ¿Hate nuestro hermano visto?
    Doña Ángela. Desde esta mañana no
ha entrado aquí.
    Don Luis.   ¡Qué mal yo
estos descuidos resisto!
    Doña Ángela. Pues deja los sentimientos,
que al fin sufrirle es mejor;
que es nuestro hermano mayor
y comemos de alimento.
    Don Luis. Si tú estás tan consolada
yo también, que yo por ti
lo sentía. Y porque así
veas no dárseme nada,
a verle voy y aun con él
haré una galantería. [*Vase.*]
                    (I, 529–542)

Page 121.

Pero aun bien no lo he creído;
porque caso extraño fuera
que un hombre a Madrid viniera,
y hallase recién venido
una dama que rogase
que su vida defendiese,
un hermano que le hiriese
y otro que le aposentase.
Fuera notable suceso,
y aunque todo puede ser.
no lo tengo de creer
sin vello.
                    (I, 553–564)

Pages 122–123.

    Isabel.   ¿Y, por tu vida,
irás?
    Doña Ángela. Un necio deseo
tengo de saber si es él
el que mi vida guardó;
porque, si le cuesto yo
sangre y cuidado, Isabel,
es bien mirar por su herida,
si es que segura del miedo
de ser conocida, puedo
ser con él agradecida.
Vamos, que tengo de ver
la alacena; y si pasar
puedo al cuarto, he de cuidar
sin que él lo llegue a entender,
desde aquí de su regalo.
    Isabel. Notable cuento sería;
mas, si lo cuenta . . .
    Doña Ángela.   No hará,
que hombre, que su esfuerzo iguala
a su gala y discreción,
pues que de todo ha hecho
noble experiencia en mi pecho
en la primera ocasión,
de valiente, en lo [ar]restado,
de galán, en lo lucido,
en el modo de entendido,
no me ha de causar cuidado
que diga suceso igual;
que fuera notable mengua
que echara una mala lengua
tan buenas partes a mal. [*Vanse.*]
               (I, 623–652)

Pages 123–124.

y porque el instrumento de la herida
en mi poder no quede,
pues ya agradarme ni servirme puede,
bien como aquel criado

que a su señor algún disgusto ha dado,
hoy de mí le despido.
Ésta es, señor, la espada que os ha herido;
a vuestras plantas viene
a pediros perdón, si culpa tiene.
Tome vuestra querella
con ella en mí, venganza de mí y de ella.
>   (I, 672–682)

Pages 124–125.

Cuando en un libro leo de mil fuentes
que vuelven varias cosas sus corrientes,
no me espanto, si aquí ver determino,
que nace el agua a convertirse en vino.
>   (I, 723–726)

Page 125.

Hallé la propia; buena está y rebuena,
pues aquesta jornada
subió doncella y se apeó preñada.
Contarlo quiero [*aunque*] es tiempo perdido,
porque yo, ¿qué borregos he vendido
a mi señor para que mire y vea
si está cabal? Lo que ello fuere, sea.
>   (I, 764–770)

Page 125.

Salirme un rato es justo
a rezar a una ermita. ¿Tendrás gusto
desto, Cosme? – Tendré. – Pues, Cosme, vamos,
que antes son nuestros gustos que los amos.
>   (I, 777–780)

Pages 125–126.

> *Doña Ángela.* ¿Qué es esto?
> *Isabel.*   Muchos papeles.
> *Doña Ángela.* ¿Son de mujer?
> *Isabel.*   No, señora,
> sino procesos que vienen

cosidos, y pesan mucho.
    Doña Ángela. Pues si fueran de mujeres
ellos fueran más livianos.
Mal en eso te detienes.
    Isabel. Ropa blanca hay aquí alguna.
    Doña Ángela. ¿Huele [bien]?
    Isabel.   Sí, a limpia huele.
    Doña Ángela. Ése es el mejor perfume.
    Isabel. Las tres calidades tiene,
de blanca, blanda y delgada.
Mas, señora, ¿qué es aqueste
pellejo con unos hierros
de herramientas diferentes?
    Doña Ángela. Muestra a ver. Hasta aquí, loza
de sacamuelas parece
mas éstas son tenacillas,
y el alzador del copete
y los bigotes estotras.
    Isabel. Item, escobilla y peine.
Oye, que, más prevenido,
no le faltará al tal huésped
la horma de su zapato.
    Doña Ángela. ¿Por qué?
    Isabel.   Porque aquí la tiene.
        (I, 824–848)

Page 127.

No en vano sois tan valiente
como sois, si habéis de andar,
desnuda la espada siempre.
saliendo de los disgustos
en que este loco os pusiere.
        (I, 950–954)

Pages 127–128.

    Cosme.   Muy bien está
pensado; mas mi temor
pasa adelante. Confieso
que es su dama, y el suceso

te doy por bueno, señor;
pero ¿ella cómo podía
desde la calle, saber
lo que había de suceder,
para tener este día
ya prevenido el papel?
   Don Manuel. Después de haberme pasado,
pudo dárselo a un criado.
   Cosme. Y aunque se le diera, ¿él
cómo aquí ha de haberle puesto?,
porque ninguno aquí entró
desde que aquí quedé yo.
   Don Manuel. Bien pudo ser antes de esto.
   Cosme. Sí; mas hallar trabucadas
las maletas y la ropa,
y el papel escrito, topa
en más.
   Don Manuel. Mira si cerradas
esas ventanas están.
   Cosme. Y con aldabas y rejas.
   Don Manuel. Con mayor duda me dejas,
y mil sospechas me dan.
   Cosme. ¿De qué?
   Don Manuel.   No sabré explicallo.
   Cosme. En efeto, ¿qué has de hacer?
   Don Manuel. Escribir y responder
pretendo, hasta averiguallo,
con estilo que parezca
que no ha hallado en mí valor,
ni admiración ni temor;
que no dudo que se ofrezca
una ocasión en que demos,
viendo que papeles hay,
con quien los lleva y los tray.
   Cosme. ¿Y de aquesto no daremos
cuenta a los huéspedes?
   Don Manuel.   No,
porque no tengo de hacer
mal alguno a una mujer,
que así de mí se fió.

Cosme.   ¿Luego ya ofendes a quien
su galán piensas?
Don Manuel.   No tal,
pues sin hacerla a ella mal.
puedo yo proceder bien.
                    (I, 1018–1062)

Page 129.

Cosme.   No, señor; más hay aquí
de lo que a ti te parece :
con cada discurso crece
mi sospecha.
Don Manuel.   ¿Cómo así?
Cosme.   Ves aquí que van y vienen
papeles, y que jamás,
aunque lo examines más,
ciertos desengaños tienen :
¿qué creerás?
Don Manuel.   Que ingenio y arte
hay para entrar y salir,
para cerrar, para abrir,
y que el cuarto tiene parte
por dónde. Y en duda tal,
el juicio podré perder;
pero no, Cosme, creer
cosa sobrenatural.
                    (I, 1063–1078)

Pages 129–130.

Cosme.   En fin, ¿qué has determinado?
Don Manuel.   Asistir de noche y día
con cuidados singulares
(aquí el desengaño fundo),
sin creer que hay en el mundo
ni duendes ni familiares.
Cosme.   Pues yo, en efecto, presumo
que algún demonio los tray,
que esto y más habrá, donde hay

quien tome tabaco en humo.

                    (I, 1093–1102)

Pages 134–135.

    Don Juan. Pesame que hayan de ser
lisonjeros y agradables,
como para vos mis gustos,
para mí vuestros pesares;
pues es fuerza que no sienta
desdichas que han sido parte
de veros; porque hoy amor
diversos efetos hace,
en vos de pena, y en mí
de gloria, bien como el áspid,
de quien si sale el veneno,
también la triaca sale.

                    (II, 45–56)

Page 135.

Disgustada con mi padre
vengo: la culpa tuvisteis;
pues aunque el galán no sabe,
sabe que por el balcón
hablé anoche, y mientras pase
el enojo, con mi prima
quiere que esté, porque hace
de su virtud, confianza.

                    (II, 64–71)

Page 135.

cuidado con su huésped
me dió, y cuidado tan grande,
que apenas sé de mi vida . . .

                    (II, 105–107)

Page 136.

que los ingenios más grandes
trabajaron en hacer
que en un bufete de jaspe

se tuviese en pie, y Juanelo
con sólo llegar y darle
un golpecillo, le tuvo?
Las grandes dificultades,
hasta saberse lo son:
que sabido, todo es fácil.

(II, 156–164)

Page 136.

pues el pensar
que soy dama suya, hace
que me escriba temeroso,
cortés, turbado y cobarde;
y, en efeto, yo no tengo
de ponerme a ese desaire.

(II, 185–190)

Page 137.

Escucha,
y sabrás la más notable
traza, sin que yo al peligro
de verme en su cuarto pase,
y él venga, sin saber dónde.

(II, 192–195)

Page 137.

Isabel.   Pon otro hermano a la margen,
que viene Don Luis.

(II, 196–197)

Page 137.

Doña Beatriz.   ¡Qué desiguales
son los influjos! ¡Que el cielo
en igual mérito y partes
ponga tantas diferencias
y tantas distancias halle,
que, con un mismo deseo,
uno obligue y otro canse!
Vamos de aqui, que no quiero

que llegue Don Luis a hablarme.
(II, 198–206)

Pages 137–138.

Doña Beatriz. Tan cortésmente os quejáis,
que, aunque agradecer quisiera
vuestras penas, no lo hiciera.
sólo porque las digáis.
Don Luis. Como tan mal me tratáis.
el idioma del desdén
aprendí.
Doña Beatriz. Pues ése es bien
que sigáis; que en caso tal.
hará soledad el mal
a quien le dice tan bien.
[*Quiere irse y detiénela* Don Luis.]
Don Luis. Oye, si acaso te vengas,
y padezcamos los dos.
Doña Beatriz. No he de escucharos. Por Dios,
amiga, que le detengas.   (*Vase.*)
Doña Ángela. ¡Que tan poco valor tengas
que esto quieras oír y ver!
Don Luis. ¡Ay hermana! ¿Qué he de hacer?
Doña Ángela. Dar tus penas al olvido :
que querer aborrecido
es morir y no querer.
[*Vase con* Isabel.]
Don Luis. [*A Doña Ángela al marcharse.*]
Quejoso ¿cómo podré
olvidarla? ¡Qué es error!
Dila que me haga un favor,
y obligado olvidaré :
ofendido no; porque
el más prudente, el más sabio
da su sentimiento al labio;
si olvidarse el favor suele,
es porque el favor no duele
de la suerte que el agravio.
(II, 249–278)

Page 139.

    Don Luis. Si ayudaros a servir
puedo en algo, ya sabéis
que soy, en cualquier suceso,
vuestro.
    Don Manuel. Las manos os beso
por la merced que me hacéis.
    Don Luis. Ved, que no es lisonja esto.
    Don Manuel. Ya veo que es voluntad
de mi aumento.
    Don Luis. [*Aparte.*] Así es verdad
porque negocies más presto.
                (II, 328–336)

Pages 139–140.

                pues ya vi
que, aunque es verdad que es aquélla,
no es su dama; porque él
despreciado no viviera,
si en su casa la tuviera.
Ya es mi duda más cruel.
Si no es su dama ni vive
en su casa, ¿cómo así
escribe y responde? Aquí
muere un engaño y concibe
otro engaño. ¿Qué he de hacer?
Que soy en mis opiniones
confusión de confusiones.
¡Válgate Dios por mujer!
                (II, 380–392)

Page 140.

    Don Manuel. Pues ¿qué tienes?
    Cosme.   Miedo.
    Don Manuel. ¿Miedo un hombre ha de tener?
    Cosme. ¡No le ha de tener, señor!
Pero ve aquí que le tiene,
porque al suceso conviene.
    Don Manuel. Deja aquese necio humor,
y lleva luz, porque tengo

que disponer y escribir,
y esta noche he de salir
de Madrid.
    Cosme. A eso me atengo,
pues dices con eso aquí
que tienes miedo al suceso.
             (II, 399–410)

Page 141.

    Doña Ángela. Si tras desto consigo
que me vea del modo que te digo,
ni dudo de que pierda
el juicio.
    Doña Beatriz. La atención más grave y cuerda
es fuerza que se espante.
Ángela, con suceso semejante;
porque querer llamalle
sin saber donde viene, y que se halle
luego con una dama
tan hermosa, tan rica y de tal fama,
sin que sepa quién es, ni dónde vive
(que esto es lo que tu ingenio le apercibe),
y haya, [vendado] y ciego,
de volver a salir y dudar luego,
¿a quién no ha de admirar?
             (II, 639–653)

Page 142.

        estando en casa
tú, como a mis hermanos les abrasa
tu amor, no salen della,
adorando los rayos de tu estrella;
y fuera aventurarme,
no ausentándose ellos, empeñarme.
             (II, 660–664)

Page 142.

    Doña Beatriz. Que ha de ser para mí de tanto gusto.
    Doña Ángela. Y luego, ¿qué diremos

de verte aquí otra vez?
                          ¿Pues no tendremos
(¡qué mal eso te admira!)
ingenio para hacer otra mentira?
    Don Luis. [*Aparte.*]
Sí tendréis. ¡Que esto escucho!
Con nuevas penas y tormentos lucho.
    Doña Beatriz. Con esto, sin testigos y en secreto
desde notable amor veré el efeto;
pues estando escondida
yo, y estando la casa recogida,
sin escándalo arguyo
que pasar pueda de su cuarto al tuyo.
                    (II, 690–702)

Pages 142–143.

                          que el fuego que me abrasa
ya no tiene otro medio;
que el estorbar es último remedio
de un celoso. Valedme, ¡santos cielos!,
que, abrasado de amor, muero de celos.
                    (II, 720–724)

Page 143.

    Don Manuel. ¡Válgame el cielo! Ya es
esto sobrenatural;
que traer con priesa tal
luz, no es obra humana.
    Cosme.   ¿Ves
cómo a confesar viniste
que es verdad?
    Don Manuel. ¡De mármol soy!
Por volver atrás estoy.
    Cosme. Mortal eres: ya temiste.
                    (II, 911–918)

Pages 144–145.

    Don Manuel. Aguarda, que a los reflejos
de la luz todo se ve;

y no vi en toda mi vida
tan soberana mujer.
¡Válgame el cielo! ¿Qué es esto?
Hidras, a mi parecer,
son los prodigios, pues de uno
nacen mil. ¡Cielos! ¿Qué haré?
    Cosme. Despacio lo va tomando.
Silla arrastra.
    Don Manuel. Imagen es
de la más rara beldad,
que el soberano pincel
ha obrado.
    Cosme. Así es verdad
porque sólo la hizo él.
    Don Manuel. Más que la luz resplandecen
sus ojos.
    Cosme. Lo cierto es
que son sus ojos luceros
del cielo de Lucifer.
    Don Manuel. Cada cabello es un rayo
de sol.
    Cosme. Hurtáronlos dél.
    Don Manuel. Una estrella es cada rizo.
    Cosme. Sí será; porque también
se las trajeron acá,
o una parte de las tres.
    Don Manuel. ¡No vi más rara hermosura!
    Cosme. No dijeras eso a fe,
si el pie la vieras; porque éstos
son malditos por el pie.
    Don Manuel. ¡Un asombro de belleza,
un ángel hermoso es!
    Cosme. Es verdad, pero patudo.
    Don Manuel. ¿Qué es esto, qué querrá hacer
con mis papeles?
    Cosme. Yo apuesto
que querrá mirar y ver
los que buscas, porque aquí
tengamos menos que hacer:
que es duende muy servicial.

Don Manuel.   ¡Válgame el cielo! ¿Qué haré?
Nunca me he visto cobarde,
sino sólo aquesta vez.
    Cosme.   Yo sí, muchas.
    Don Manuel.   Y calzado
de prisión de hielo el pie,
tengo el cabello erizado.
y cada suspiro es,
para mi pecho un puñal,
para mi cuello un cordel.
Mas ¿yo he de tener temor?
¡Vive el cielo que he de ver
si sé vencer un encanto!
                    (II, 929–977)

Pages 145–146.

Que no es bien que des la muerte
a una infelice mujer.
Yo confieso que lo [soy],
y aunque es delito el querer,
no delito que merezca
morir mal, por querer bien.

                .   .   .

Fuerza el decirlo ha de ser;
porque no puedo llevar
tan al fin como pensé
este amor, este deseo,
esta verdad, esta fe.
                    (II, 1049–1054; 1058–1062)

Page 146.

Como sombra se mostró,
fantástica su luz fué;
pero como cosa humana;
se dejó tocar y ver.
Como mortal se temió;
receló como mujer;
como ilusión se deshizo;
como fantasma se fué.
Si doy la rienda al discurso,
no sé, ¡vive Dios!, no sé,

ni qué tengo que dudar,
ni qué tengo de creer.
                    (II, 1123–1134)

Pages 146–147.

Aquí llegó una mujer
(al oír y al parecer)
y a oscuras y por el tiento,
de aposento en aposento,
sin oír, hablar, ni ver,
me guió. Pero ya veo
luz; por el resquicio es
de una puerta. Tu deseo
lograste, amor, pues ya ves
la dama; aventuras leo.
                    [*Acecha por la cerradura.*]
¡Qué casa tan alhajada!
¡Qué mujeres tan lucidas!
¡Qué sala tan adornada!
¡Qué damas tan bien prendidas!
¡Qué beldad tan extremada!
                    (III, 26–40)

Pages 147–148.

Aunque agradecer debiera
discurso tan cortesano,
quejarme quiero (no en vano),
de ofensa tan lisonjera;
pues no siendo ésta la esfera,
a cuyo noble ardimiento
fatigas padece el viento,
sino un albergue piadoso,
os viene a hacer sospechoso
el mismo encarecimiento.
No soy alba, pues la risa
me falta en contento tanto;
ni aurora, pues que mi llanto
de mi dolor no os avisa;
no soy sol, pues no divisa
mi luz la verdad que adoro,
y así, lo que soy ignoro;

que sólo sé que no soy
alba, aurora o sol; pues hoy
ni alumbro, río ni lloro.
Y así, os ruego que digáis,
señor Don Manuel, de mí
que una mujer soy y fuí,
a quien vos sólo obligáis
al extremo que miráis.
                    (III, 91–115)

Pages 148–149.

un enigma a ser me ofrezco,
que ni soy lo que parezco
ni parezco lo que soy.
Mientras encubierta estoy,
podréis verme y podré veros;
porque si a satisfaceros
llegáis, y quién soy sabéis,
vos quererme no querréis,
aunque yo quiera quereros.
Pincel que lo muerto informa,
tal vez un cuadro previene,
que una forma a una luz tiene,
y a otra luz tiene otra forma.
Amor, que es pintor, conforma
dos luces, que en mí tenéis;
si hoy a aquesta luz me veis,
y por eso me estimáis,
cuando a otra luz me veais,
quizá me aborreceréis.
Lo que deciros me importa
es, en cuanto a haber creído
que de Don Luis dama he sido,
que esta sospecha reporta
mi juramento, y la acorta.
                    (III, 132–155)

Pages 149–150.

   Don Manuel. [*Aparte.*] De mi cruel
duda salí con aquel

descuido; agora he creído
que una gran señora ha sido,
que, por serlo, se encubrió,
y que con el oro vió
su secreto conseguido.

(III, 174–180)

Page 151.

¡Ay de mí! ¡Cielos piadosos,
que queriendo neciamente
estorbar aquí los celos,
que amor en mi pecho enciende,
celos de honor averiguo!
Luz tomaré, aunque imprudente,
pues todo se halla con luz,
y el honor con luz se pierde.

(III, 461–468)

Page 152.

Yo he de buscar ocasión,
verdadera o aparente,
para que pueda en tal duda
pensar lo que debe hacerse.

(III, 605–608)

Page 152.

Don Manuel. ¿Eres ilusión o sombra,
mujer, que a matarme vienes?
Di, ¿cómo has entrado aquí?
  Doña Ángela. Don Manuel . . .
  Don Manuel.   Di.

(III, 665–668)

Pages 152–153.

y torpes mis sentidos,
prisión hallan de seda en mis vestidos.
Sola, triste y turbada,
llego de mi discurso mal guiada
al umbral de una esfera,

que fué mi cárcel, cuando ser debiera
mi puerto o mi sagrado.

(III, 689–695)

Page 153.

que ya resisto, ya defiendo en vano
decir quién soy, supuesto
que el haberlo callado nos ha puesto
en riesgo tan extraño.
¿Quién crêrá que el callarme haya hecho daño
siendo mujer? Y es cierto,
siendo mujer, que por callar me he muerto.
En fin, él esperando
a esta puerta estaba, ¡ay cielo!, cuando
yo a sus umbrales llego,
hecha volcán de nieve, Alpe de fuego.
Él a la luz escasa
con que la luna mansamente abrasa,
vió brillar los adornos de mi pecho
(no es la primer traición que nos han hecho)
y escuchó de las ropas el ruido
(no es la primera vez que nos han vendido).
Pensó que era su dama,
y llegó, mariposa de su llama,
para abrasarse en ella,
y hallóme a mí por sombra de su estrella.

(III, 700–720)

Page 154.

¿Quién de un galán creyera
que, buscando sus celos, conociera
tan contrarios los cielos,
que ya se contentara con sus celos?
Quiso hablarme, y no pudo;
que siempre ha sido el sentimiento mudo.
En fin, en tristes voces,
que mal formadas anegó veloces
desde la lengua al labio,
la causa solicita de su agravio.
Yo responderle intento

(ya he dicho cómo es mudo el sentimiento),
y aunque quise, no pude;
que mal al miedo la razón acude,
si bien busqué colores a mi culpa;
mas cuando anda al buscarse la disculpa,
o tarde o nunca llega;
más el delito afirma que le niega.
                    (III, 721–738)

Page 155.

"Ven, dijo, hermana fiera,
de nuestro antiguo honor mancha primera;
dejaréte encerrada
donde segura estés y retirada,
hasta que cuerdo y sabio
de la ocasión me informe de mi agravio."
                    (III, 739–744)

Page 155.

Por haberte querido,
fingida sombra de mi casa he sido;
por haberte estimado,
sepulcro vivo fuí de mi cuidado;
por que no te quisiera,
quien el respeto a tu valor perdiera;
por que no te estimara,
quien su pasión dijera cara a cara.
Mi intento fué el quererte,
mi fin amarte, mi temor perderte,
mi miedo asegurarte,
mi vida obedecerte, mi alma hallarte,
mi deseo servirte,
y mi llanto, en efecto, persuadirte
que mi daño repares,
que me valgas, me ayudes y me ampares.
                    (III, 747–762)

Page 156.

    Don Manuel. [*Aparte.*]
Hidras parecen las desdichas mías

al renacer de sus cenizas frías.
¿Qué haré en tan ciego abismo,
humano laberinto de mí mismo?

.   .   .

si pretendo
librarla, y con mi sangre la defiendo,
remitiendo a mi acero su disculpa,
es ya mayor mi culpa,
pues es decir que he sido
traidor, y que a su casa he ofendido,
pues en ella me halla.
Pues querer disculparme con culpalla,
es decir que ella tiene
la culpa, y a mi honor no le conviene.
Pues ¿qué es lo que pretendo?
si es hacerme traidor si la defiendo;
si la dejo, villano;
si la guardo, mal huésped; inhumano,
si a su hermano la entrego.
Soy mal amigo si a guardarla llego;
ingrato, si la libro, a un noble trato;
si la dejo, a un noble amor ingrato.
Pues de cualquier manera
mal puesto he de quedar, matando muera.
                              [A Doña Ángela.]
No receles, señora;
noble soy, y conmigo estás ahora.
                    (III, 763–766; 771–792)

CHAPTER 8. THE MAGNANIMOUS PRINCE AND THE PRICE OF CONSCIOUSNESS: *LIFE IS A DREAM*

Page 161. *La vida es sueño*, edición, estudio y glosario de Augusto Cortina (Madrid: Espasa-Calpe, S. A., 1955)
                              La puerta
(mejor diré funesta boca) abierta
    está, y desde su centro
nace la noche, pues la engendra dentro.
                    (I, i, 69–72)

Page 165.

Pues que ya vencer aguarda
mi valor grandes victorias,
hoy ha de ser la más alta
vencerme a mí.
                    (III, xiv, 1065–1067)

Page 165.

Nace el bruto, y con la piel
que dibujan manchas bellas,
apenas signo es de estrellas
gracias al docto pincel,
cuando atrevido y cruel,
la humana necesidad
la enseña a tener crueldad,
monstruo de su laberinto:
¿y yo con mejor instinto
tengo menos libertad?
                    (I, ii, 133–142)

Page 166.

Fuera más que muerte fiera,
ira, rabia y dolor fuerte;
fuera muerte: desta suerte
su rigor he ponderado,
pues dar vida a un desdichado
es dar a un dichoso muerte.
                    (I, ii, 237–242)

Page 167.

    Hipogrifo violento
. . . parejas con el viento,

                .   .   .
    . . . rayo sin llama,
al confuso laberinto
destas desnudas penas . . .
                    (I, i, 1–7)

Page 168.

Mujer, vengo a persuadirte
al remedio de mi honra,

y varón, vengo a alentarte
a que cobres tu corona.
Mujer, vengo a enternecerte
cuando a tus plantas me ponga,
y varón, vengo a servirte
con mi acero y mi persona.
Y así, piensa que si hoy
como mujer me enamoras,
como varón te daré
la muerte en defensa honrosa
de mi honor, porque he de ser,
en su conquista amorosa,
mujer para darte quejas,
varón para ganar honras.
                    (III, x, 715–730)

Page 168.

ni te miro, porque es fuerza,
en pena tan rigurosa,
que no mire tu hermosura
quien ha de mirar tu honra.
                    (III, x, 821–824)

Pages 169–170.

                    pues estamos
en mundo tan singular,
que el vivir sólo es soñar;
y la experiencia me enseña
que el hombre que vive sueña
lo que es hasta dispertar.
            .   .   .
    Yo sueño que estoy aquí
destas prisiones cargado,
y soñé que en otro estado
más lisonjero me vi.
¿Qué es la vida? Un frenesí.
¿Qué es la vida? Una ilusión,
una sombra, una ficción,
y el mayor bien es pequeño;

que toda la vida es sueño,
y los sueños, sueños son.
>   (II, xix, 1165–1170; 1191–1200)

Pages 173–174.

¿Qué os admira? ¿Qué os espanta,
si fué mi maestro el sueño,
y estoy temiendo en mis ansias
que he de despertar y hallarme
otra vez en mi cerrada
prisión? Y cuando no sea,
el soñarlo sólo basta;
pues así llegué a saber
que toda la dicha humana,
en fin, pasa como un sueño . . .
>   (III, xiv, 1114–1123)

Page 174.

>   quien miente y engaña
es quien para usar mal dellas
las penetra y las alcanza.
>   (III, xiv, 978–980)

Notes

CHAPTER 1. A BEGINNING

1. Some fairly recent ones may be cited, though all are fragmentary or frankly surveyish in intent. Everett W. Hesse, *Calderón de la Barca* (New York, Twayne, 1967); Angel Valbuena Briones, *Perspectiva crítica de los dramas de Calderón* (Madrid, Ediciones Rialp, 1965); Micheline Sauvage, *Calderón: Dramaturge* (Paris, L'Arche, 1959); Albert E. Sloman, *The Dramatic Craftsmanship of Calderón: His Use of Earlier Plays* (Oxford, Dolphin, 1958).

2. The term *comedia* refers not to comedy but to any play in general where stress is laid on the characters being rewarded or punished as they deserve.

3. *Auto sacramental* is an allegorical one-act play, like the English medieval morality play. Its sacramental nature, symbolized in the Eucharist, confirms the miracles by which God's grace is bestowed upon mankind.

4. The *silva* is made up of rhymed couplets with alternating lines of seven and eleven syllables; the tone is lyric but the measure can be used for dialogue. The *décima*, as the term implies, is a ten-line stanzaic form in irregularly rhymed patterns; it is reserved for speeches involving complaints or arguments and is typically used in soliloquies. *Romance*, the commonest measure, used mainly for narration, is based on an eight-syllable line with assonantal rhymes of alternating vowels: A-E, I-O, E-A, E-E, E-O, and so forth, in almost limitless combinations. The *quintilla*, like the *décima*, is framed on set line-units; its five lines are octosyllabic but only two lines may rhyme, and no three consecutively. The measure is reserved

for complimentary dialogues. The *redondilla* is a quatrain form of octosyllabic lines rhyming *abba* and employed to incorporate fast-moving dramatic action. *Octavas* are eight-line octosyllabic units, used to mark off portentous events or speeches; the lines rhyme *abababcc*, like a little sonnet.

5. Bruce W. Wardropper believes the puns in Calderón are especially significant. Discussing the famous one in the opening of *Life Is a Dream*, "*apenas llega cuando llega a penas*" ("she hardly arrives before hardship arrives"), Wardropper insists, "The paronomasia is pointless, and the ambivalent interpretation impossible, unless one understand the stranger to be a newborn child." From this he concludes, "Thus what textual critics have intended to dismiss as a literary convention of the period — pointless punning or punning as rhetoric — acquires significance as the keypiece to the whole puzzle" ("Apenas Llega Cuando Llega Apenas," *Modern Philology*, 57 (1960), 244).

CHAPTER 2. HONOR SEEKS ITS OWN LEVEL

1. "Two medieval Spanish codes of laws, the *Fuero Juzgo* of the Visigoths and the later *Fuero Real,* specifically gave a husband power to kill an unfaithful wife and her lover, so long as he killed both. This provision, along with many others of the *Fueros,* was incorporated into the *Nueva recopilación de las leyes de España* (New Compendium of the Laws of Spain) compiled in 1567, and was thus part of the law of the land during the lifetime of the *comedia*" (Margaret Wilson, *Spanish Drama of the Golden Age* [Oxford, Pergamon, 1969], p. 46).

Américo Castro notes that in the laws of Alfonso Sabio, Christian women are condemned "who sleep with Moors or Jews." After the third offense "they are condemned to death. If it was a case of a married woman, the husband could do as he wished in the matter — kill her or forgive her" (*The Structure of Spanish History* [Princeton, Princeton University Press, 1954], p. 527).

2. According to Castro, the Spaniard in the eleventh century "was ready to adopt Arabic ways of expressing personal value (*fijodalgo*), or what there was good in Arabic actions

(*fazañas*). Fazaña, 'feat, prowess,' originally 'model of goodness, generous act,' comes from the Arabic *hasanah* (good act,
generosity)." Castro, *Structure of Spanish History*, p. 629.

3. This is partly paraphrased from Lope de Vega's *Los
Comendadores de Córdoba:*

> Honra es aquella que consiste en otro;
> ningún hombre es honrada por sí mismo,
> que del otro recibe la honra un hombre;
> ser virtuoso hombre y tener méritos,
> no es ser honrado.

4. Identity, a convenient social and psychological fiction, is
also part of a sexual fiction which has been called *machismo*.
In this regard, the honorable man is always trying to vindicate
an image of himself which can never be made visible since it
so largely depends on his own imagination — as that imagination is made to work or is worked on by others. The best-known
acrobat of honor, who knows how to manipulate others, and
who is outside the Calderonian framework in this sense, is the
sexual athlete, Don Juan Tenorio.

5. Norman Maccoll, *Select Plays of Calderón* (London,
1888), p. 375.

6. Ibid., pp. 381–382.

7. Like Ben Jonson's, Calderón's dramatic art has been
poorly understood, and for similar reasons. Taking Jonson's
humor theory as a rigid application to drama of a medieval
psychological principle, critics missed the fruitful purpose
it served in the development of an art based on character
typology. And they were thus prevented from seeing how the
logical requirement of his aesthetic came to flower in his allegorical and mythological masques. Similarly with Calderón.
The critics who give limited approval to the art of realistic
portraiture in *The Mayor of Zalamea* or *The Phantom Lady*
are like the critics who commend the Jonson of *Volpone* or *The
Alchemist*. They do not see that the realism overlays a deeper
typological design which they object to when the realistic
patina disappears in the dramatists' other works. Jonson's
mythological plays and masques are natural developments of
an earlier typological realism much as Calderón's mythological
plays and *autos* are condensations and fulfillments of a domi-

nant symbology at work in his earlier honor plays and well-known cape-and-sword plays.

CHAPTER 3. HONOR AND THE COMIC SUBVERSION

1. A. A. Parker, "Towards a Definition of Calderonian Tragedy," *Bulletin of Hispanic Studies,* 39 (1962), 227–228.

2. Prosser Hall Frye, *Romance and Tragedy* (Lincoln, Neb., University of Nebraska Press, 1961), pp. 311–312, 314.

3. Noted and translated by E. C. Riley, *Cervantes's Theory of the Novel* (Oxford, Oxford University Press, 1962), p. 182. I am particularly indebted to Professor Riley in these pages for his richly detailed and lucid account of Cervantes's self-reflective devices in the *Quijote.*

4. Ibid., pp. 201–202. This is Riley's adaptation of the designated passage in the *Quijote.*

5. See A. Irvine Watson, "*El pintor de su deshonra* and the Neo-Aristotelian Theory of Tragedy," *Bulletin of Hispanic Studies,* 40 (1963), 17–34.

6. E. M. Wilson regards *Secret Vengeance* as a disguised miracle play (*"una especie de disfrazada comedia de santos"*), in which the principal characters are made to enact typical roles. The vital displacement, according to Wilson, is that honor is substituted for religion, which makes Don Lope "a mystic of honor," Don Juan a believer, but indiscreet, Doña Leonor, another believer but a sinner overthrown by her passions, and Don Luis, who only indulges his whims and desires, "an apostate of honor" ("La discreción de Don Lope de Almeida," *Clavileño,* 2 [1951], 1–10).

CHAPTER 5. A STRANGE MERCY PLAY:
DEVOTION TO THE CROSS

1. Albert Camus, "Avant-Propos," *La Dévotion à la croix* (Paris, Gallimard, 1953), p. 12.

2. I have summarized elsewhere J. J. Bachofen's view of such a situation: "Archetypal situations of this sort apparently involve the dynamic interplay of two broad, antagonistic prin-

ciples. One might say the conflict between these principles is nearly pervasive enough to affect every emotion and every move a person makes or thinks of making. Together these principles engender the dichotomies of art evolving out of authoritarian religion and relate to the biases of artistic expression we call classical or romantic, rational or enthusiastic. One principle is the dominance of woman and the natural virtues imputed to her, which are culturally shaped into the matriarchal ideals of love, equality, peace, mercy, fecundity, the reassuring periodicity of nature, human freedom, brotherhood, and the world as an earthly paradise. In opposition is the powerful and now triumphant principle of male authority, which encompasses all the virtues of civilized life: law, conscience, justice, military heroism; the concepts of hierarchy, primogeniture, and individualism; and the material conquest over nature" (Edwin Honig, *Dark Conceit: The Making of Allegory,* [New York, Oxford University Press, 1966], p. 35).

CHAPTER 6. HONOR HUMANIZED:
THE MAYOR OF ZALAMEA

1. See the discussion comparing the two plays in Albert E. Sloman, *The Dramatic Craftsmanship of Calderón* (Oxford, 1958).

2. Norman Maccoll, *Select Plays of Calderón* (London, 1888), p. 252.

CHAPTER 7. FLICKERS OF INCEST ON THE FACE OF
HONOR: *THE PHANTOM LADY*

1. The answer to why and how such plays by Calderón influenced English comedy might show that the generic aim of romantic comedy is to liberate the overidealized and overprotected woman from social bondage so that she may freely assert her nature to act as an individual. This is the subject of Calderón's Coriolanus play, *Las armas de hermosura,* 1652 (The Weapons of Beauty), one of the later plays which deals with the rights of women.

2. Francis Cornford, *The Origin of Attic Comedy* (Cambridge, Eng., Cambridge University Press, 1934), p. 33.

3. Colin Still, *Shakespeare's Mystery Play* (London, C. Palmer, 1921), pp. 235–236.

CHAPTER 8. THE MAGNANIMOUS PRINCE AND THE
PRICE OF CONSCIOUSNESS:
LIFE IS A DREAM

1. Suggestive of such complexity are two observations of Professor Entwistle's made, however, not about this play but about *Devotion to the Cross*. "The evidence of the senses is not denied, but it is checked and corrected. The world of phenomena is, admittedly, a dream, but there is a network of realities immediately underneath the surface and embracing the correlated postulates of all the sciences. It is this world which Calderón reveals in a number of his great plays." Accordingly, Entwistle sees (borrowing Calderón's own term) that *Devotion* is "a representable idea. The characters are individual exponents of leading principles. They are seen, so to speak, beneath the epidermis, in their essential structure. As infrared photographs eliminate the superficial differentiae without confounding different individuals, so Calderón's actors lose something of the personality conferred by a thousand superficial details without ceasing to be individual entities" (William J. Entwistle, "Calderón et le théâtre symbolique," *Bulletin Hispanique*, 52 [1950], 41–54).

One can apply these observations to *Life Is a Dream*. The first, in pointing to Calderón's moral realism, leads to one definition of the theme — the triumph of consciousness in experience — in a play which is dramatically formed by a series of actions and soliloquies imitating a dream vision. The second observation, about the subcutaneous nature of the moral life, leads one to look for the life of impulse, which when followed even superficially in this play tells a good deal about the intricate emotional dynamics that make it such an absorbing document of psychological realism.

2. I am indebted here to Albert E. Sloman's discussion of the two plays in Chapter 10 of *The Dramatic Craftsmanship of Calderón* (Oxford, 1958).

CHAPTER 9. AN ENDING

1. Peter N. Dunn, "Honour and the Christian Background in Calderón," *Bulletin of Hispanic Studies*, 37 (1960), 75–105.

2. Northrop Frye, "Mythos and Logos," *Yearbook of Comparative and General Literature*, no. 18 (1969), p. 15.

3. Ibid., p. 18.

4. Aristotle, *Politics*, I, ii–iv (Bywater translation).

5. Franz Kafka, *Letter to His Father*, trans. Ernst Kaiser and Eithne Wilkins (New York, Schocken, 1966), pp. 87, 29, 37, 123.

6. Ramón Menéndez Pidal, "Del Honor en el Teatro Español," in *De Cervantes y Lope de Vega* (Madrid, Espasa-Calpe, 1940), p. 152.

7. A. L. Constandse, *Le Baroque Espagnol et Calderón* (Amsterdam, Plus Ultra, 1951), pp. 61, 48, 50.

8. Alexander A. Parker, "The Father-Son Conflict in the Drama of Calderón," *Forum for Modern Language Study*, 2 (April 1966), 99–113.

9. Kafka, *Letter to His Father*, pp. 101, 105.

10. Edward M. Wilson [with W. J. Entwistle], "Calderón's *Príncipe constante:* Two Appreciations." *Modern Language Review*, 34 (1939), 207–222; "Calderón and the Stage Censor in the Seventeenth Century: A Provisional Study," *Symposium* (Fall 1961), pp. 165–184; "The Four Elements in the Imagery of Calderón," *Modern Language Review*, 31 (1936), 34–47.

11. Peter N. Dunn, "Introduction," *El alcalde de Zalamea* (Oxford, 1969), pp. 1–28; "Patrimonio del Alma," *Bulletin of Hispanic Studies*, 41 (1960), 90–105.

12. Alexander A. Parker, *The Allegorical Drama of Calderón* (Oxford, Dolphin, 1943).

13. Alexander A. Parker, "Metáforo y símbolo en la interpretación de Calderón," in *Actas I*, ed. F. Pierce and C. A. Jones, Congreso Internacional de Hispanistas (Oxford, 1964), pp. 140–160.

14. Albert E. Sloman, *The Dramatic Craftsmanship of Calderón* (Oxford, 1958), p. 284.

15. Alan K. G. Paterson, "The Comic and Tragic Melancholy of Juan Roca: A Study of Calderón's *El pintor de su*

deshonra," *Forum for Modern Language Studies,* 5 (1969), 244–261.

16. *The Confessions of St. Augustine,* III, 2, trans. Rex Warner (New York, New American Library, 1963), p. 53.

BIOGRAPHICAL NOTE

1. Gerald Brenan, *The Literature of the Spanish People* (New York, Meridian, 1957), p. 277.

Index